A BUREAUCRAT FIGHTS BACK

PRADIP BAIJAL studied at the Indian Institute of Technology, Roorkee, and trained at Oxford University in the privatization of public enterprises and the process of reforms. After completing assignments in the steel, power, finance and disinvestment sectors, he served as chairman of the Telecom Regulatory Authority of India. Later, he acted as a consultant to the World Bank and the International Telecommunication Union on telecom and broadband reforms.

PRAISE FOR THE BOOK

This is an honest account of the journey of one of India's finest civil servants. History will credit Baijal as being at the forefront of India's great telecom revolution. Yet the unravelling of the 2G scandal has left scars on those who have relentlessly served the nation with their impeccable work. The book offers a first-hand narrative of the reforms needed in the telecom sector. But more telling is the urgent need to revamp the government's watchdog agencies. It is a clarion call to stop witch hunting practices, otherwise Baijal may well be amongst the last of his tribe to have had the courage to carry out big and bold reforms. The India of today cannot afford this. For any India watcher, this is a must-read.

DEEPAK PAREKH, Chairman, HDFC Limited

I have known Pradip Baijal for long and a great deal of that association has been professional. Much before the so-called 'reforms' started, there were those, in particular Pradip, who were ready to change the way we govern ourselves. John Maynard Keynes famously said, 'Sir, when the facts change I change.' Pradip has endeavoured to do so even at great personal cost.

V.K. SHUNGLU, Former CAG

Pradip Baijal's book is a tour-de-force about where there is a will, there is a way. The institutional foundations of the telecommunications revolution in India were set under his stewardship as chairman of the Telecommunications Regulatory Authority of India, and this process is described in the book, warts and all. Under his direction, India went from a chronically communication-poor country, to one where democratization of communications happened almost overnight, as if by a miracle. What requires such phenomena to occur is a combination of common sense and the ability to break the mould of stale thinking that has often permeated Indian thought and policy. Pradip Baijal's approach is described in the book, which ought to become one widely referred to in understanding contemporary India and its technological possibilities.

SUMIT MAJUMDAR, Professor of Technology Strategy, University of Texas Dallas, USA; author of *India's Late, Late Industrial Revolution*

This book is a must-read for those interested in governance and regulation in an era of private sector infrastructure provision. Mr Baijal played a significant, and a not so well-known, role behind the boom in Indian telecommunication. India's relatively less significant experience with privatization under his guidance yielded more revenues than the larger public disinvestments in China and Russia. This book reveals an important facet of private sector competition promotion in India—that a capable executive and bureaucratic arm is equally significant for good governance. These accounts are key to understanding why India grows rapidly at some times and not at others.

RAHUL MUKHERJI, Associate Professor, National University of Singapore; author of *Globalization and Deregulation: Ideas, Interests and Institutional Changes in India, Political Economy of Reforms in India, India since 1980s*

Both China and India have witnessed telecommunication revolutions. Among developing nations, these countries have taken advantage of globalization to extend telecommunication infrastructure and services well beyond urban cities into the rural countryside. Their paths to globalization and development differ markedly; and in this formidable book, Pradip Baijal, introduced to me as India's foremost privatizer and regulator, weave a tale of grit and determination, the power of ideas, and partisan politics to reveal India's story. Motivated by what he viewed as unjustified attacks on his good name, this story of the salacious palace intrigue behind the constructing of second generation (2G) telecommunications networks contextualizes the growth and development of India's telecommunications within the country's market reforms. What makes this book an exceptional read is that Baijal, an esteemed officer of the Indian Administrative Service, parallels the breathtaking history of India's post-Independence development as it intersects with globalization, with his personal story. This book humanizes in the process the people and Government of India and the trajectory of their political economic development in the last several decades.

ROSELYN HSUEH, Assistant Professor, Department of Political Science, Temple University, Philadelphia; author of *China's Regulatory State : A New Strategy for Globalization*

The book is a first-hand account of the major events and policies that brought about the phenomenal growth of Indian telecom sector—the most outstanding reform in post-Independence India. Baijal wrote the script as chairman, TRAI, and implemented the change after its approval from the government. The most outstanding achievement of Baijal as the telecom regulator was to enable the process of tariff competition and causing it to become the cheapest in the world, thereby making it affordable to the poorest Indian. The asymptotic growth of the telecom sector in India can be traced to this single decision. One cannot afford to miss this book if one wants to learn the trials and tribulations of a committed reformer in India.

S.D. SAXENA, Director (Finance) (Retd), BSNL; author of *India Connected*

A BUREAUCRAT FIGHTS BACK

The Complete Story of Indian Reforms

PRADIP BAIJAL

HarperCollins *Publishers* India

First published in India in 2016 by
HarperCollins *Publishers* India
Building No 10, Tower A, 4th Floor, DLF Cyber City, Phase II,
Gurugram – 122002
www.harpercollins.co.in

1 2 3 4 5 6 7 8 9 10

P-ISBN: 978-93-5177-755-7
E-ISBN: 978-93-5177-756-4

Typeset in 11/14.5 Electra LT Std by
R. Ajith Kumar

To my mother who taught me to fight adversity and keep going forward and to my wife, son and erstwhile colleagues who never lost faith

By Panju Ganguli
REFORMS
CMP ALWAYS KEEP LEFT
OTHERWISE
I HAVE SPOKEN TO THE LEFT. WHAT THEY WANT IS TO GO FORWARD BUT TAKE ALONG THE SECTIONS OF PEOPLE WHO HAVE BEEN NEGLECTED
THE TELEPHONE HAS TO BE RECOGNISED AS THE POOR MAN'S INSTRUMENT FOR CONNECTIVITY
P. CHIDAMBARAM
Union Finance Minister
PRADIP BAIJAL
Chairman, TRAI

Contents

Foreword

It was in pursuance of the commitment given by the Government of India to the World Trade Organization (WTO) in 1995 that two years later an independent regulator, the Telecom Regulatory Authority of India (TRAI) was set up. Not long after it became functional, the government of the day became unhappy both with its independence as also with its regulatory functions. No wonder those who constituted the first Authority (B. K. Zutshi, N. S. Ramachandran and I) ran into a headwind with resultant conflicts with the government. That however is another story for another day.

The author, Pradip Baijal, took over as the third chairman of TRAI in 2003. TRAI was at the regulatory crossroads at that time. While the sector was crying out for strong regulatory intervention, the government and its operators were resistant to change. Change was looked upon as anti-establishment and pro-private business. It was in this situation that TRAI led by Baijal had to take tough decisions, many of which are recounted in his book, *A Bureaucrat Fights Back*, which makes for interesting reading. Like him or not, Baijal could not be ignored—sometimes acerbic, but always decisive.

Baijal is correct when he says in that a regulator should have thorough knowledge of regulatory law and the capacity to have the orders and directions of TRAI approved by the appellate authority, courts and the Parliament; else one such element being set aside may lead to the entire scheme collapsing. The book shows that he carried out this task with diligence and was successful in getting his orders approved. In most cases, the Supreme Court supported him. Without this support India could not have achieved revolutionary growth in telecom. Baijal led TRAI with the aplomb it so needed, paving the way for the telecom revolution in India. Baijal's book gives an insight into the goings on in the world of telecom during his tenure and even beyond. This book would be an interesting addition to the reading list of those who have anything to do with telecom and reforms in India.

Justice S. S. Sodhi
former and first chairman of TRAI

Preface

Reform has been accepted as an instrument of growth all over the world. We, in India, have also been travelling on this path for around three decades. There have been positive and negative consequences of reform. I have been a practitioner in this area and have seen reforms from within the Central and the state governments. I am writing this book for those who want to study, understand or participate in the reform process in India, or in countries like India, and learn about the enormous benefits of economic reforms, and also their pitfalls, and the means to avoid these.

We are perhaps the only large country having huge viable infrastructural and industrial gaps which need to be filled for development and growth. These can be filled by public investments, private money and by FDI (Foreign Direct Investment). There are gaps in indigenous resources available to the government for investment and an abundance of FDI and FII (Foreign Institutional Investor) money, besides the private money from within the country waiting to be invested in viable projects for accelerating India's development. The first phase of reforms has led to many private projects in different sectors languishing owing to lack of clearly defined rules. The private sector is not keen to invest in such an environment, leading to a stagnant growth rate. China took advantage of these resources by carefully structured reforms, but of a different format. This book is an attempt to understand the impact of our efforts so far and to carefully structure the future. I look at the future by first looking at the process of reforms through the 2G (Second Generation Wireless Telephony) reforms I was intimately connected with. These reforms led to unparalleled growth in India and later to a huge scam which led to the ruling party being routed in elections.

When reforms pose such challenge to the polity, should political parties attempt reform and not continue the centrist policies we have always practised? This is the story of reforms in India—damned if you do and damned if you don't. This is also applicable to those involved with reforms.

India was one of the first countries to start a telephone line in 1850. It grew to a tele-density of 0.02 per cent in 1947—after about a hundred years of telephony we had a few thousand phones with most phones only for the government. Post-Independence and post-reform growth has been analysed in Chapter 2, when the sector grew to more than a billion phones today.

The 2G scam shook the nation. There were several charges pressed against me and these have been dealt in Chapter 3. The charges, though fraudulent, started a chain of inquiries and the ministry claimed that some key documents were 'missing'. On the basis of the available facts, the UPA (United Progressive Alliance) government used similar modus operandi—removing and misinterpreting files, and in some cases blaming the previous government—for the scams during their period. In the recent Ishrat Jahan case, reports of the NIA (National Intelligence Agency) were suppressed and misinterpreted. Then the CBI (Central Bureau of Investigation) was directed to prosecute on the lines dictated by the UPA-II. The CBI director obliged despite knowing the uncomfortable truth. Even in the Coalgate scam, then coal minister Sriprakash Jaiswal admitted that some crucial files relating to the investigation between 1993 and 2004 had gone missing. Two could be a coincidence but three definitely makes a pattern. I have given a detailed account of this method of deceit as was used against me.

Chapter 4 and 5 explain the reformers' dilemma. If you do not reform, you are not doing your job; if you do, you may be forced into conspiratorial inquiries aided and abetted by some political parties, corporates, and the incumbents.

With the introduction of private sector in the network, huge litigation ensued. Chapter 6 describes the consequent telecom litigation and the role of the courts, particularly the Supreme Court, in interpreting the regulatory law in its true spirit. Later, the Supreme Court saved the sector from scamsters when they tried to extract the surpluses of the reforms for their own pockets. All investors therefore ask for transparent regulatory regimes with judicial guidance.

I have moved to other sectors that I dealt with while in service—power and disinvestment—in Part II. Power sector reforms were started in a hurry, without preparatory work, legislation and restructuring, unlike the telecom sector. The results were disastrous and continue to be so, despite many legislative changes. Reforms in disinvestment started with the setting up of the Disinvestment Commission and saw a lot of success. These success stories though were investigated on flimsy charges. Part III deals with the various government-led inquisitions in disinvestment cases such as VSNL (Videsh Sanchar Nigam Limited) and the Laxmi Vilas Hotel case. Through this section, I highlight with examples, how the CBI filed cases without reading the documents carefully.

Implementation of reforms created major problems for the Indian government and political parties in power. Why pursue reforms then? I have tried to answer this in Part IV. The book also deals with the inevitability of reforms for growth in an increasing globalised and interconnected world. I also discuss the importance of Digital India, Smart Cities and the Internet of Things, and how with the proper implementation of these programmes, India will experience a growth curve no country has witnessed before.

Part V of the book is an autobiographical account of my induction into the Indian bureaucracy. It includes nuggets from my postings, interactions with politicians and hopes to offer a glimpse into the world of a bureaucrat. I have often wondered why I chose to work in assignments, both at the Centre and in the states, which revolved around reforms, despite having problems in each assignment, inevitable in a conservative polity.

When I faced intense, unfair and almost conspiratorial inquiries, many years after the assignments in the government, I started wondering what I had done to deserve this. Perhaps, I had not understood the power of money on human affairs. It is the enormous strength of the Indian polity that nothing could harm me and even the reforms were implemented.

PART I

REFORMS IN INDIA AS SEEN THROUGH TELECOM

1

The History of Telecom, Corruption and Politics

Telecom reforms, unlike other reforms, were carefully structured with issuance of policy documents, new legislations like the TRAI Act of 1997 and 2000 which created institutions like TRAI and TDSAT (Telecom Disputes Settlement and Appellate Tribunal). TRAI was declared the broadcasting regulator in 2004. There was another futuristic initiative—the Convergence Bill 2001—but this was not implemented as the government came up with the Unified Access Service Licence (UASL) 2003, which did not require new legislation. Most of the problems of the Indian telecom sector today are due to this unfinished initiative. The sector also remained dormant for 145 years after its start in 1850 due to the telephone being treated as an instrument of the elite and monopoly in the public sector. It was only in 1995, when private players were introduced, and later, the initiation of sectoral reforms in 1997, that the sector started growing. After aggressive reforms in 2003, the sector exploded in numbers.

The Bofors scam highlighted that the Indian voter, economically deprived and poor, is sensitive to corruption. The Howitzer was a brilliant gun, carefully chosen, and it showed its worth during the Kargil war. However, the deal was not fully examined by the courts, nor did the full facts regarding the deal ever come out. The scam affected future defence purchases adversely. More importantly, the allegations of kickbacks destroyed a Congress government headed by a young, dynamic and technologically savvy prime minister elected in 1984 with a massive majority.

Second-generation wireless communication technology, commonly known as 2G, had started being adopted across the world in mid-1980s. As with many other new technologies, everyone opposed its entry in India until 1995. Even when the mobile technology first entered in 1995 through CDMA (Code Division Multiple Access) technology, its wings were clipped and it was only allowed to service a fixed telephone. Another 2G technology, GSM (Global System for Mobile Communications) which came later and, after auctions, was allowed full mobility. These however failed to grow as regulations did not provide competition on a level playing field between technologies and operators.

Both technologies were allowed full mobility in 2003 and the regulatory regime enforced a level playing field between operators and technologies. Both these factors led to the unparalleled growth in this sector which not even the most optimistic analysts or the government ever imagined.

This reform changed India forever, and mobile tele-density rose from 1.0 per cent in 2002 (achieved after seven years of its introduction and five years of regulation) to almost 80 per cent in 2011, perhaps the fastest technology dispersal in the world. India's mobile penetration increased at a rate three times that of China, prompting authors Assa Doron and Robin Jeffrey to refer to India as a 'cell-phone nation mobile telephony revolutionizing business, politics and ordinary life' in *The Great Indian Phone Book*. In the view of many experts and economists, the rapid growth of mobile telephony in India ranks inarguably as one of India's greatest success stories. Cheap telephone connectivity empowered individuals in myriad ways and has served as a massive productivity multiplier for the economy by collapsing communication costs.

The impact of reforms can only be understood when we look at the evolution of the sector since its start in India in 1850, incidentally amongst the first countries in the world to start a telephone.

Let's trace the sector's evolution process in detail below.

The Pre-Independence Story

We were one of the first countries in the world to have telecom.

In 1850, the first telegraph line was opened in Calcutta for the use of the East India Company (EIC). It is remarkable to note that the British recognized the power of communication as early as in 1850 when the EIC started establishing its base in India. The British had realized that to rule a vast country like India, they needed advanced systems of communication and conveyance.

Little wonder then, that the railways, road, post offices and telecommunication started growing at a fast pace to cater to the needs of the administration and for establishing a quick foothold in India. It is necessary to note that the growth was made only to the extent of catering to the need of the ruling elite and not for the public.

This process could have been altered after Independence to cater to the fast and pressing need of infrastructure for the growth of Indian economy; however, some of this was lost in the debate of essential necessity wherein telecom was treated as a luxury and was neglected in the process of long-term planning.

Till 1995, telecom also remained a totally government effort and did not grow.

The first telephone exchanges were opened in the year 1881 in Calcutta, followed by Bombay and Madras. These were operated by a private telephone company which was granted licence by the British government.

A number of initiatives were taken to establish a sturdy

infrastructure of communication to aid the British administration in India. In this regard, the telephone and telegraph lines linking Calcutta, Madras and Delhi are worth mentioning. The maintenance of this primitive technology to keep the communication running is a matter of folklore. These lines were continuously maintained by runners. The first direct link between India and Britain was established as early as in 1927.

Telecom Post-Independence

In post-Independence India, major changes happened in terms of establishing Indian Telephone Industries Ltd or ITI as the manufacturing company for the telephone instruments and later telephone exchanges. For the modernization of the telecom system, automated exchanges were introduced—first the Strowger Exchanges and subsequently the Cross-Bar Exchanges—in collaboration with AT&T (American Telephone and Telegraph) Belgium. These changes were introduced in the mid-1950s and 1960 respectively.

Indian telecom suffered neglect in terms of infrastructure while the Planning Commission kept on talking about rapid growth. There were limited funds from the government for telecom infrastructure and these funds too were often poorly utilized in the monopoly environment.

The need for rapid expansion was felt by citizens, and long waiting lists were a feature in that period as people wanted to use the technology as early as possible. Corruption in getting telephone connections, and even in keeping the connections alive and in working order, was commonplace and was one reason why growth was stunted. Artificial demand–supply mismatches and the resultant benefits helped some in 'control' positions.

In order to reach the rapid expansion targets, the government started a cable manufacturing company, Hindustan Cables Ltd (HCL). However, the production of cable was too far below the demand and ultimately the cable sector was deregulated bringing in a number of manufacturers. This brought in significant change in the growth rate of the telecom sector. Unfortunately, with the rapid changes in technologies, the demand for cables subsided resulting in a glut in the cable industry.

The major landmark in the growth of telecom was the introduction of the electronic switching system in collaboration with the French telecom manufacturer CIT Alcatel.

The Indian experience in this respect was a repetition of the French experience. It was said that as late as in 1970, half the population of Paris was waiting to get a telephone line and the others who had a telephone used to wait for the dial tone. From such a situation, the French introduced the system of public borrowing, thereby making available huge resources for the growth of telecom sector in France. The net result was that by the end of 1970, the French telecom system became the most advanced system in Europe.

The Indian telecom story followed a similar trajectory. When Mahanagar Telephone Nigam Limited (MTNL)—the public sector undertaking (PSU) formed for the city of Delhi and Bombay—was allowed to raise resources by the issuance of telecom bonds it created a major impetus for the growth of the Indian telecom industry and also gave a dividend to the public who earned higher returns on these bonds.

CIT Alcatel was also licensed for the manufacture of the new-generation switches in India at the newly established factory for the switching system at Mankapur in Uttar Pradesh (a remote area of eastern UP). The remoteness of the factory added to the cost of manufacturing and the switches manufactured in India turned out much costlier than similar switches manufactured elsewhere in the global market, leading to this company not performing well.

In 1982, a major change happened in the form of the Sarin Committee which was set up to study ways and means to develop systems for faster growth of the Indian telecom. As an outcome, Sam

Pitroda, an NRI, made a presentation for the quick growth of the sector which resulted in the setting up of the Centre for Development of Telematics (C-Dot). C-Dot manufactured electronic telephone exchanges for the first time. It was set up as an R&D organization to develop state-of-the-art switching systems indigenously in India to suit local requirements. C-Dot developed rural automatic exchanges (RAXs) which brought about a faster change in rural connectivity and a growth in demand, as the rural population started enjoying the benefits of telecom technology.

The impact of the C-Dot RAX reduced the cost of this technology by half, resulting in the cost-effective yet marginal growth of telecom in rural India due to faulty implementation. The growth was still dependent on government support and the allocation of funds was low. India also had to build up the long-distance network which was operating on cables and the low-capacity microwave network. The huge demand for long-distance calls made it necessary to develop the network at a fast pace.

Two major developments created growth opportunities in this regard. The first was the digital exchanges based on CIT Alcatel technology manufactured at the Palghat factory of ITI in Kerala. The second was additional long-distance capacity added by the ISRO (Indian Space Research Organization) satellite launched in the early 1980s called the INSAT (Indian National Satellite System) series of satellites. These long-distance channels augmented the quality of service.

Despite all these government efforts—about 140 years of the British Raj and about forty-seven years after Independence—the tele-density remained a paltry 1.09 per cent even by 1994. No one in India could at that time visualize that a scientifically structured reforms programme, with public–private cooperation and new technology which was previously disallowed, could lead to 100 times the earlier growth. It would also provide huge income to the government instead of the expenditures sponsored by the Planning Commission or the Ministry of Finance. Most importantly, reform would provide telecom access to everyone and would reach everywhere.

Several international players entered the market and penetration continued to grow. Growth in urban and rural areas skyrocketed and billionaires were created in the prevailing business environment despite plummeting tariffs. The government started earning huge monies from telecom, rather than making huge expenditures and achieving apologetic growths. Could a developing poor country ask for more?

There were no complaints against regulatory and licensing changes made in the beginning of 2004. After 2006, the rulers started breaking all rules and thought they could make personal profits from the surpluses of the growing sector. They sensed the increasing value of the spectrum—due to the explosive growth in mobile subscribers—and, instead of realizing this value to the government coffers, diverted it to their pockets. When complaints started, the erstwhile UPA government tried to put the blame on the Vajpayee-led NDA government. This was done by manufacturing contrived reports by suppressing facts. The entire conundrum is analysed in detail in subsequent chapters.

2

India's Unusual Telecom Growth

The mere passing of reform acts leads to nothing. They have to be implemented. And with barriers created by incumbents enjoying monopoly and high profits, despite their inefficient operations, implementing reforms often becomes an impossible task. However, if implemented, one can grow from 10 to 1,000 million mobiles in little more than a decade, sometimes at 500 per cent of Government of India's targeted growth rate and with most of the funds provided by private players. Contrary to popular belief and sectoral experiences, telecom reforms even worked in spurring growth in rural telephony. Penetration grew from a stagnant 0.43 per cent in 1998 to 2 per cent in 2007 to about 50 per cent today in rural areas after implementation of rural reforms in 2006 proposed by TRAI in 2004. In the power sector, a similar network sector, the reforms were not implemented in the spirit provided in the Electricity Act 2003, leading to Government of India's conservative targets being missed by half for more than three decades. Of course, such models, as those shown in Indian telecom, have to be saved from scamsters wanting to encash the surpluses of reforms for themselves and convert reforms into crony capitalism.

Early Reform

Around 1994, the government had realized that telecom growth can be best achieved by bringing in private operators and capital to open up the sector. With the 1991 reforms having been ushered, this was possible.

The process was a long and tardy one as the government was always apprehensive about the strategic importance of telecom and the nagging fear that private operators may allow information to leak to unwanted agencies. The privatization of telecom in the UK served as an example and also acted as a catalyst in speeding up the process of bringing in private players in the Indian sector.

The year 1994 was a major milestone in the history of the Indian telecom sector since the National Telecom Policy was issued in 1994 and the year witnessed the entry of the private sector in the basic services space which earlier was restricted to the Department of Telecommunications (DoT). It also saw the allotment of mobile licences to private operators. The process adopted for award of these licences was competitive bidding, and it saw mind-boggling figures being quoted as licence fees. The process led to licences being given to eight Cable Modem Termination System (CMTS) operators in the four metros, fourteen CMTS operators in eighteen state circles, six Base Transceiver Station (BTS) operators in six state circles, and paging operators in twenty-seven cities and eighteen state circles. The winner in these auctions was the small equipment manufacturer Himachal Futuristic Company Limited (HFCL) in partnership with Bezeq, an Israeli government-controlled company. It won nine licences for its bids totalling Rs 85,000 crore.

Soon after the results of the bids were declared, the government announced that it had decided to invoke the provision in the tender documents that gave it the right to limit or 'cap' the number of licences. It announced that no company would be allowed to retain more than three licences for the Type A circles which was considered to have the maximum commercial potential. This meant HFCL had to forgo all but three of its A circle licences. This marked the beginning of policy manipulation. Theoretically, the government also lost huge possible revenues, but the action led to more competition in the sector.

Subsequently, these licensees approached the government seeking relaxation in payment of the licence fee which then led to the government initially granting an extension in payback period and the concession of allowing migration from a fixed-licence fee regime to a revenue-sharing regime. In the bargain, the government introduced more competition by doing away with duopoly—again a step which led to doing away with a sector which could have led to cartelization. Had the government not changed the policy and introduced the National Telecom Policy 1999, the sector would have consisted of many sick companies, no competition and, consequently, high tariffs and no growth. While the exact figure of this waiver was never made public, conservative estimates peg it to be of the order of over Rs 40,000 crore. In addition to this waiver, these licensees never paid a rational entry fee, and instead the outstanding payments were treated as the one-time fee and their licences migrated to NTP 1999.

This action of the government attracted the attention of the CAG, which under its audit report, categorically mentioned: 'The special audit reports in chapter 4 also include paragraphs on migration of the existing licensee from fixed licence fee regime to revenue sharing regime and non-charging of one-time entry fee from them. The amount of loss on these accounts could not be quantified at this stage.'

When I joined as chairman of the third telecom regulator in 2003, I had an ideal team consisting of D.P.S. Seth, the first chairman of BSNL (Bharat Sanchar Nigam Limited), and P.K. Sarma, a seasoned bureaucrat, former chairman of CBDT (Central Board of Direct Taxes). The part-time members appointed were: S.G. Dhande, director of IIT, Kanpur, and Arvind Virmani, chief economic advisor to the Government of India. The sector had received its full dose of telecom reforms. Two reform acts had been passed, the regulator had started working, orders and regulation had been issued, but yet we had not been able to improve upon the 'Hindu rate of growth' of around 3 per cent. The entire sector was in litigation and almost all operators were incurring losses. No one was investing money into the sector.

Fortunately, Arun Shourie, with whom I had worked for two and a half years in the Ministry of Disinvestment, took over as the telecom minister around the same time. He had a vision for the sector. We in TRAI also saw the huge need for reforms in the sector. Courtesy the Government of India, and unlike other bureaucrats, I had the formal training in reforms and privatization from a one-year course at the University of Oxford and previous experience of reforms in other sectors. The other members also had similar experiences relevant for reforms. Very early in our working, we decided that we would never have TRAI's decisions with a note of dissent and therefore debated issues for long periods till we reached consensus.

Much later, in 2010 when the CBI inquiries were started against TRAI officers, had it not been for the telecom minister's insistence on being questioned by the CBI in the 2G case, I would not have been fully able to comprehend his vision. But understanding his reply and TRAI's actions requires the context on what happened in the sector prior to 2003. I start with the facts at TRAI's end, as I understood them.

The Results of the Reforms

The first National Telecom Policy was issued in 1994 with the objective of bringing changes in ownership, service and regulation of telecommunications infrastructure. The policy introduced the concept of telecommunication for all, and its vision was to expand facilities to all the villages in India. Private operators started their operation somewhere in 1995. But they could not connect with the existing network since there were no regulations for interconnections and termination of telephony, and TRAI had to be set up in 1997 under a Court order. Its mandate was reducing the interference by the government in deciding tariffs and policymaking. The first tariff order was issued in 1998. There were several problems with NTP 1994 and the TRAI Act 1997. The NTP 1999 and the TRAI Amendment Act 2000, rationalized things further by establishing job-focused institutions. TRAI's adjudication and dispute settlement function was transferred to the TDSAT for strengthening the regulatory framework. Moreover, any direction, order or decision of TRAI could be challenged by appealing in the TDSAT. Despite these measures the tele-density was apologetic. From 1998 to 2003, it increased from 1.94 per cent to 5.11 per cent, at a rate of 0.6 per cent per year, still much below government targets in comparison to the miserable pre-reform period rate of 0.04 per cent.

The post-2003 changes bringing Unified Access Service Licensing led the sector to explode in growth numbers. This was courtesy the fall in tariffs due to increased competition in a level playing field and technology-agnostic licensing. The regulator's decision of leaving the tariffs to operators, after making many pro-growth regulations, also helped. As was seen in the previous phases, litigation also multiplied. However, reforms could change the sector as a Unified Access Licensing regime was approved by the government, and litigation was quickly settled through discussions with stakeholders and operators in 2003. All litigations were withdrawn by operators. The Supreme Court also approved TRAI's regulations.The growth in 2003–04 and 2004–05 was more than 2 per cent; higher than the fifty years' total growth up to 1998. Later, the growth kept accelerating in a no-litigation environment at a rate no one had anticipated.

Unified Access Licensing alone could not bring growth. There were many other distortions which had to be managed. The first was the Access Deficit Charge (ADC) of Rs 5.20 per minute on each call, of which the major portion was imposed on fixed lines in the beginning of 2003 by the regulator. This would have meant a much higher tariff for fixed lines, to subsidize fixed lines that were being challenged by new technology and to help them survive during the initial years. However, this measure would have actually killed fixed lines further.

I asked TRAI officers and the economists attached to TRAI the rationale behind such an ADC. No one could explain it. One of the outspoken advisors told me that the ADC regulation was virtually dictated by the representative of one of the mobile operators. Being new to the telecom sector, and only understanding cross-subsidies with my limited knowledge of power regulation, my questions to all telecom experts yielded no results till one of the advisors brought to me the World Bank's manual on regulation, InfoDev's *Telecommunication Regulation Handbook*, that explained all the concepts of telecom regulation and the best practices in the world. I also went to the UK to understand the nitty-gritty of reforms with the practitioners in Ofcom (The Office of Communications), the UK regulator, and also had similar meetings with the staff of FCC (Federal Communications Commission), the US regulator. These interactions helped hugely, since the nature of the network, technologies and the regulatory issues were the same the world over.

The InfoDev book explained that the purpose and concept of ADC was meant to be a temporary measure for three to five years at the beginning of telecom reforms, to allow the incumbent to withstand the pressure from new technologies and operators. ADC was normally below -10 per cent of the sectoral turnover, but in our case TRAI had imposed a cross-subsidy of 30 per cent of the sectoral turnover, mostly on fixed lines (thus raising their tariff enormously), which would have ruined the sector and rendered the fixed-line operation, for which it was meant, unviable.

Fortunately, the incumbent BSNL protested against the scheme that the resultant high tariffs would kill the fixed lines, and this representation gave us the opportunity to modify the ADC scheme to around 10 per cent of the sectoral turnover, with the majority of the ADC being imposed on mobiles, the new technology whose introduction was the rationale for this cross-subsidy. The subsidy was also limited to five years, reducing every year.

Further, we did not want the fixed telephones to go down. As a matter of fact, in this period all countries wanting to be aggressive on introduction of broadband—like South Korea, China, Vietnam and many others—were taking measures to increase fixed telephony, the only vehicle for broadband at that time, with wireless broadband not yet having stabilized. But we could not increase fixed lines, perhaps on account of the need for taking too many permissions from all kinds of insensitive agencies.

The second and the third problems were the high carriage and termination charges. Since these elements of the telecom network were in the nature of monopolies, we reduced these charges to the bone and allowed operators to fix call initiation charges on their own, since at this level there was plenty of competition. Later, this change enforced in India was recommended to all European countries by the European Commission (now the European Union). We also made significant changes in the regulations, consistent with the best practices around the world, as compiled and explained in the InfoDev book.

Most of these measures were challenged in the TDSAT, which often declared them illegal. We took such cases to the Supreme Court and ultimately won all cases.

Had the regulator's actions not been approved by the SC, we would have had apologetic reforms and a poor sector growth, only catering to the incumbent's interests. It is normal that a regulator studies the powers enumerated in the Act, reads the best practices around the world, and enforces the best practices consistent with the network by means of issuing orders and regulations. If, subsequently, some of the regulations/orders are set aside only after interpreting the Act in parts, reforms have no future in any sector. As detailed in Chapter 5, the telecom sector owes most of its growth in India to the enormous time spent by the Supreme Court interpreting the provisions in the totality of the reform act. The incumbents who opposed the progressive regulations were so powerful that the government, which had issued the reform act, censured me for going to the Supreme Court too often to ask for the act's final interpretations. We were lucky that the Supreme Court invariably ruled in favour of the regulator's powers to intervene, and found our interventions legal.

These measures and the UASL increased competition in India and brought tariffs to the minimum, thus making mobile networks affordable so that they could reach the masses. The high subscriber numbers led to profits by mobile operators, even at rock-bottom tariffs.

Another problem was the high handset prices. We removed the minimum price regulation of this equipment, the sector having matured and government reduced import duty. This led to handsets becoming very inexpensive and affordable to the poorest. The consequent explosion in mobile numbers changed the environment and encouraged the TV channel Aaj Tak to do a programme, *Roti, Kapda aur Mobile*.

The best practices in telecom reforms in different countries, as identified in the *Telecommunication Regulation Handbook*, Module 1: Overview of Telecommunication Regulation, by InfoDev, were:[1]

- Increasing evidence that more liberalized telecommunications markets were growing and innovating faster and serving customers better.
- The need to attract private sector capital to expand and upgrade telecommunications networks, and to introduce new services.

- Growth of the Internet, which caused data traffic to overtake voice traffic in many countries, and led to the introduction of many new service providers.
- Growth of mobile and other wireless services, which provided alternatives to fixed networks and introduced new service providers to telecommunication markets.
- Development of international trade in telecommunication services which are increasingly provided by transnational and global service providers.

The book also explained the widely accepted regulatory objectives as:

- Promote universal access to basic telecommunication services.
- Foster competitive markets to promote efficient supply of telecommunication services, good quality of service, advanced services and efficient prices.
- Where competitive markets do not exist or fail, prevent abuses of market power such as excessive pricing and anti-competitive behaviour by dominant firms.
- Create a favourable climate to promote investment to expand telecommunication networks.
- Promote public confidence in telecommunication markets through transparent regulatory and licensing processes.
- Protect consumer rights, including privacy rights.
- Promote increased telecommunication connectivity for all users, through efficient interconnection arrangements.
- Optimize use of scarce resources, such as radio spectrum, numbers and rights of way.

These objectives were an important signpost for us at TRAI. It is important to note that the objective of the policy was not revenue maximization alone—as the press and the CAG have narrowly defined sometimes—but rather the fast growth and broader health of the sector and the various stakeholders. As I explain further in the book, we adopted many of these objectives when scripting our 2003 recommendations and regulations.

While the overall sector grew faster as the benefits of reform kicked in, rural tele-density continued to be a huge problem. It had grown from a mere 0.43 per cent in 1998 (despite huge government commitment and expenditure) to only 2 per cent in 2007. The phones installed were often non-functional and had to be periodically replaced at government expenditure. Everything changed when TRAI's proposals of 2005 for rural telephony, mainly extending mobile telephony and shared and subsidized towers to rural areas, were accepted with modifications by the government in 2006. Penetration grew from a stagnant 0.43 per cent in 1998 and 2 per cent in 2007 to about 50 per cent today in rural areas. Again, most of the funding requirements was being picked up by the private sector.

The Indian telecom sector became the best performing sector in India and the world, leading to huge private investments.

Telecom reforms started in 2003, allowing a level playing field among operators. Consequently, private operators started investing more. The sector-wise capital employed for the years 2005–06 and 2010–11 are given below (Table 2.1).

Table 2.1: Increase in Private Investment vis-à-vis Public Investment

Particulars	2005–06			2010–11		
	Public	Private	Total	Public	Private	Total
Capital Employed	1,05,784	64,303	1,70,087	89,066	2,40,866	3,29,932
Gross Block	1,26,546	73,297	1,99,843	1,97,339	2,71,018	4,68,356

Note: The 'capital employed' represents the funds necessary for a business to function or the funds deployed to operate the business. Capital employed is sum of net block, capital work in progress and working capital.

Source: TRAI book *Telecom Sector in India: A Decadal Profile*.

- The capital employed by public and private sector companies has shown a decrease of 16 per cent and growth of 275 per cent respectively, over the period of 2005–06 to 2010–11.
- The gross block has shown growth of 134 per cent.
- The gross block of public and private sector companies has shown an increase of 56 per cent and 270 per cent, respectively.

This has not happened in any other infrastructure sector in India. It is pertinent to mention that this reform allowed the operators to remain afloat and brought explosive growth, resulting in much higher earnings for the government than in the earlier entry-fee regime, as shown in Table 2.2 below.

Table 2.2: Government's Revenues from Telecom

Statement of revenues received by the Central government in comparison to revenues foregone (Rs in crore)

Year	Auction fees foregone	Government revenues	Cumulative Total
1999–00	1,603	–	–
2000–01	2,270	–	–
2001–02	2,734	–	–
2002–03	2,456	5,467	5,467
2003–04	2,470	9,098	14,565
2004–05	2,511	7,856	22,421
2005–06	2,591	8,620	31,041
2006–07	2,680	9,128	40,169
Total	19,314		
2007–08	–	11,911	52,080
2008–09	–	13,214	65,295
2009–10	–	13,588	78,883
2010–11	–	13,891	92,774

Year	Auction fees foregone	Govt. revenues	Cumulative Total
2011–12	—	16,011	1,08,784
2012–13	—	16,701	1,25,486
2013–14	—	18,766	1,44,252
2014–15	—	20,998	1,65,250

Sources: Column 2—1999–00 to 2006–07: Indicators for telecom growth, Study Paper No. 2/2005, TRAI; Column 3&4—2002–03 to 2009–10: Performance Audit Report on the Issue of Licences and Allocation of 2G Spectrum by the DoT, CAG; Columns 3&4—2010–11 to 2014–15 are from the TRAI website.

Before these reforms, there was very low mobile growth like in the fixed lines. Many of the operators did not give up the litigation path even then. For one small benefit or other, they went to the TDSAT and got most of the TRAI orders set aside on minor technical grounds. This continued till a Supreme Court bench comprising Justices Ruma Pal, B.N. Srikrishna and Dalveer Bhandari said: 'Limiting TRAI's powers to enforcing TTO (Telecom Tariff Order) would mean consequently, the entire scheme of the TRAI Act would become unworkable.'

Had TRAI not fought these cases, it would have become another toothless regulator, unable to bring growth or enforce competition. And the UPA government of eminent economists and reformers tried its best to ensure that TRAI would not take its fight to the Supreme Court.

Advent of 2G and the Birth of TRAI

Mobile with 2G technology came into India in 1995 after the launch of NTP 1994. Interconnection with the public operator was not easy. Consequent to multiple disputes, the high court asked the government to appoint a regulator in 1997, and the TRAI Act 1997, had to be promulgated. TRAI was appointed as the regulator under this Act.

In 2000, an amendment had to be passed for enforcing judicial review of TRAI decisions and for taking dispute issues out of TRAI's jurisdiction. TRAI got connectivity for mobiles with great difficulty. In 2002, the mobile tele-density—five years after setting up TRAI, seven years after introduction of private operators and almost a decade after Sam Pitroda left India—was 1 per cent. I mention this— as telecom literature often talks of Pitroda bringing in the mobile revolution. Nothing can be further from the truth. Prior to 1995, the Indian policymakers, including Sam Pitroda, had actively opposed the introduction of mobiles in this poor country. Thus, there were hardly any mobiles for nearly seven years after the induction of private players, and particularly none in villages. In the late 1990s, tariff was Rs 32 at both ends of the call. By 2002, we were adding 0.2 million subscribers a month and tariffs were Rs 4 per minute. Long-distance and international long-distance tariffs were up to Rs 80 per minute; telecom was an instrument of the rich and rural areas had almost no telephones. The few rural phones were placed at high cost to the government and rarely worked since most were defective and could not be maintained, being almost a single phone in a village.

The geographical coverage of mobile infrastructure in India was 20 per cent in 2002, in comparison to about 100 per cent in most developed countries, and much higher coverage in most African countries too. Today the mobile coverage in India is more than 80 per cent, which can easily be upgraded to mobile broadband coverage as most other countries have done.

Mobiles were introduced in most countries in the 1980s. Our policy planners blocked them till mid-1990s because they were supposedly expensive for our poor. The technology itself was not expensive. Poor density and numerous surcharges, similar to many other sectors, made it appear so. Early in the first decade of the millennium, no telecom manufacturer was prepared to look at India. The minuscule numbers of mobile handsets were mostly smuggled in by our rich. The fixed tele-density was always around 3 to 4 per cent for the decade before 2003, and is even so now.

Even when CDMA (Code Division Multiple Access) was allowed in 1995 to be operated by MTNL in Delhi, our service-wise licensing allowed this for a licensed fixed telephone only. Thus, we locked the phones so that they could not move outside the house. This was irrational since technology allowed mobility, but our locked mindset and licensing regime did not allow movement.

The scheme did not work and ultimately limited mobility in a local area was allowed to make the operators viable. This led to a war in the TDSAT and the Supreme Court between different classes of licensees. After some time, the rules were further changed in 2003, to allow full movement by the operators. This was done with the same payment conditions as for mobiles (one operator who had breached limited mobility rule in spirit was also fined heavily), and the sector again got embroiled in litigation in the Supreme Court between operators.

The disputes between the two classes of operators was successfully negotiated by Arun Shourie with the help of advice from the then solicitor general, leading to all cases in the Supreme Court and other courts being withdrawn, and the sector finally settled down. Increased competition and the benefits of scale for the individual operators led to reduced tariffs and, consequently, even faster growth. After all the Supreme Court cases were withdrawn by the operators, monthly additions jumped from 0.2 million to 2 million in 2004 and to 6 million in 2006 after further measures were taken by TRAI to encourage growth.

TRAI's proposals of 2005 for rural telecom were accepted with modifications for encouraging mobile telephones in rural areas in 2006. Rural tele-density jumped from 2 per cent to 20 per cent in two years, and to 50 per cent in 2015, and all at minimal subsidies. With mobile phones going into rural areas, the monthly additions jumped to 20 million, 100 times the growth rate of 2002–03 and three times the growth rate China ever achieved. Since the sector and competition had matured, TRAI allowed tariffs to be fixed by operators in 2003, and with increased competition, our telecom tariffs became almost the lowest in the world in 2003–04. They gradually fell even further. China was amazed at these developments in India and consulted TRAI to replicate such growth.

Despite the fall in tariffs, the operators made profits due to the huge growth in the number of subscribers. By 2010, most operators were making profits.

In 2001, to respond to the needs of convergence and draw advantage, the government had approved the Convergence Bill prepared with the help of the legal luminary Fali Nariman. This bill was referred by the Parliament to a Parliamentary Committee headed by Somnath Chatterjee, who was also a legal heavyweight. From the proceedings of the Committee it appeared that there was resistance to the bill by the incumbents. The bill was ultimately approved by the Committee in 2004 with some changes, but the timing of the implementation was left to the government. It has not been converted into an Act so far, as the Unified Access Licensing having been implemented it was thought that content could be left to another operator. With increasing digitization and evolution of many services on the Net that could never be anticipated earlier, it is time that the Convergence Bill is looked at again. TRAI gave its recommendations on Unified Access Licensing in October 2003. When these were approved by the cabinet, the cabinet asked TRAI to bring full Unified Licensing in six months (See Annexure 1).

During his oral evidence to the Joint Parliamentary Committee (JPC) on 14 September 2011, Vinod Vaish, the then secretary DoT, submitted that the concept of Unified Access Service Licensing regime was part and parcel of the TRAI recommendations. He drew attention to the summary of recommendations of TRAI dated 27 October 2003: 'In the interest of consumers of the telecom sector and to promote and ensure orderly growth of the telecom sector, the

Authority recommends that the country should migrate to Unified Licensing Regime for all telecom services. As a preparatory step, Unified Access Service Licence will be implemented for access services in each circle. Finally, within six months, Unified Licensing through an authorization process for all services...'

He also said that UASL evolved for the purpose of tackling the field level problems where service specific licences transgressed into the area of the other, and added that the cabinet had approved the UASL regime. In fact, the National Telecom Policy was amended to add Unified Access Licensing as a class of licence plus Unified Licence as well. It was mentioned that UASL was for a transition period of six months. As per Vaish, whatever the DoT did was with the understanding that what they were doing was for a transition period of six months. After this period, TRAI recommendations on pricing and allocation of spectrum would be received, and the rest of action would take place at that point of time.

The implementation of UASL along with reforms in regulations brought explosive growth to telecom by allowing all the technologies to provide voice telephony, reducing cross-subsidies and connection charges, and allowing operators to compete in a level playing field and giving them freedom to fix tariffs. The recommendations of TRAI on Unified Licences were given to the government in early 2005 but were not acted upon for a long time. This was the beginning of the 2G scam and led to many problems for the government, and its ultimate downfall.

The recommendations of the Somnath Chatterjee Committee were also not pursued, perhaps on account of opposition from some stakeholders, and also because the government moved to an alternative Unified Access Service Licence–Unified Service Licence route.

The government, through a notification in 2004, also brought broadcasting reforms within TRAI's jurisdiction, thus implementing partial unification of broadcasting without a legislative change. However, with increasing digitization of the medium and evolution of many more services on the Net (transmission medium), it is urgent that we consider far more seamless convergence of services again, as has been done in most other countries, to ensure far greater utilization of scarce resources in the sector, and a much higher demand on them.

DoT's action on UASL's recommendation of TRAI

We thought that the job was over when we gave a recommendation on Unified Access Licensing (UAL) in October 2003. Arun Shourie's reply to the CBI in 2011 allowed me to understand that the government had a much tougher job to pilot the change in the telecom sector following TRAI's recommendations.

Let me first try to explain the complexities of the problem and the job done at the government level in 2003.

Regulation under the NDA government

The context and the challenges of the sector are often forgotten when one tries to compare policy decisions across eras. Media pundits and the experts forgot the state of the sector and the economy when comparing policies being adopted by Maran and A. Raja after 2006 versus what had been done in 2003. They also forgot that the old regime could not continue after TRAI's specific recommendations on these issues in 2005. But these recommendations were not examined and were kept hidden in an almirah while Dayanidhi Maran and A. Raja ensured that business continued as usual.

When the controversies broke, and later became unmanageable in 2010, Raja perhaps had no choice but to state that he was only following Baijal's policies as recommended by TRAI in 2003. No one challenged him or asked him whether he had considered the subsequent 2005 TRAI recommendations. Maran did the same in 2006, after I left.

It is critical to understand the state of the telecom sector in 2003 before judging any of the TRAI recommendations at that time and the decisions the NDA government took.

- The sector was in a precarious condition, recovering from the high burden of the excessive bids operators had made for the licences in the 1990s. The shift to the revenue-sharing model had rescued it from collapse, but several questions remained on the viability of the sector.
- Few corporates or international companies were coming forward to enter the sector or to extend the coverage of the services that they were providing. One of the principal objectives of the government was to steer the sector on to a growth path and make it a compelling investment opportunity.
- The breadth of services being provided was concentrated in the relatively well-to-do parts of the country. Several circles like the north-east, Jammu and Kashmir (J&K), or even less-developed states like Bihar, were not seen as 'investible'. In fact, apart from BSNL, no operator had come forth to provide services in the J&K circle. In some circles (like Assam, Bihar, the north-east, Orissa, Madhya Pradesh) there was only one licensee, or a second operator had taken the licence but was hardly providing any service. There was not much of growth even in Calcutta (now Kolkata). Circles like Bihar, Haryana, Rajasthan, Punjab, Uttar Pradesh (East), were also suffering from slow growth. As a result, one of the principal concerns of the government was to extend communication services to these underserved areas.
- The sector was paralysed by litigation. The Wireless Local Loop (WLL) operators with CDMA technology and the mobile operators with GSM technology were at each other's throats. Almost nothing could be done that would not be challenged by one side or the other in the TDSAT, the high courts and the Supreme Court. The operators would file cases not just against each other but against the government also.

- As an example, no sooner had the cabinet decided to integrate the WLL and full-mobility services, the GSM operators moved the Supreme Court to stay any order that the government might issue in this regard.
- A major concern of the government, therefore, was to lift the sector out of this quicksand of litigation, and speed was of the essence to avoid a stay. It was also becoming apparent that the licensing system was being rendered obsolete by the advancement in technology, and the government had not been able to pass the Convergence Bill 2001, to deal with this.
- This was specifically noted in the National Telecom Policy of 1999. The Policy Paragraph 1.3 of NTP 1999 is cited in Paragraph 2.5 of TRAI 'Recommendations on Unified Licensing' October 2003. In particular, the NTP 1999 statement noted, 'Convergence now allows operators to use their facilities to deliver some services reserved for other operators, necessitating a re-look [sic] into the existing policy framework.'
- This is why the government set up the group on telecom and IT convergence in 2001. The way that technological advances were cutting the rationale of the licensing system, and also the way that the licensing system in turn was holding back the adoption of newer technologies, thereby harming the interests of consumers and the country, were the major themes of the TRAI report of October 2003, and the principal reason it recommended that government should replace the plethora of licences with a Unified Licence.

While the government had been able to establish the bidding route firmly in disinvestment, the experience with bidding in the telecom sector had not been altogether a happy one. When the sector had been first opened up and private operators had been invited to bid, they had filed grossly excessive bids as a result of which the sector had all but collapsed, and had to be rescued by abandoning the obligations ensuing as a result of the bids. Even though the fourth cellular licences were given as a result of a multistage bidding process in 2001, tele-density had not changed much since the bids in 2001. The bidding policy, with all its associated benefits of transparency and revenue maximization for the government, was sometimes myopic and counterproductive. It is only now that auctioning is being seen as the only mechanism to allot natural resources, bolstered by the CAG's recent view. The situation was different in 2003. Several areas of the country had not been taken up by any operator when the bids were invited for the fourth cellular operator. In March 2003, bids were again invited for these areas. As it became evident that not a single bid was going to be received, the government called off the entire exercise.

The changes implemented by the government after the TRAI recommendations were: an amended NTP 1999 and reduced revenue share. These brought all operators to the discussion table and convinced them to agree to the new scheme, leading them to withdraw all litigation in the Supreme Court and in other courts. This helped the sector rise from the morass it was in to become the best performing sector in the world.

The job of convincing multiple and litigant stakeholders to one scheme, and implementing the new scheme with everyone's consent in a no-litigation environment and without having to legislate, has no parallel in the Indian governance. The only parallel in the world is the job done by the New York commissioner/legislator, who ages back and without any litigation, divided New York into parallel streets and avenues, and changed the city for ever.

What did we achieve?

It is a matter of great pride for all of us who were involved that these steps more than fulfilled the objectives that the government had sought to pursue.

- The country's need at the time was to put the sector back on to a path of rapid growth.This was especially so in the underserved and unserved areas, as the contrast between the absence of services in these areas and the parts of the country in which services were growing was giving rise to the grouse that the former was being neglected. The turnaround was absolute, and 20 per cent geographical coverage in the past is 90 per cent today, and that too mostly at private sector expense.

- The sector was on the verge of collapse and the government had to adopt measures like shifting to revenue sharing, etc., in place of fixed annual licence fee based on bids to bring it back to normal.
- From being a rich man's toy, the mobile has become an adjunct of everyman's daily life. It has enabled the poorer craftsmen, small businesses and service providers, etc., to improve their businesses. It has enabled migrant labour to keep in touch with their families. In a word, it has been a boon to the poor as much as to the rich.
- At that time, operators used to charge Rs 28 to 32 per minute, since both the caller and the person called had to pay. Today, our rates are the lowest in the world.
- Our tele-density was far below the world average. Our position was 122nd in the list of countries with mobile telephones. Today, the Indian telecom network is the second largest network in the world.
- The sector was mired in a host of legal cases with private operators fighting each other, and every decision of the government was being challenged in court; now, litigation was brought to an end.
- Earlier, the government had to spend an amount close to Rs 20,000 crore every year for growth of telephone services in the country. Now, the telecom sector is contributing to the exchequer more than Rs 50,000 crore every year by way of licence fee, spectrum charges, service tax and other corporate taxes.

Reactions to the New Indian Telecom Policy of 2003

The growth model that evolved in India surprised many, and foreign governments and universities invited the chairman and members of TRAI to seminars around the world to explain the model. As the chairman of TRAI, I was invited to a seminar in Beijing University. By this time, I had incurred the displeasure of the telecom minister by disagreeing to his suggestion of not giving the Unified Service Licence recommendation, as directed by the cabinet in November 2003. I was not allowed to go I sent the secretary, TRAI (I had powers to approve his tour programme). He reported that the seminar was attended by four central ministers of the Chinese government, who were surprised at how India, a poor cousin of the Chinese growth model, could evolve a model which led to huge telecom growth.

Later, their operators visited TRAI to understand the model leading to the higher growth in India as compared to China as shown in Figure 2.1.

All this had been achieved by the government, working effectively along with the regulator, by taking hundreds of decisions in public

Figure 2.1: India–China Performance

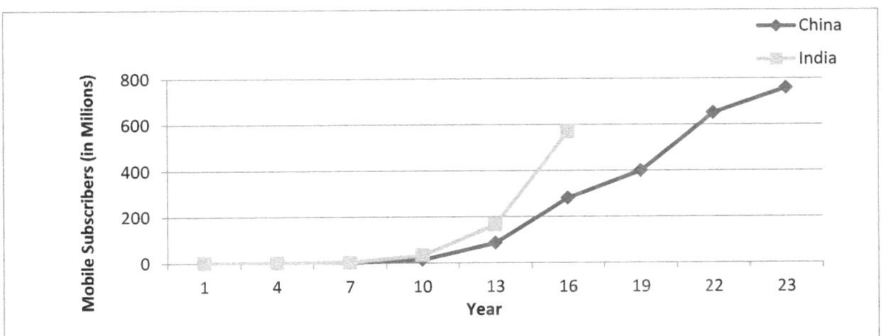

China Year* 1: 1988, Year 23: 2010

India Year* 1: 1995, Year 16: 2010

* When mobile telephony was started.

interest. There has been no such progress in any other network sector because aggressive decisions have not been taken and we continue to stagnate in growth in these sectors. Despite conservative plan targets in other sectors, we continue to underperform. Tariffs continue to remain high, further impacting affordability and inhibiting growth.

In 2010, the telecom sector overachieved the targets set by the government itself by over 300 per cent for both overall and rural tele-density and with heavily diminishing rural subsidy.

Consequently, there are huge balances in the Universal Service Obligation Fund (USOF), which can and are being used for the launch of rural broadband. Ironically, we have not yet given good roads or public transport to rural areas. Hopefully, it will be rural broadband that will join the millions of Indians who live in the hinterland to the international mainstream, if the sector's regulations are made growth friendly. At present they are not, though TRAI/ government has taken some initial steps.

International Recognition

TRAI's success gained international praise. The enormous growth in mobile numbers and steep fall in tariffs were noticed globally, and various regulatory institutions acknowledged the contributions made by TRAI.

a. Shosteck, a research group based in the US, wrote in 2004, 'This study analyzes the Indian mobile market to understand the lessons that it might offer the rest of the world. It concludes that India's "Unified Licence"—with which any operator can offer any access technology, whether landline or wireless—has enabled for more robust competition than otherwise would be possible.'
b. On 29 September 2005, the US regulator was quoted on Indiantelevision.com: 'When I look at all the steps that have been taken to encourage investment and innovation, if you look at where India is compared to other countries, it is one of the

shining stars. And a lot of that is owed to the head of regulator, Pradip Baijal. I think he has taken a bit of stick in India, but that is normal because most of the time when you are a regulator you're thinking about where you want your country to be in five or ten years while everyone else is thinking about today.'

c. A 2005 report titled 'The Indian Telecom Industry', produced by the Indian Institute of Management (IIM) Calcutta, said: 'Indian telecommunications today benefits from among the most enlightened regulation in the region, and arguably in the world. The sector, sometimes considered the "poster-boy for economic reforms" has been among the chief beneficiaries of the post-1991 liberalization...Despite several hiccups along the way, the Telecom Regulatory Authority of India (TRAI), the independent regulator, has earned a reputation for transparency and competence.'

d. Wharton Business School, in an article titled 'A Tale of Two Sectors: What Can Indian Telecom Firms Teach the Power Industry about Reforms?', complimented the efforts of the telecom regulator and drew a list of parallel measures which could be implemented in the power domain to replicate the success of the Indian telecom sector. It stated: 'India's telecom sector started out with many of the same drawbacks as power...when reforms began, the telecom sector was also the exclusive domain of inefficient, government-owned monopolies. It, too, needed competition and a massive infusion of private and foreign capital to improve efficiency. When reforms began in 1991, telephones were a luxury in India—the waitlist for one could stretch for years. As late as 1995, four years into liberalization, only one in a hundred Indians had a telephone, compared to two out of a hundred in Indonesia, four in China and eight in Thailand. Yet, though telecom reform started later than power, it has been far more successful. Between 2000 and 2005, India added about 18 million fixed phone lines and nearly 73 million mobile connections. Tele-density grew more than three-fold to 11.5 per cent; in urban areas to 34.7 per cent. Foreign companies such as Singapore Telecommunications and Vodafone have poured billions into Indian telecom, as have large Indian companies such as Reliance and the Tata Group. In 2005 alone FDI announcements for the telecom sector amounted to 2.5 billion dollars.'

e. The Frost & Sullivan Asia-Pacific Technology Awards 2004 were held in Singapore. An international panel of judges examined the performance of various regulators in the region and judged the TRAI as the Asia-Pacific Regulator of the Year, 2004. TRAI won the award for creating a regulatory environment which reduced uncertainty and discord.

f. The InfoDev *Telecommunication Regulation Handbook,* 2011, published by the World Bank, mentioned the impact of India's regulatory reforms on mobile penetration and price. It concluded: 'The implementation of an effective regulatory framework has resulted in greater economic growth, increased investment, lower prices, and better quality of service, higher penetration, and more rapid technological innovation in the sector. In fact, investors consider the regulatory environment to be a critical factor in their analysis of whether or not to invest in a country. Telecom Regulatory Authority of India (TRAI) has made a comprehensive reform (2003) of the regulatory framework to promote technological neutrality and take advantage of inter-modal competition. These regulatory efforts have brought economic growth to the sector and produced a marked increase in mobile subscribers and a fall in mobile tariffs.'

The Impact of India's Regulatory Reforms on Mobile Penetration and Price

Figure 2.2: Trends in IUC Mobile Tariffs and Subscriber Growths

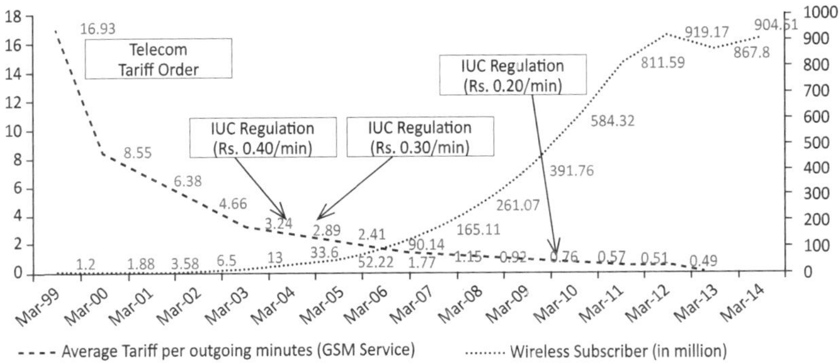

Source: InfoDev, *Telecommunication Regulation Handbook*, 2011 (modified to 2014 as per TRAI figures)

Grand Reversal

Fast forward to 2010, everyone responsible for this revolution faced well-publicized inquisitions in India for three years, though it was clear very soon after the inquiries started that there was no case against the actions taken in 2003–04. As explained earlier, within a few months, TRAI filed an affidavit in the Supreme Court, and the finance minister's report to the prime minister certified that no wrong was done during 2003–06. Yet the government's left hand intentionally did not know what the right was doing. The inquiries went on to confuse the public and undermine the truly revolutionary work conceptualized and implemented by the NDA (National Democratic Alliance) government and TRAI in 2003. I will deal with this in detail in the next chapter. But before going to the period from 2010 onwards, let me record that the licences were given during the NDA period in the most transparent manner, and in consultation/knowledge of all operators, leading to 'nil' complaints in this highly litigant sector. The complaints were only generated by the UPA government in 2010.

The Diversion: Licences issued in the NDA regime

To divert attention from the wholesale corruption that marked the process, allegations were made regarding the licences that were given during November 2003 and May 2004, when the NDA government was in office. In particular, the allegation was that the Tatas and Reliance were favoured. As chairman of TRAI, the CBI initiated proceedings against me and started a preliminary inquiry. To do so, against me as the regulator—a purely recommendatory figure—was surprising. I found myself trying to explain things that happened a decade ago and required a lot of nuanced knowledge of the sector and reform processes as pursued by the government. I did not have most of this knowledge till Arun Shourie jumped into the inquiry at his own discretion. Unfortunately, neither the media nor the investigative officers appeared to have the patience or domain knowledge to understand the issue at hand. The media trial which ensued was personally painful, and at times frightening.

This is what transpired.

Applications from the Tatas were pending for sanction to provide basic services in four circles since September. Letters of intent were issued to them in the normal course. These were sent out by the Licensing Cell (Basic Services Group) on 7 November 2003. Meanwhile, the government announced the guidelines for UASL on 11 November 2003. Tatas, by their communications dated 18 December 2003, surrendered the LoIs that had been given, and instead applied for and got UASLs. None of the four LoIs had been in Type A circles. They were all for Type B circles (basically the unwanted non-remunerative circles).

Tata Teleservices applied for UASLs in eight service areas on 12 November 2003. These were Bihar, Orissa, Rajasthan, Madhya Pradesh, Himachal Pradesh, Kolkata and Uttar Pradesh (East). These were all underserved and unpopular areas with very low tele-density.

Bharti applied for UASLs in six service areas, namely Bihar, Orissa, Rajasthan, UP (East), West Bengal, including Andaman and Nicobar Islands, and J&K. Once again, all these were underserved and unpopular areas with very low tele-density. Till the NDA demitted office, Bharti acquired the following licences: Bihar, J&K, Orissa (now Odisha) and UP (East) on 10 February 2004 and West Bengal on 11 February 2004.

Out of these five service areas, apart from BSNL, no other operator had ventured forth to provide services. While Bihar, Orissa and West Bengal circles were offered during the 2001 auction, no bidder had expressed any interest. In March 2003, DoT had again tried to auction these service areas. As it became evident that there would be close to nil response from possible operators, the auction process was abandoned at the last moment.

Vodafone Essar got two LoIs on 28 November 2003 and 13 February 2004 respectively. These were for UP (West) and West Bengal—both of which were underserved areas.

Dishnet Wireless got seven LoIs on 5 February 2004. These were for Assam, Bihar, Himachal Pradesh, J&K, the north-east, Orissa and West Bengal. Each and every one of these areas was so ill-served that there were charges of neglect by government of these poorer areas.

A glance at the tele-density in some of these circles for which data was available will show the situation that prevailed then as compared to 2010.

Table 2.3: Increase in Tele-density in Areas with Poor Connectivity

Service Area	Tele-density in per cent (2003)	Tele-density in per cent (2010)
Bihar	1.3	32.94
Jharkhand	1.6	
Jammu and Kashmir	2.5	50.69
Orissa	2.2	43.32
Uttar Pradesh	2.1	40.97
West Bengal	3.7	52.87
Andaman and Nicobar	9.6	
Assam	0.2	36
Rajasthan	0.6	62.6
Madhya Pradesh	0.79	44.8
NE excluding Assam	0.7	50.7

On the general question of licences given during that period, recall the facts that were set out earlier.

Today, there is a rush for licences; at that time few were coming forward to enter the sector or to extend the coverage of the services that they were providing. This is evident from the following table:

Table 2.4: No Rush for Limited Licences Given

Application Received (Month–Year)	No.	LOIs Issued (Month–Year)	No.
Nov–03	18	Dec–03	18
Dec–03	0		
Jan–04	0		
Feb–04	1	Mar–04	1
Mar–04	7	Apr–04	7
Apr–04	1	Apr–04	1
May–04	0		
Jun–04	1		

Application Received (Month–Year)	No.	LOIs Issued (Month–Year)	No.
Jul–04	0	Aug–04	1
Aug–04	0		
Sep–04	0		
Oct–04	0		
Nov–04	0		
Total	28		28

Second, such services being provided were concentrated in the relatively well-to-do regions of the country. As noted above, it is a matter of pride that the decisions of the government were implemented with such fairness and transparency, and the migration and other licences were given with such fairness and transparency that not a single objection was raised by any party—and this in a sector in which every step of the government had hitherto been challenged and denounced by one side or the other, in media or before courts.

Not a single question was raised in Parliament over what was done. When they saw the fairness and openness with which cabinet decisions were being implemented and licences being granted, the petitioners who had filed a petition in the Supreme Court to stay the implementation of the UASL regime withdrew the petition. The media also, otherwise very alert, did not see any problem in the changes being made.

'First-Come, First-Serve': Was it the wrong policy?

The policy principle of 'first-come, first-serve' has been in vogue for long, certainly before the time I joined the TRAI. It has been a fair mechanism to allocate natural resources across the globe and had been widely used even in India. Even the telecom sector had its own share of examples:

a. Guidelines for Issue of Licence for Basic Service, No. 10-2/2000-BS-II, Ministry of Communications, Department of Telecommunications, Licensing Cell (Basic Service Group), Sanchar Bhavan, New Delhi, dated 25th January, 2001.

   Clause 26 of this document reads in part: '. . . For Wireless Access Systems in local area, not more than 5+5 MHz in 824-844 MHz paired with 869-889 MHz band shall be allocated to any Basic Service Operator including the existing ones on first come first served basis. The same principle shall be followed for allocation of frequency in 1880-1900 MHz band for Micro cellular architect based system system.'

b. Procedure for Allocation of Spectrum on First Come First Served Basis, No: 10-2/2000-BS-II, Ministry of Communications, Department of Telecommunications, Licensing Cell (Basic Service Group), Sanchar Bhavan, New Delhi, dated 23rd March, 2001.

   Paragraph 1 of this document states, 'As per Guidelines issued for Basic Telephone Service providers, the spectrum for WLL service in the frequency of 824-844 MHz paired with 869-889 MHz is to be allocated on first come first served basis.'

Later that year, the Group on Telecom and IT Convergence submitted its report on limited mobility. The Group was headed by the then finance minister, Yashwant Sinha, and it elucidated the meaning of the principle 'first-come, first-serve' in regard to allocation of spectrum. Paragraph 25 of this report stated:[2]

> The Group noted that the description of 'first-come-first-served' used in the Guidelines of January 2001 was not an accurate description of the content of policy as announced and as implemented with reference to existing Fixed Service Operators. It does give the impression that immediately on application the applicant would become eligible for a spectrum licence, whereas

> in fact the Guidelines—especially when read with the spectrum allocation procedure of 23 March 2001, which stipulates the conditions under which the spectrum would be allocated—clearly require that the Operator seeking spectrum must have established a Point of Presence (POP) in an SDCA (Short Distance Charging Area) in order to be eligible for the first tranche of spectrum; further instalments of spectrum being given subject to fulfilment of roll out obligations which would include the obligation now mentioned in this advice, and to ensure that the spectrum already given has been optimally utilized.
>
> The 23 March 2001 Procedure also stipulates that in the event of roll out obligations not being fulfilled the spectrum allocated would revert back to the government. Hence, 'first-come-first-served' on a true interpretation only means that allocation of spectrum is and must be considered inextricably linked to performance.

The Group noted that the quantum of spectrum to be allocated to the fixed service providers for WLL with limited mobility is in accordance with the recommendations of TRAI.

In a word, 'first-come, first-serve' was a well-established and recognized method of processing applications.

In the report 'Recommendations on Unified Licensing' that TRAI submitted in October 2003, Paragraph 7.29 stated:

> . . . The allotted spectrum varies from 4.4+4.4 MHz to 10+10 MHz depending upon the number of subscribers in each service area. Existing BSOs [Basic Service Operators] shall be allocated 5+5 MHz in 824-844 MHz paired with 869-889 MHz bands on a first come first served basis. The same principle shall be followed for allocation of frequency in the 1800-1900 MHz band.

In contrast to what happened during Raja's time—when the finance ministry repeatedly objected to what he was proposing to do—during 2003, no objection was ever raised by the ministry.

In particular, the record on file establishes that the member (finance)—who represents the finance ministry on telecom affairs—specifically approved the decision that the 'first-come, first-serve' principle shall be observed.

In my view, 'first-come, first-serve' was a perfectly reasonable principle. It was never the sole criterion: the applicant was to have fulfilled a number of other requirements and these requirements were known to all at the time they submitted the applications. Only after they had fulfilled those requirements, would this criterion come into play.

Licensing Regime: The Migration to UASL

At TRAI, we were of the view that we slowly needed to create a unified licensing policy, whereby we would become technology-agnostic and promote convergence of services. Experts from the field had advised us of the upcoming convergence—and we wanted India to be able to benefit, and perhaps leapfrog the West through a forward-looking policy. Our recommendations had the following salient features:

i) Within six months Unified Licensing regime should be initiated for all services covering all geographical areas using any technology.
ii) Unification of access services at circle level should be taken up forthwith. For this consultations with various stakeholders had already been completed. This should be immediately followed up with steps to set out the guidelines and rules for Fully Unified Licensing/Authorization Regime by gathering details of international practices and through the consultation process (Paragraph 7.6 of the TRAI recommendations).
iii) To determine the benchmark of the entry fee for the UASL regime, TRAI had considered the option of inviting bids from existing as well as new prospective players and concluded that this option would be time-consuming and that it would delay the implementation of Unified Licensing. Accordingly, we had advised against it.

TRAI recommended that instead the existing entry fee of the Fourth Cellular Operator be accepted as the basis for fixing the entry fee for migration to Unified Access Licensing regime for Basic and Cellular services at the Circle level (Paragraphs 7.16 to 7.20).

iv) TRAI had stated that it would give its recommendations on efficient utilization of spectrum, its pricing and spectrum allocation procedure in the near future. We had done so to optimize spectrum allocation and price discovery, but believed that given the recent failed auction and the need to promote services in the underserved areas, opting for a payment similar to the fourth operator was the most prudent.

v) We, at TRAI, had stated that it was not in favour of high spectrum pricing since such a regime would make the services more expensive and the desired growth would not take place in telecommunications.

vi) TRAI advised that the formulation of an appropriate environment for growth, regulation and strategy had to be based on the single priority of the moment, viz., increasing the availability of phone connections at affordable costs and tariffs and ensuring fast roll-out of services. Indeed, that was the objective of the government. Growth of tele-density, it said, revolved around developing access networks and making access to them available at low cost.

vii) To achieve 100 million wireless subscribers, the TRAI team had estimated that an investment of the order of Rs 50,000 crore would be required, and that for investment of this order to come forth, a sector free of litigation was a prerequisite (Paragraph 6.5).

viii) TRAI had recommended that induction of new cellular mobile operators should preferably be done under the 'Unified Licensing Regime' expected to come into being (Paragraph 7.37).

ix) Yet two paragraphs later, TRAI recommended that if adequate spectrum was available, then in the *existing* Licensing Regime, government *may* introduce additional players through a

> multistage bidding process as was followed for the Fourth Cellular Operator.

There was a lot of confusion with respect to this paragraph, when looked in isolation. Did the TRAI recommend multistage bidding even in 2003? As is evident from the reading of the full recommendation, the recommendations were clear on the migration of existing basic service licence providers, and the fact that they had to pay equal to the fourth operator. In addition, it also stated that if the government wanted to ignore the UASL regime being recommended, it could continue with the bidding process in the pre-UASL regime, which was indeed the existing regime at that moment.

In its meeting on 31 October 2003, the cabinet decided:[3]

> The recommendations of TRAI with regard to implementation of the Unified Access Licensing Regime for basic and cellular services be accepted. DoT be authorized to finalize the details of implementation with the approval of the Minister of Communications and IT in this regard including the calculation of the entry fee depending upon the date of payment based on the principles given by TRAI in its recommendations.
>
> The recommendations of TRAI in regard to the course of action to be adopted subsequently in regard to the implementation of the fully Unified Licensing-Authorization Regime be approved. DoT be authorized to finalize the details of implementation with the approval of the Minister of Communications and IT on receipt of recommendations of TRAI in this behalf.

The cabinet decision clearly recognized that, as recommended by TRAI and by the Group of Ministers, the process of implementation would be in two phases. In the first phase, the Unified Access Licensing Regime would be introduced. In the second phase, after recommendations of TRAI in regard to a fully Unified Licensing

Regime had been received and approved by cabinet, that regime would be introduced.

In both phases, the details of implementation of the UASL regime and of the fully Unified Licensing Regime were to be worked out by the DoT with the approval of the minister of communications and IT.

As I read some of these documents after ten years, it was clear that TRAI's recommendations for the UASL regime were duly accepted and approved by the cabinet. The DoT was given all the powers to implement the recommendations as they saw fit. As I have mentioned earlier, the fact that the UPA was targeting me, the regulator, was surprising—I had only recommendatory powers and had not taken any decision. Further, all my recommendations were scrutinized and accepted by the industry, the various stakeholders (after the amicable settlement in particular), the DoT and the cabinet.

Further, as will be evident from both—the recommendations of TRAI and the decision of the cabinet—the UASL regime was a transitional phase. It was to be the first step towards putting in place a fully Unified Licence Regime. During this transitional phase, the DoT was to proceed with its usual duties using the price paid by the fourth cellular operator as the benchmark.

The cabinet never intended that the department should halt all expansion of services and, to take one instance, leave the unserved areas in a state of neglect.

What happened as a consequence was that an addendum was included—nothing was subtracted from NTP 1999—and two additional categories were introduced: henceforth, the DoT could issue licences not just for Basic Services, NLD (National Long Distance), ILD (International Long Distance), etc. It could in addition issue UASL and Unified Licences.

Had the cabinet directed the DoT to stop all further steps for extending services waiting for the final Unified Licensing Regime to come, the sector would have per force been frozen for over a year.

No sooner had the cabinet decided to introduce unification of licences, the cellular operators filed an application in the Supreme Court seeking a stay on the implementation of the UASL regime. This application became part of the appeal that had been filed earlier by the cellular operators against the TDSAT order of August 2003 in the limited mobility case.

Implementation of the cabinet decision therefore required careful handling of the litigation before the Supreme Court. DoT accordingly proceeded with the following objectives in mind:

a) Ensure that the decision of the cabinet regarding the UASL regime is not stayed as a result of the petition of the cellular operators; and
b) Implement the UASL regime in so transparent and fair a manner that the sector would indeed become litigation-free.

Through the law ministry, the services of the then solicitor general became available and were availed of by the DoT for handling this matter.

Implementation

The sequence of events in the implementation process was as follows:

i) Since there were pending applications for Basic Service Licences, these were dealt with in accordance with the usual procedure. Tata Teleservices had applied for providing Basic Service in four service areas in September 2003. LoIs were issued against these applications in the normal course for Basic Services on 7 November 2003
ii) On legal advice, including that of the solicitor general, in the guidelines for issue of UASLs resulting from migration, it was provided that all new applications for Access Services would be in the UASL category. The rationale for this was manifest: issuing of service-based licences, as was the practice till then, would have perpetuated the very aberrations which were sought to be

corrected by the UASL regime that the cabinet had directed the DoT to implement.

These guidelines were issued on 11 November 2003. This meant that henceforth neither applications for Basic Services nor new cellular mobile operators would be entertained. The new operators for access services could only be of the UASL category.

Going in for bidding for the new UASLs would have required determination of slots for auction in each service area in the CDMA technology and separately for those involving GSM technology. The bidding process would have been time-consuming. The government also had before it the fate of the bidding process that it had initiated as recently as in March 2003 when bids had been invited for the vacant slots for the fourth cellular operator, based on GSM technology, but no bids had been received and the process had to be cancelled at the last moment.

The main reason for this lack of response was evident to the government: the telecom sector had got entangled in litigation and, except for the existing lot of service providers, new entrants were not forthcoming. There was another important aspect which could not be ignored. Had all further permissions been stopped, and Reliance had proceeded to migrate on the basis of the cabinet decision of 30 November 2003, the government would have been open to the charge that it had favoured Reliance by stopping its competitors.

Apart from being unfair, such an outcome would have definitely resulted in the courts staying the TRAI report regarding multistage bidding process related to the introduction of additional cellular operators under the pre-UASL regime. As per the explanation provided by the ministry, they clearly argued that if it had been intended for new UASL operators, it would have been worded differently and the words 'existing regime' would not have been used. Thus there was no violation of the cabinet decision in this regard.

It is in this background that clarification was sought from TRAI by the then secretary, DoT, about how the new applications for UASLs were to be dealt with. The clarifications sought by the DoT were ratified by the entire TRAI, as was the process at that time. However, this too became an area of huge controversy. The CAG was not allowed to review all the available papers and presumed that I had given the clarifications individually in reply to a 'telephonic conversation' to secretary, DoT. This was not a surprising conclusion, since files had apparently been removed at the time of audit. When all the documents were later reviewed, it was clear that as per TRAI process, the issue had been discussed at length and ratified by the TRAI board. I do not blame the CAG since the conspirators had removed the files at the time of audit. Either way, the fact that the media was getting suspicious about two senior government officials seeking clarifications over the phone was hilarious, at least now in hindsight. As Shourie rightfully told the media once this controversy sparked off, 'What other means of communication would you expect the Secretary of the Department of Telecommunications to use! In any case, everyone knew that time was of essence with the stay application being heard in the Supreme Court.'

The entry fee recommendation which was benchmarked to that paid by the fourth cellular operator and which had been adopted for the purpose of migration in November itself had to be used for others also—otherwise the latter would at once get a ground for charging the government with tilting the playing field in favour of one or the other operators. Even the majority of the TDSAT in its judgment delivered as recently as in August 2003 had held that, while the introduction of WLL had been legal, it had upset the level playing field.

Tata Teleservices, who were the major competitor of Reliance, the cellular operators, Bharti and Hutch, who had applied for new UASLs, would, justifiably not have agreed to anything which would have put them at a disadvantage vis-à-vis Reliance. On this basis, in accordance with the recommendations of TRAI, a procedure was adopted for dealing with applications for new UASLs; and the new applications, which were few in any case and which were from operators with great experience in the sector, were dealt with.

The procedure adopted and the decisions taken were so manifestly fair and transparent that there was no controversy or allegation by anyone of any discrimination. No one challenged the approach or decisions in any court. No objections were raised in Parliament. There was no criticism in the media. And this position continued for six years in a highly litigious sector.

The procedure adopted for grant of new UASLs was simple and straightforward. The entry fee payable was based on the same principles as were followed for migrating from Basic Services to UASL. In November itself, Reliance migrated in eighteen service areas; Tata Teleservices in six areas; Bharti, HFCL and Shyam in one area each.

The applications were dealt with on a first-come, first-served basis, with date of application being the reference point for determining the priority. The procedure adopted had the concurrence of the member (finance) in DoT, and as required by the decision of the cabinet, it was approved by the minister of communications and IT.

There have been assertions that the procedures adopted for new UASLs were not notified and therefore were not transparent, and that many likely applicants were denied the opportunity to enter the field. However, it is clear that whatever actions were being taken in DoT at that time were in the public domain and were being closely watched by the media, the apex association representing the cellular operators, namely, the Cellular Operators' Association of India (COAI) and the apex association representing the basic service operators, namely, the AUTSPI (Association of Unified Telecom Service Providers of India) , previously known as the ABTO (Association of Basic Telecom Operators).

Litigation in the Supreme Court was being actively contested and all decisions of the DoT were under close watch. Everyone—including those who may be presumed to have been interested in entering the sector—was fully aware of what was being done.

The fact is that at the time, the sector was in a precarious condition and new entrants were not interested in entering it. There was also the pending litigation which had created considerable uncertainty in the minds of entrepreneurs.

Since no restrictions had been put on the number of operators in any particular licence area, anyone applying for the UASL could hope to be considered. No waiting list was created. The applications for new UASLs were from the well-known service providers. There was nothing surprising in Tata Teleservices trying to catch up with the other major CDMA service provider, namely, Reliance; or in Bharti trying to enter some more service areas so as not to lose market share of the mobile cellular market to Reliance and Tata Teleservices who, by availing of migration, were on the way to becoming full-fledged cellular mobile operators in their respective areas.

These aspirations of the existing set of operators were not unreasonable and were fulfilled without any issue of level playing field getting raked up, and no one was able to get stay orders from the Supreme Court on implementation of UASL.

The goal was to promote a litigation-free environment in the telecom sector which would lead to greater investments and facilitate its faster growth with healthy competition so as to attain a target of 100 million mobile phones by the end of 2005. The steps taken to implement the UASL regime were completely in harmony with the cabinet decision. The UASL regime was implemented and the court cases were withdrawn.

The granting of new UASLs did not favour any particular operator; it was done by general application. Only well-established operators submitted applications for new licences, and this position continued till the end of 2004 by when only twenty-eight LoIs were issued. In fact, no applications were received in the period from July to November 2004. The fact that there was no rush to get the licences and no waiting list for several months in the latter half of 2004 amply demonstrates that the UASLs were not found to be cheap and that there were not many takers of these licences in CDMA or GSM platform.

On the other hand, delay in processing the new applications or any decision which entailed applying any other principles for determining the entry fee would have opened the government to the charge of favouring one or the other of the operators and blocking the path of other competitors. As noted earlier, this would have certainly led the court to stay the operation of the UASL regime and thus thwarted the decision of the cabinet.

In addition to attending to the routine tasks that had to be implemented during the interim period, we began exchanging views about elements of the unified licensing regime. Should the bids be single-shot bids as was the case in disinvestment? Or should the bidding be multistage? Should the bids be conducted by the DoT—a department that had itself been dragged into much litigation, and was the object of strident allegations—or should they be conducted by an independent agency? How should incentives be built into the bidding process to induce optimal use of the spectrum, and penalties for hoarding or inefficient use? What should be the stance of the government if, once again, the competitors overbid and then could not sustain their operations at the high prices they had paid? Should they be rescued as had to be done when the sector was first opened up? Or had the sector become mature enough by now so that firms that overbid should be allowed to go under?

These were the sort of questions on which DoT had begun work in the wake of the six-month framework suggested by TRAI.

Then the government changed, and the advance towards the

unified regime was halted despite a clear cabinet order, which no one openly tried to reverse. The procedures which were only to be followed for an interim period of six months were made permanent, and TRAI's recommendations of January 2005 were not considered.

TRAI regulates one of the most competitive and largest markets of the world. Both the government and TRAI contributed to this performance, by playing their respective roles with unlike what happened in other sectors. When I retired, it was the proudest moment in my career as a government officer. Others in service recognized this. Several senior UPA ministers, corporate chiefs and government officials personally congratulated me. It was perhaps this reason that getting investigated for those same decisions was all the more difficult to accept personally. It is surprising that while inquiries went on against me and the then minister for three years, no one in government or the CAG has yet bothered about the conspiracy of removing papers from government/TRAI files.

What would have happened if the government had not replaced the huge entry fee by revenue share? What would have happened if unified access licensing had not been introduced? Perhaps the rest of the book will help the reader in finding answers.

3

The TRAI Cases

At the heart of the 2G case against me was the mysterious disappearance of crucial government and TRAI files. The facts were withheld from the CAG by some people in the government. The missing files raised questions on the nature of decisions taken by the TRAI, and the CAG was tricked into erroneously submitting an adverse remark against me regarding some decisions TRAI took in 2003. A. Raja, the then minister for telecom and the chief accused in the 2G scam, swore through a false affidavit, believing that the truth would never come out before the Supreme Court, and tried to pin the blame of his actions of 2008 on recommendations made by me, and not TRAI, in 2003. I believe that the people in the DoT decided to play up this irregularity to create a diversion. Yet the CBI pursued its inquiry with enormous publicity, perhaps at the behest of interested corporate, government and non-government players. Truth, unfortunately for intriguers, has a tendency to come out in all its glory along with the documents. Maran's letter to the prime minister in 2005 indicates he was party to the conspiracy. Ministers do not pressurize bureaucrats beyond a point if they do not comply with the political executive's illegal oral directions. I did not understand for years why this was not so in this case. It was only recently that I understood the rationale for this illogical behaviour—the huge amounts of havala transfers that the CBI discovered in 2G transactions. These were perhaps too tempting for the political executive to resist. An analysis of the conspiracy will prevent similar attempts in future.

At the beginning of this chapter, let me state that I have not written anything which is not supported by documents. I have only narrated the facts sequentially to conclusively prove the conspiracy and the rationale of the actions of the scamsters. The four-year inquiry in this case, and the other cases that followed, forced me to hunt for documents and files in the government with the help of old colleagues, and through other sources, mostly the press. I am grateful to the government, and the incompetence of its advisors, who despite knowing that the truth was on my side, believed that they could suppress facts in an open society, press and the right to information (RTI). Today, perhaps, I know more about the 2G scam than its perpetrators.

The Inquiry against Me

Soon after the much publicized inquiries against me were started in November 2010, I met Yashwant Sinha at a social function. He warned me that the inquiries did not have much to do with me and were actually aimed against Arun Shourie and the NDA. He said that the UPA ministers did not have the guts to start inquiries against Arun Shourie directly and had picked on me. Of course there could be other reasons. Maran had told me that I should not give recommendations for Unified Licensing as directed by the cabinet in December 2003, but I had not obliged. The prime minister had also asked me to cooperate with him, but I had told them that if

I do not give recommendations the spectrum may be sold at old rates, and there would be a scandal too big to handle. This is what happened in the 2G scam after I left TRAI, and they were perhaps upset with my non-cooperation. If I had cooperated, I felt that the entire blame would fall on me for not having complied with the cabinet's orders. All senior political leaders would have sidestepped as they did in Coalgate and other scams leaving most of the blame on bureaucrats, and leaving me with no choice—damned if you do, damned if you don't.

When the inquiry started, as advised by Yashwant Sinha, I tried to meet Arun Shourie. But he had left active politics and was living in a cottage in Lavasa. I rang him up and with his permission, met him at Lavasa with all the documents and spent time with him discussing the case. He immediately understood that if the conspirators were successful against me, mud would also fall on him and the NDA. Without further ado, he jumped into the fray by writing to the CBI director that the UASL was planned, supervised and executed by him, and there was no point in examining the secretary, Vinod Vaish, and the chairman. He had to be called for evidence and he attended it in a blaze of media attention, with journalists at the gates of the CBI office at the time of his arrival and departure. On similar occasions, and during the CBI raid on my house and my bank locker, I had felt embarrassed with journalists and TV cameras all around. But Arun Shourie said that we must go proudly to the CBI office and face them; after all we were trying to help the state to find out the truth. He was also of the view that those called should send their written statements to the CBI with documents, immediately after the event, lest any oral statement is later misinterpreted or not written properly.

Another politician who stood by me during my ordeal was the late N.K.P. Salve, my former minister in the Ministry of Steel and Power and a Member of Parliament from Betul, when I was collector, Betul, in 1973. After the controversy broke, he himself asked me to visit him at his New Friends Colony house. He told Harish Salve (his son) to help me, and that he would pay my fee if Harish charged it. He knew I could not have afforded his son's fee. Salve's advice to me was enormously helpful. He also rang up P. Chidambaram and told him that he would advise not to initiate inquiries against me, since knowing me well he was sure that I would never commit an irregularity or be careless on file. He also said that an inquiry, if started against me, would be embarrassing for the Congress party later. It took me five years to prove him right. Arun Jaitley, with whom I had worked when he was disinvestment minister and an eminent lawyer, also helped my team of lawyers to deal with the case.

The Background to the Conspiracy

We achieved unparalleled growth in the telecom sector after 2003. While we were basking in the encomiums being showered on us from around the world, little was I aware, except some indications given to me in 2006 itself, by the late G.L. Sanghi, a senior Supreme Court advocate who was our lawyer in many TRAI cases, that a conspiracy was being hatched to discredit me and these reforms. He was so concerned about this conspiracy that he telephonically requested Sri Khan, an eminent criminal lawyer in the Supreme Court, that he should advise me in his absence if any case was started against me. He was at that time going to the USA on a holiday. He unfortunately never came back and had a heart failure at Frankfurt airport. The third TRAI completed its term in March 2006, and I forgot what had happened earlier.

The complaints on 2G reforms done by the NDA, the articles written by many journalists, including the article by J. Gopikrishnan on the fraudulent structuring of bidding companies, the letter written by Subramanian Swamy to the prime minister on frauds during spectrum allocation, and the PILs filed by Subramanian Swamy, Prashant Bhushan and others, the agitations by Baba Ramdev and Anna Hazare, the CAG reports and the SITs set up by the Supreme

Court in 2010 spread panic in the UPA-II. They were earlier overconfident that no one could touch them. Since there seemed to be an open-and-shut case against Maran and A. Raja, and also their collaborators in the government, a conspiracy was implemented which could deflect the criticism on to the previous government for the carefully implemented scams after 2006. Let us examine the different aspects of this conspiracy.

The Conspiracy

First, some files of TRAI were removed, leading to an erroneous conclusion in the CAG report,[1] Paragraph 3.1.7, of November 2010:

> 3.1.7-—The DoT's action of applying the rates approved for the existing operators for migrating to UAS regime, to new applicants also by relying on the clarification of the Chairman TRAI in his individual capacity was inconsistent with the recommendation of the TRAI (2003) and went beyond the authority given by the Cabinet.

Immediately after tricking the CAG into giving this adverse remark against me, A. Raja on 8 November 2010 filed a false affidavit in the Supreme Court and made public statements saying that all he had done was follow the recommendations given by me in 2003. At this stage, the content of the CAG report had not come out in the press, but obviously Raja was keeping track. There was urgency to unveil the conspiracy on account of the enormous criticism of 2008's 2G scam in 2010. The CBI inquiry against me started immediately thereafter, and I received the notice on 22 November 2010. His plea of innocence was that he was misguided by my actions, which were illegal as per the CAG's report. The government immediately followed this up with a high-profile CBI inquiry which made repeated headlines in all the newspapers. The case they were trying to present was simple: We did not auction the spectrum and applied the same rates as applied by the previous NDA government to new applicants. Don't blame us; the real fault, if any, lies with the previous government/TRAI chairman.

This can only be described as a travesty of truth for several reasons. First, TRAI is only a recommendatory body and it is the government which has the powers to accept or reject the recommendations. Thus, the policies were approved by the government, on the basis of TRAI recommendations. If Raja had said that as a minister, he only followed the policy approved by Arun Shourie, the telecom minister from 2003 to 2004, and the cabinet during the NDA regime, he would have at least been technically correct even if factually inaccurate. Instead, he spoke about following Baijal, which was absolutely fallacious.

The CAG in the paragraph quoted above had said that the Department of Telecommunication's action relied on the clarification of the chairman, TRAI, in his individual capacity. This was incorrect, and everyone in DoT knew that all decisions in TRAI were taken/endorsed in the Authority's meetings. The crucial file simply went 'missing', as did many other files, as explained in a finance ministry note of 25 March 2011 (See Annexure 2). That this omission was not an innocent mistake is clear from the fact that as per regular procedure when the draft CAG report was sent to the DoT for comments, none of its officers pointed out that the paragraph of the draft report was wrong. The officers were obviously under pressure to stay silent, and did not chose to side with the known truth. That the government can compromise files of DoT and TRAI, sent to the CAG is a serious matter, and should be investigated further for remedial and criminal action.

TRAI comprises five members. Apart from the chairman, there are two full-time and two part-time members. As per standard procedure, action on any urgent matter can be taken after obtaining concurrence of the chairman and full-time members on file. The decision is then placed before the full body by the advisor concerned in the next monthly meeting for confirmation. Thus, any urgent decision taken in anticipation of TRAI approval has to be ratified in the next meeting after the advisor concerned makes a presentation. The rationale for this arrangement was that if TRAI had to take a decision urgently, it did not need to wait for the monthly meeting. Such arrangements are the norm in all multi-member bodies, including the cabinet. After all, TRAI could not tell its stakeholders that it took policy decisions only once a month. This was precisely the procedure adopted for the approval under question, in a case everyone knew the SC was hearing on a day-to-day basis, and required immediate clarification to the government.

The letter of 14 November 2003—which was alluded to in the CAG report and which was the lynchpin of the case against me in the CBI and the Joint Parliamentary Committee inquiry—is reproduced below:

> Pradip Baijal
> Chairman TRAI
> November14, 2003
>
> My Dear Vinod,
>
> Kindly refer telecon regarding entry fee of the new unified licensees.
>
> In this regard I am reproducing para 7.18, 7.19 and 7.20 of our recommendations:
>
> 7.18 The 3rd alternative is that the existing entry fee of the fourth Cellular Operator would be the entry fee in the new Unified Access Licensing Regime. BSOs would pay the difference of the fourth CMSP's existing entry fee and the entry fee paid by them. It may be recalled that, even in the past, entry to cellular and basic services has been on fixed fee basis, e.g. for metros in the case of cellular and the second BSO.
>
> 7.19 It is recommended that the 3rd alternative as mentioned

in para 7.18 above may be accepted for fixing the entry fee for migration to Unified Access Licensing regime for Basic Cellular services at the circle level.

7.20 In service areas where there is no fourth operator—viz. Bihar, Orissa, W.B. & A.N. and Assam etc.—no extra entry fee would be charged from the existing operators migrating to the Unified Access Licensing Regime, since in these areas operators did not see a potential market at the time of repeated bidding for the 4th cellular operators.

It would be clear from the above that entry fee of the new unified licensee would be the entry fee of the 4th cellular operators and in service areas where there is no 4th operator - the entry fee of the existing BSO fixed by the government (based on TRAI's recommendations). Incidentally, in such states where no 4th cellular operator came in, the entry fee for BSOs was fixed by the government and as per our recommendations in para 7.20 above, it will be the same for new or existing unified licensee.

With regards,
Yours sincerely,

(Pradip Baijal)

Soon after the CBI inquiry started, I was shown the letter in the CBI office in November 2010. From the trend of questioning, it was clear that they were making a case on the following lines:

a. That I had issued the clarification which the CAG in para 3.1.7 of its 2010 report said I had issued in my individual capacity without requisite ratification as there were no ratification papers.
b. The clarification helped the Tatas.
c. I had joined the Tatas after retirement which proved quid pro quo.

Based on this line of inquiry, the CBI officers confidently asserted that this was an open-and-shut case since they had sufficient material to register an FIR and to arrest me.

I told the investigating officer (IO) that there had to be a file showing the approval of all members of TRAI on the clarification mentioned in the letter. I was shocked when the CBI officers said there were no such files or papers. When I asked the CBI officials to give me access to the files they had with them which supposedly proved their case, they refused. They said that all documents would be provided when the charge sheet was filed, and it would be filed soon.

Flummoxed by the reply, I went through the papers kept by me after retirement. Sure enough, I found two letters and an agenda note that clearly showed TRAI's approval had been obtained. Here, I must express my gratitude to the former Attorney General Ashok Desai and the UK power regulator, Prof. Stephen Littlechild, who had warned me that if one faced an inquiry after retirement, one would not be given access to any files and papers, and therefore, it was important to prepare for inquisitions during service itself by keeping copies of important papers. Ashok Desai had also warned me that some of the documents may be removed later. I had taken his advice and kept some important papers. I was fortunate that I did so because in this case, the same happened.

The two letters and an agenda note conclusively proving my case are reproduced below:

D.O. No. 101-35/2003-MN November 19, 03

Subject: Recommendation of the TRAI on issues relating to Spectrum

Dear Shri Gupta,

Please refer to TRAI's recommendations dated 27.10.2003, para 7.30 of the recommendation states that efficient utilization of spectrum by all service providers is of utmost concern to the Regulator. TRAI has further mentioned that it will shortly provide recommendations on efficient utilization of spectrum pricing, availability & spectrum allocation procedures. DoT vide their letter No. 848-1139/2003-VAS/5 dated 12.11.2003 had asked TRAI to submit its opinion on spectrum-related issues at the earliest.

In para 7.31 of TRAI recommendations, it was mentioned that while operators may be issued unified access licence they should continue to provide wireless services in the already allocated contracted spectrum and no additional spectrum would be allocated only because of migration. It has been further recommended that there shall be no change in spectrum allocation procedure as part of migration process then the principle is that the prevailing spectrum allocation procedures should continue till fresh guidelines are issued by DoT. This principle can be applied in the interim period for the new entrant also.

Thus in the interim period before the TRAI recommendation on efficient utilisation of spectrum etc. become available, if the licensor has to issue any Unified Access Licence to new applicants, TRAI feels that spectrum to new licensees may be given as per existing terms & conditions relating to spectrum in the respective licence agreement. This implies that even though Unified Access licence is service and technology neutral, spectrum under the new unified licence for offering mobile services may be allocated in the interim period on the technology used for offering these services. For example, if a new unified access provider is offering wireless mobile services using GSM technology then the allocation/contracted spectrum to existing cellular mobile licences may be provided and for those CDMA technology spectrum allocation as per the provision of basic service operators licence can be considered.

Regarding entry fee to new unified access licensees, the matter has already been clarified Chairman TRAI's d.o. letter 14th November, 2003 (copy enclosed)

This issues with the approval of Authority.

Harsh Vardhana Singh

Shri J.R. Gupta.
Sr. DDG (VAS)

Clearly, this letter of 19 November not only confirms the content of the letter written by me, but also confirms that this has been issued with the approval of the Authority (TRAI). The second letter also references the letter written on 14 November and again confirms that the reply was approved by the full Authority.

No 101-29/2003-MV-Vol (1)

Date: 4th December, 2003

Shri A.S Verma, Director (VAS-II)
Department of Telecommunications

Sub:- Issues relating to Entry Fee for Unified Access Services Licence (UASL)
Ref:- DoT's letter no. 842-439/2003-VAS dt. 21st November, 2003

This is with respect to above referred letter of DoT, which seeks a clarifications regarding entry fee for the new Unified Access Licensee in West Bengal (excluding Kolkata).

The above matter has been addressed in Clause 7.24 of the TRAI's Recommendations dated 27th October, 2003.

Relevant extract of Clause No. 7.24 of TRAI's recommendations on Unified Licensing Regime dated 27th October 2003 are as follows:-

'Since the service area for unified licensee will be as per existing CMSPs, it means existing BSOs in Maharashtra, Tamil Nadu and West Bengal will get two unified licences (one for Metro city Mumbai and the other for the rest of Maharashtra and so on). The difference of entry fee to be paid by them will be divided between Metro city licence and the rest for the circle on pro rata basis of entry fee of the 4th cellular operators.

In West Bengal, there is no fourth cellular operator, so while migrating to Unified Access Licensing Regime, the BSO in West Bengal will not pay any extra entry fee. The same BSO in Kolkata, if it so desires, will have a separate Unified Access Licensing Regime by paying the difference in the entry fee paid by him for West Bengal and the entry fee of the fourth Cellular operators.'

On this basis the entry fee for Kolkata is (Rs 78 crore–Rs 25 crore= Rs 53 crore) and for rest of West Bengal is zero. Since for Cellular Services Andaman & Nicobar is part of West Bengal (Excluding Kolkata), for Unified Access Service Licence also the service area will be West Bengal (excluding Kolkata) and including Andaman & Nicobar will be Rs 1 crore. Please also refer to TRAI's letter dated November 14, 2003 wherein the issue of entry fee for new Unified Access Service Licence (UASL) has been explained.

Considering the above, as already specified in TRAI's recommendations and subsequent clarification dated November 14, 2003, the entry fee for new UASL in West Bengal including Andaman and Nicobar is Rs 1 crore.

This issues with the approval of the Authority.

(Ashish Narayan)
Dy. Advisor (MN)

In the final JPC report,[2] the chairman also observed: 'Regarding the background of the D.O. letter dated 14 November, 2003 written by the former Chairman, TRAI, the Committee have been informed that the letter had the ex-post facto approval of the Authority'. There was thus no adverse comment on TRAI or me in the JPC report. I also found the agenda note for ratification dated 17 November 2003, reproduced below, further proving that TRAI approval was obtained:

> Vide our letter dated 14th November, 2003 it was clarified to DoT that the entry fee of the 4th cellular operator and in service areas where there is no 4th operator-entry fee of the existing BSO fixed by the government (based on TRAI recommendations). Incidentally, in states where no 4th operator came in, the entry fee for BSO's was fixed by the government and as per TRAI recommendations, it will be the same for new or existing unified licensee.
>
> This issues with the approval of Advisor (MN).
>
> Sapna Sharma, Technical Officer (MN).

It was then that I realized that the adverse remarks of the CAG against me had been engineered by suppressing these crucial papers from them. I am also grateful to the then CBI, who gave me two occasions to explain, and then many more before filing an FIR (which was ultimately not filed).

Armed with the papers which clearly disproved that I acted in my individual capacity, I marched into the CBI office for a second meeting. When I showed the CBI officials the documents in my possession, I could see that they were extremely disappointed. They obviously had a brief from their 'masters'. This time they showed me the files, albeit with great difficulty. I was able to find the same documents, as shown above, in different files and also letters written to the government that the matter was ratified by TRAI. The letters were available in a number of files as it is normal government practice to mark copies of such letters to all concerned. Thus, any government letter gets attached to different files. The main file continues to be missing even today.

Despite having demolished the basis of the inquiry against me in 2010 itself, the inquiries continued, including a well-publicized CBI raid on my house later in mid-December 2010, with a large number of TV cameramen accompanying the CBI team. It was then that I realized that I was not facing an inquiry, but a carefully designed conspiracy by the 'who's who' in UPA-II.

Though this was not relevant to the inquiry, I was quizzed about joining the Tatas. I told the CBI that this was totally baseless as I had never joined the Tatas. I had only acted as a consultant to Tata Teleservices and Tata Steel on specific issues. The Tatas were amongst a large number of entities including World Bank, International Telecommunication Union (ITU), foreign governments, Indian companies and MNCs who had given me consultancy assignments. I gave them a list.

What I found amusing was the misunderstanding that the clarification, which was at the centre of the case, had not helped the Tatas or Reliance. However, I did not expect the policemen to understand the complexities of telecom regulation. I explained to them and later to the JPC, and also gave the JPC a written statement, that the Tatas and Reliance being fixed operators could be given licences and spectrum under the UASL approved by the cabinet. The 14 March 2003 clarification, if at all, had helped Airtel and Vodafone. I also explained that the entire scheme was approved in the presence of all operators in a meeting taken by the telecom minister. Again, they were disappointed.

This was not the end. Truth repeatedly came out, as it usually does, but it did not prevent CBI and the UPA government continuing with the inquiry and initiating more inquiries that were even more fraudulent.

Arun Shourie told me during the inquiry that TRAI had also filed an affidavit (See Annexure 3), in February 2011, before the Supreme Court in the case filed by Subramanian Swamy[3] against the Union of India, Ministry of Communications and Information Technology and others—Writ Petition (C) No. 10/2011—an application by the petitioner for impleading eleven persons, to whom licences were given in 2008 in respect of 2G spectrum. TRAI had stated that whatever we in TRAI (during 2003–06) or the government had done was right. TRAI, which had much better access to all papers, had filed the following affidavit in the SC in Swamy's writ petition.[4] Paragraphs 15 and 16 of the affidavit, relevant to this case are reproduced below:

Year 2003:- CAG not right

Paragraph 15

New entrant decision was taken by TRAI as authority on 19.11.2003.

Cabinet endorsed TRAI recommendation for migration on 4th operators price:- (CAS Comp. Vol. II, Pg.46-74) [Once migration to UASL at 2001 price approved, then New UASL at the same time could not be issued at the different price. Difference would give entrenched player an advantage in the same time space and would have breached Article 14]

Cabinet said UASL be worked out on the principles set by TRAI in rules. So the clarification by TRAI could be accepted. [The other part of Cabinet decision relating to 'Spectrum Pricing formula' does not relate to entry fee. It pertains to spectrum charge].

However TRAI has no role in executive decision making of government and if it is felt that Cabinet decision was required then it was for DoT to ensure it.

Paragraph 16

Considering the 2003 situation of nascent development, the backdrop of two migrations, introduction of UASL as a first step towards fully unified licence and Cabinet approval to this, the initiation of the consultation process by TRAI for unified licence, the stage of development then, as well as the long passage of time the Legality of grant of licence in year 2004 should be accepted.

Arun Shourie felt that the inquiry would cease immediately after this affidavit. However, the CBI and JPC continued with their inquiries and adverse publicity, clearly revealing that the main idea behind the inquiries was not the inquiries themselves, but the adverse publicity including the oft-repeated news of my likely arrest. The owner of one TV channel told me that the source of the news was CBI. Despite the length of the inquiry, the CBI in its wisdom did not deem it fit to question TRAI on the affidavit filed by them in the Supreme Court holding everything right despite CBI vigorously pursuing a fraudulent inquiry; nor did the media make the connection and dig out the affidavit. The TRAI chairman, J.S. Sarma, himself told me that the CBI had not questioned him. God bless the late J.S. Sarma for having the courage to file this affidavit. I asked him why he submitted it in such an adversarial environment. He replied that suppressing the truth always proves costly, since ultimately it always comes out in the open. Whenever new truths came out courtesy activists, some journalists sometimes gave me copies. I kept them carefully, and used them during the conspiratorial inquiry. However, those who gave me papers said that they did not have the courage to openly confront the government/ CBI with these documents. The inquiries continued.

As had been predicted by the late J.S. Sarma, the uncomfortable truth came out, this time in the finance ministry report to the PMO. This report clearly showed that everyone who mattered in the UPA-II government was involved in the post-2006 telecom scam, the documents kept missing, actions were not taken as per decision taken in inter-ministerial meetings, perhaps because that had become the normal practice in the government, particularly in the DoT, and the scam had no relationship with 2003–06 actions.

Unfortunately, the Shivraj Patil Committee report did not examine the issues in detail, despite the facts being known to officers of the DoT, who advised Justice Patil in writing the report and gave him documents in a closed room. I will discuss this later in the book.

Obviously, the facts in the FM's report were known well to the officers in the DoT, but were not shown to the judge, and charges were framed by the judge against many. The judge also did not care to find out from the people he was severely indicting. What justice in a report written by a retired Supreme Court judge, which led to a charge sheet against the former telecom secretary and the CBI court ruling that the charge was fraudulent!

Despite the overwhelming proof of my innocence, the inquiries continued full blast as the following would show:

a. My statement before the investigating officer on 18 July 2011.
b. D.P.S. Seth's statement before the investigating officer on 20 July 2011.
c. Rajeev Chandrasekhar's detailed letter to the CBI charging me with false and self-contradictory statements on 20 June 2011.

It is abundantly clear from the above that the intention of the inquiries was not to find out the truth, but only to publicize that an inquiry was going on. I have never in my service seen such a 'banana republic' face of the Government of India. All other lapses pointed out by the finance minister's report to the PMO were glossed over. I am fortunate that I have lived to tell the story; many bureaucrats did not.

My head also bows in reverence to the then finance minister Pranab Mukherjee, and other officers in the finance ministry, and also chairman, TRAI, who in January 2011 had the courage to state the true version of the story, despite an adversarial climate created by the government with the help of CBI raids and leaked stories against everyone who sided with the truth. I thought this was the end of the 2G story. I was surprised when I found there was much more.

The Rajeev Chandrasekhar Story

I saw the letter (See Annexure 4) from an independent Member of Parliament (MP) on a website 2Gscam.com. Kudos to the website creator who was concerned about the facts regarding 2G coming out in the open.

It was also frightening that a member of Parliament connected with telecom, and a party to the 2G scam, kept meeting and sending drafts of charge sheets and other papers to the CBI, even after all facts of the case were before the CBI, the government and the courts in March 2011. Obviously the CBI IO also did not find it worthwhile/proper to divulge its tentative findings at this stage to the non-government player. He kept guiding the CBI directly in investigating these cases on the basis of distorted facts. The letter below, whose photocopy appeared on 2Gscam.com explains this. This was at the same time when the prime minister was reluctant to see any paper about the 2G scam, including those from his own minister, while non-state actors were guiding the investigation. I am sure that Vivek Priyadarshi, SP CBI, was not repeatedly interacting with Rajeev Chandrasekhar on his own, since he got to know the whole truth in February 2011 after TRAI filed an affidavit in the Supreme Court, and everyone in CBI told me that they were aware of the affidavit, but were yet compelled to keep on questioning me with all the publicity. He was directed by someone powerful in government to meet Chandrasekhar and examine the facts presented by this non-state actor. Perhaps this was the perfect example of public–private partnership in UPA-II. It was also interesting that I saw one such other correspondence on the IO's table, when he was trying to question me from the earlier such letter quoted in June 2011 letter.

The extent of preparation of the case and due diligence by this non-state actor was remarkable, except that most of the letter was inconsistent with facts and contained jargon. I will only point out one—the letter dated 19 November 2003 cited at Annexure 12 of Chandrasekhar's letter in itself proves that the letter dated 14 November 2003 was not my personal letter as stated in the letter, but it was approved by TRAI. I have not been able to lay my hands on the other letters and the minutes of the meeting, if any. Everyone also knew the relationship this non-state actor had with powerful elements in the UPA-II government, including Chidambaram and Maran. The 2G story did not end here either. After the publication of my e-book, a journalist from *The News Minute* gave me a letter from Maran to the prime minister.

Maran's Letter to the Prime Minister

This letter, dated 03 June 2005, included a number of statements to misguide the prime minister into believing that I had not sent the USL recommendations to the government. My colleagues in the DoT warned me that the government was planning to censure me on the basis of this letter, having found nothing in the other fraudulent inquiries. The relevant extracts of this letter are reproduced below:

> Respected Prime Minister…
>
> 3. I have been observing the working of TRAI and particularly the style of working of the Chairman Mr Pradeep Baijal. Being responsible for its working, I have answered many questions in the Parliament as well as references from Hon'ble Members of Parliament and issues raised in the Department's Consultative Committee. In the case of Reliance Infocomm, just to give one example, instead of taking timely and stern action at their end, TRAI simply passed it on to the Department of Telecommunications on the ground that TRAI is not equipped to take action…I strongly suspect that in matters where his

recommendations were not accepted by my Ministry, instead of accepting the position, he has been giving unwarranted inputs to interested parties perhaps with the ulterior agenda of having his recommendations find acceptance in government by putting undue pressure on the Department. Such attitude needlessly compromises the position of the ministry. I would imagine that once TRAI has given its recommendation, the Chairman has no business to air his views in the press and media defending his recommendations as their acceptance or otherwise is the sole prerogative of the government which it would in any case exercise in public interest...

... 5. Unfortunately, TRAI inordinately delayed giving their recommendation on the specific issues. It finally gave its recommendation only in May, 2005, after a period of 18 months. Also, TRAI has included their views on some other issues, most notably that of 3G spectrum and its pricing. The government had not asked for recommendations on 3G at all. This is a sensitive issue having external policy ramifications. TRAI should have quickly given its recommendations on the specific issues raised by us...

Yours Sincerely
Dayanidhi Maran

Maran's letter to the former prime minister was also a part of the conspiracy to later start the 2G scam. In my opinion, this letter was intended to be used in defaming TRAI, and get proceedings started against me. Earlier inquiries against me had produced no results, and he expected this letter would defame me within the government, enabling him to start the 2G scam in 2005 itself by suppressing the fact that I gave the USL report in January 2005.

Earlier Inquiries against Me

There was a starred question in Rajya Sabha in December 2004. The question was why had I not inquired into the cases against RIL and imposed an ADC regime. I pointed out that since the complaint against Reliance was serious, I had sent it to the vigilance cell of DoT in January 2005 on the basis of a standing order dated 23 June 2003. The DoT had acknowledged and thanked us for sending the complaint. As a matter of fact, the DoT was concerned about illegal traffic and had issued detailed procedures to deal with these cases, which I followed. But such was the intensity of propaganda unleashed against me on this count in Parliament that the matter was later discussed in the zero hour. No one defended me or TRAI in the Parliament. An excerpt from TRAI's note is reproduced below:

> On this, TRAI in its letter F.No. 402/29/2001-FN dated 11th December, 2004, replied to the question of Shri Nilotpal Basu, the then MP Rajya Sabha. That In several specific cases of complaints received from M/s VSNL, BPL, BSNL and MTNL, TRAI had forwarded them to DoT to obtain quick results in the light of the above mentioned limitations regarding the jurisdiction of TRAI and the non-availability of staff with the Regulator. It may be recalled that during the course of deliberations of a committee appointed by TRAI to investigate and give recommendations on the matter of grey traffic and its linkage to the IUC regime, it was noted by the committee that on the operation of clandestine/illegal Telecommunications Centres/Telephone Exchanges, the DoT had already sent letter on 23rd and 24th June, 2003 setting up a mechanism for monitoring of data and had specified the Vigilance Wing of DoT to act as the nodal agency for investigation. Accordingly, when the TRAI received the complaints in August 2004 and later these were forwarded to DoT for investigation through Vigilance Wing and further action for checking the same.

> In fact, in response to our letter forwarding the above complaints. DoT responded immediately that the matter is being investigated by the DoT. Moreover, DoT did quick and good work by reaching a conclusion by 4th October, 2004 validating TRAI's expectations of the established mechanism being the quicker possible way to address the matter.

However, Maran in his letter to the former prime minister said that TRAI didn't investigate the RIL's matter deliberately and referred it to DoT. He did not tell the prime minister that TRAI had acted within the established procedure.

Later, an inquiry was conducted by the cabinet secretary against me. No prizes for guessing that the inquiry couldn't find anything amiss.

Maran also did not also reveal that he did not defend TRAI when this complaint was raised in the Parliament. This led to a lot of mudslinging on TRAI's actions and I had to defend the independent statutory body before the media. Thus, his grand plan of defaming TRAI failed. He was naturally upset at my media statements as expressed in the letter.

How the Problems Began

My problems as the telecom regulator started when Dayanidhi Maran was appointed the minister for telecommunications in the UPA-I government. I was surprised at his appointment, so were the media and other stakeholders, as it was a clear case of conflict of interest since he was a broadcaster and TRAI had been appointed as a broadcasting regulator in 2004. I expressed my misgivings to the prime minister but he dismissed these concerns with the argument that there was no conflict since TRAI was an independent regulator, and the I&B and telecom were separate ministries. There obviously was conflict. It was extensively reported in the media that he was running an illegal telephone exchange which benefited Sun TV. The media often put the question of conflict to me and I had no option but to skip the question since the prime minister had already made a statement on the matter.

I also mentioned to the prime minister that though mobile telephony had achieved phenomenal growth, broadband was not showing similar growth. The growth of broadband required a number of decisions, including early reconsideration and enactment of the Convergence Act or, alternatively, bringing the unified licence and many other measures to be taken by different ministries. The PM appointed two committees in the PMO: one headed by him and the other, a subordinate committee, headed by the principal secretary to the prime minister. Dayanidhi Maran protested against these committees, and directed his officers not to attend them. He also told me that he was 'Prime Minister, Telecom' and would take all decisions on telecom, and that I had no business meeting the prime minister. I do not know how Maran came to know about our meeting. He warned that I could come to severe harm. He was proved right, since I did face severe hardships four years after my retirement from TRAI.

Consequent to his actions, the committees on broadband in the PM's office never met. His pressurization techniques also got him out of the scrutiny of the empowered group of ministers (EGoM) on spectrum-pricing issues; a time now identified by many as the beginning of Congress's end. How could pricing issues not be examined by the finance ministry? This was also in violation of the Rules of Business, which the finance ministry raised many times.

Coming back to the Ministry of Finance's report of 25 March 2011, it conclusively proved that missing files and papers had become a norm in DoT and it is not surprising that the relevant file of 2003 about TRAI's approval was also found missing. Obviously someone was behind these missing files/papers. I was also aware in 2006, that some relatives of Maran's personal staff, who were employed in TRAI, were behaving strangely. But with no concrete evidence in hand, I took no action.

What Happened After I Retired

Maran, first, gave additional spectrum to Aircel at old rates in 2006. He then wanted to give spectrum to new companies also at old rates. He had suppressed the January 2005 recommendations. He therefore asked TRAI for recommendations on the number of access providers in each service area and for reviewing the terms and conditions. TRAI issued its consultation paper on 12 June 2007 and gave recommendations on 28 August 2007. Raja (Maran had been replaced) then asked for applications for more licences, and started giving them, thereby breaking all the rules. He also ignored the price changes which had been suggested by TRAI in Paragraph 2.95 of the 2007 recommendations. The finance ministry also wanted a clear procedure regarding the revised prices, but this was glossed over. TRAI's USL recommendations of 2005 were also not taken to the cabinet—as desired by the cabinet in October 2003—or to any other inter-ministerial forum. This led to the great 2G loot.

Surviving Multiple Inquiries

During the multiple inquiries, I got assistance from most of those who had worked with me during these assignments, but there were some erstwhile colleagues who were scared to even shake hands or take calls from me during these state-sponsored inquiries. I cannot expect any rational person to willingly get into the same vicious cycle as they would have had they been seen helping me. However, there were three exceptions. One was D.P.S. Seth. He took full part in the telecom inquiries I faced without any hesitation and fear of getting involved. The second was Rakesh Kakkar, a secretary in the Government of India, who had helped me in framing the broadcasting regulation. When the motivated inquiries against me were on in full swing, he continued helping me without any fear of consequences. The case of P.K. Basu, secretary in the Ministry of Agriculture, was even stranger. At the height of inquiries and raids against me, he instituted a 'Baijal award' in the Ministry of Agriculture for the joint secretary who delivered the most. Both Kakkar and Basu were absolutely brilliant and diligent officers. They were considered for many important post-retirement assignments but lost out, perhaps, due to their association with me. K.K. Gupta, another joint secretary in the Ministry of Disinvestment, was perhaps not made secretary due to his active involvement in a government-sponsored programme of privatization. I must recall here that in July 2002, when Basu completed seven privatizations, he collapsed in his office at 3 a.m., and had to be hospitalized. However, he did not allow any of his colleagues to tell the secretary, lest the programme slowed down.

Personally, I received many accolades, both international and national. However, once the false CBI inquiries started, everyone including the media, became a part of the inquisitors. I was advised by my lawyers not to talk. This was difficult for me since I was being attacked severely and unjustly, and it was difficult not to tell my side of the story. Some of the documents shown to me during the inquisitions were signed by some senior people in TRAI, who were then in world organizations. I did not insist that they prove the documents, though my lawyers advised me to do so, as that would have meant calling them to India for evidence in a CBI case. This could have had an adverse effect on their careers.

Regulators are intensively supervised by appellate bodies, the high courts and the Supreme Court, parliamentary committees and the government. All the regulator's decisions are taken considering the efficiencies of different and changing technologies. The examination of policy and legal issues, particularly those which are appealable, by the CAG and later by the CBI makes a mockery of the prescribed legal scrutiny in the relevant Acts. The division of work between all these agencies must be clearly demarcated in the regulatory enactments. If this is not done early, policy paralysis will continue and 'no reforms' would be the norm for a long time. These issues of defining jurisdictions have been under the scrutiny of the government for very long.

CBI Raid, Imminent Arrest and Legal Assistance

My house was raided by a CBI team during the inquiry. They did not know what they were looking for and sat for four hours despite asking for permission to leave. Yet, rumours were spread that many incriminating documents were found. Then started the news items proclaiming that I was going to be arrested. At this stage, one senior CBI officer, my lawyer and a businessman friend hinted that I should leave Delhi till things cooled down. The CBI had made out a case for custodial interrogation, alleging that I was not cooperating in their inquiry. Had they taken me for custodial interrogation, people would have been convinced that something incriminatory was found in the raid.

Then, on the DIG's orders, the team wanted to search my wife's lockers. I asked them why as there were no charges of corruption. The vague discussion with them led me to understand that the raid was made on the charge that I had Tata-Unitech's deal papers. The fact is that the Tatas had a bitter experience with their shareholding in Idea Telecom. They would not have tried for a shareholding in Unitech telecom. Besides, I could hardly be the custodian for secret papers of the Tatas, if any. Even if they had some papers, they could have kept them at thousands of their locations in the country, and not at my residence.

I left Delhi a few days after the raid and only came back after a fortnight, when people told me that CBI had got busy in many other and bigger cases.

Perhaps, I was a target also because I was advising the Tatas on spectrum and iron ore allocation and in the process had finalized many drafts assisting them in filing HC/SC cases against arbitrary allocations. The Tatas were not given these resources, perhaps because they did not pay speed money though they were the first in the legal queue. We therefore advised them to take recourse to the obvious remedy—file cases against wrong allocations in courts and write well-documented letters about the injustice to stakeholders. These actions of theirs and ours led to only partial results, but it aided the 2G and Coalgate scam exposure.

The frame-up leading to the telecom inquiry led to a lot of embarrassment and huge financial loss to me. I was forced to close my consulting business due to the massive adverse publicity. I also had to resign from independent directorships, consulting assignments of the World Bank, ITU and FIIs. It also led to a considerable expenditure on lawyers.

When the CBI increased the heat on me in the newspapers in 2010, my son, working in the private sector for an American company, got nervous and retained U.U. Lalit as my senior lawyer. His juniors told me later that I was wasting money on their fees since there was no case against me. Subsequently, the CBI approached him for representing them. With my consent, he started work with the CBI. The next day, I was surprised to find a cheque from him returning the entire amount of the retainer and consulting fees. Through his juniors I protested that he did not have to return the fee and the clerkage, but he insisted. It brought me a great deal of joy when he was appointed a judge of the Supreme Court in 2014.

The Minister's Zero Loss Theory

To protect the UPA government in 2009, Kapil Sibal, minister, DoT, came up with the zero-loss theory. This theory made him a laughing stock as the actual auction amounts received were much higher. However, perhaps to protect Maran and Raja, he set up a roving inquiry on all policy issues, etc., in the DoT during 2001–09. There were no complaints on decisions taken in the NDA government time, yet to confuse matters, he set up the inquiry for the entire period; it was similar to what was done in my case where the DoT tried to put the blame on me for illegalities committed during Maran/Raja period.

I had warned many in UPA-II that all inquiries against me and others would lead back to the prime minister as he had indeed approved the actions of ministers and ministries in his government. This is precisely what happened later. Had I cooperated, I would not have been able to save myself from numerous inquiries. Since I did not cooperate, Maran and Raja had to ignore TRAI's UASL reports, and therefore I was squarely blamed by them for the 2G scam, which was initiated after my retirement. Of course, I was subjected to baseless inquiries to teach me, and perhaps through me others, not to insist that they should act as per law but as per the minister's illegal instructions. I am lucky nothing could be proved against me and that I recovered documents of the file which were removed by the scamsters. It is sad that some officers couldn't withstand the pressure.

Why Multiple Inquiries

I did not understand, from 2008 to 2014, why fraudulent inquiries were started and so vigorously pursued against me. Normally, ministers in a government do not pressurize officers if they are unwilling to follow illegal oral instructions.

I saw some newspaper reports which give me a clue to what was happening. *Business Standard* in an article[5] on 10 July 2015 titled '2G scam money went to tax safe havens via Surat: ED' reported: 'Investigations by the Enforcement Directorate (ED) into Rs 5,395-crore hawala scam has revealed that operators were also involved in sending 2G scam money to tax safe havens such as Switzerland via Surat based firms which were created to run the racket...' Also, in his book, 2G *Spectrum Scam*, Subramanian Swamy had assessed the size of bribes paid to be Rs 60,000 crores.[6]

Moneycontrol, a business website, published an article on the same date titled, 'ED unearths India's biggest hawala trail in 2G case'.[7] The article wrote: 'The ED has, as of now, found evidence of Rs 10,000 crore being routed out of India. Some arrests have also been made by the agency in connection with the case...'

Perhaps the slush money involved was so huge that the political executives could not resist the temptation of making huge monies by selling spectrum as per old procedures/prices. Also, while huge money was being made, some companies like the Tatas were not cooperating, and they had to be made to fall in line. Perhaps that was the reason that the Tatas were also persecuted by false inquiries, and then there was always the issue of conflict of interest with Sun TV.

However, the Congress achieved at least one goal. Only few, like Arun Shourie, spoke about the huge success of telecom, IT, broadcasting and disinvestment reforms during the NDA government of Atal Bihari Vajpayee. Others, perhaps not sure of the facts after the well-publicized inquiries initiated by UPA-II, did not speak out.

4

UNRAVELLING OTHER CONSPIRACIES

> I suffered the consequences of conspiratorial inquiries against TRAI's actions. I could never believe that the state itself could be a conspirator, and realized that I faced a conspiracy, not an inquiry. Gradually, I got to know the nature of most other scams, and then inquiries in other sectors convinced me that these operations were similar to those against TRAI. I am not venturing any guess about where this central planning agency was located.

There were no inquiries in any of the deals or decisions I had taken during my career. The one illegal inquiry that I did face was closed by the prime minister on Arun Shourie's prodding during UPA-I. To see the same prime minister later behave helplessly bewildered me. Or was this helplessness simply a façade?

When I got to know the details of my case better, I also saw that there were many similar cases against Shyamal Ghosh and P.C. Parakh. This pattern of persecution, I realized, was the result of highly centralized planning of first implementing scams in different sectors, and then covering them up through different devious means. I state this because sequences of events and the strategy in all these cases were strikingly similar. Let me show this in the three cases of Shyamal Ghosh, the Coalgate and the Commonwealth Games.

The Shyamal Ghosh Story

The government woke up to scams when there was intense public backlash in 2007. In telecom cases, it was planned that the blame should be put on the NDA government and its officials. To put further blame on the DoT in the NDA government prior to 2004, Kapil Sibal first stated that there was zero loss in UPA actions, and when that statement brought ridicule, he appointed the Justice Patil Committee with the following terms of reference:[1]

> Subject: Setting up of a One-Man Committee to look into certain issues relating to Department of Telecommunications as per Terms of Reference.
>
> It has been decided by the competent authority to constitute a One-Man committee comprising Hon'ble Justice Shivraj V. Patil, retired Judge of the Supreme Court to examine the appropriateness of procedures followed by the Department of Telecommunications in issuance of licence and allocation of spectrum during the period 2001-2009. The Terms of Reference of the Committee are as per Annexure.
>
> 2. The Committee shall be vested with the following powers:
>   I. To call for any records in the Department of Telecommunications.
>   II. To call any officials of the DoT to get a briefing on any matter relevant to the TOR of the Committee.
>   III. To call any official of the DoT to assist in obtaining or explaining any record.
>   IV. To seek any additional administrative assistance or manpower required for the discharge of its functions.

3. The Headquaters of the committee will be at New Delhi.
4. The committee shall submit its report within a period of one month.
5. The Hon'ble Justice Shivraj V. Patil—One Man Committee will be entitled to facilities as per government norms commensurate to the position held.

Terms of Reference

1. To study the circumstances and developments in the Telecom Sector that led to the formulation of the New Telecom Policy 1999 and subsequently, introduction of 4th Cellular Telecom Mobile Services (CMTS) licence in 2001.
2. To examine the internal (intra-departmental) procedures adopted by DoT during the period 2001–2009 for
   - Issue of telecom access service licences and
   - Allocation of spectrum to all telecom access services licensees during the above period.
3. To examine whether these procedures were in accordance with extant policies and directions of DoT/government.
4. To examine whether these procedures were followed consistently and if not, identify specific instances of:
   - Deviation from laid down procedures
   - Inappropriate application of laid down procedures
   - Violation of underlying principles of laid down procedures.
5. To examine whether the procedures adopted were fair and transparent and were in keeping with the principles of natural justice and if not, identify the specific instances of lack of fairness and transparency.
6. To identify the deficiencies, if any, in the procedures as formulated and identify the public officials responsible for such deficiencies.
7. To identify the shortcomings and lapses, if any, in the

implementation of the laid down procedures and identify the public officials responsible for such lapses.

8. To suggest remedial measures to avoid in future
   - Deficiencies in formulation of procedures and
   - Lapses in implementation of laid down procedures.

It can be seen from the above terms of reference that this was a committee that was supposed to examine all the changes that were made in the telecom sector in the last eight years. Anyone, even one vaguely familiar with the telecom sector, would have known that these changes were enormous and had been a subject matter of long and protracted cases in the high courts and the Supreme Court. The Committee was supposed to examine policies, procedures and deficiencies at all levels in a one-month period. Further, the Committee had to restrict itself to the files given to it, and talk only to serving officers. The Committee also had to identify people for deficiencies and lapses. The Committee was thus asked prepare charge sheets even for the period there were no complaints, and which had been adjudicated extensively in courts before 2009. Basically, the Committee was asked to lock itself in a room, examine thousands of files along with serving officers, without asking for any clarification against whom charges were framed. That a retired Supreme Court judge could be given the work of such an auditor, and that the judge could have accepted such an assignment surprises me, and also the fact that it could and did submit its report with only an extension of one month. Such a report could only be written by serving officers, working under the pressure of the minister, and the Supreme Court judge signing the report.

I had learnt that natural justice was important for such committees. To highlight this, the Madhya Pradesh case which I experienced as an undersecretary in 1969 comes to mind. I prepared a summary of the reports of the Nagarkatti Commission and Justice V. R. Sen

Commission against Pt Dwarka Prasad Misra, the former chief minister. Justice Sen had held the Nagarkatti Commission report void since it had not given an opportunity to the accused to present their case. While Justice Patil had not been appointed under the Commission of Inquiry Act, it was very surprising to see a retired judge of the Supreme Court ignoring this basic canon of natural justice.

I am also told that the then telecom secretary, armed with this report and other papers, made a presentation before the JPC and devoted almost all his time on the NDA government's actions and barely a fraction of the presentation was focussed on UPA-II's actions. He knew that all the illegalities were post-2006 and not during NDA's time. Such was the pressure from the telecom minister.

However, again either the scamsters did not do their homework or there was divine intervention. Justice Patil's report found many irregularities in the NDA period and some from Maran and Raja's time. The report went to CBI for further action. When doing scrutiny, the CBI found only two cases from the NDA time worth pursuing, namely, the case involving Shyamal Ghosh, Sunil Mittal and Vodafone regarding extra spectrum; and both Maran and Raja cases of UPA-II time. The UPA-II period cases are at advanced stages of prosecution while the most prosecutable case in Justice Patil's report for NDA period was found to be based on fraudulent grounds as per the findings of the CBI court, I can only make guesses about the facts of other cases. Of course, the judicial system once again gave justice. That one fraudulent case put one of the most outstanding officers of the service, who had helped bring about the telecom revolution, through immense pain, loss of reputation, and financial loss. Shyamal Ghosh even tried to sell property to meet lawyers' costs at one stage. The case against me and others could not reach even the FIR stage, and continued with intensive inquiries for four years. It was ultimately closed down.

Could a Supreme Court judge, not knowing the sector, and without talking to anyone, produce such a report in approximately six weeks? I leave it to the other eminent jurists in the country and telecom experts to judge. The facts are so glaringly simple that even a layman can judge. Here, I give some glimpses of the Patil Committee report for the NDA period.

The Patil Committee Report

Deviation: Despite recommendations of TRAI dated 27 October 2003 that the new entrants in UASL regime could be permitted /introduced through a multistage bidding process, the recommendation was also accepted by Union cabinet on 31 October 2003, in deviation from the same, a procedure was promulgated on 17 November 2003 to accept applications for UASLs in the form prescribed for BSLs (Basic Service Licence), for which approval from the Telecom Commission (TC) was not taken. Procedure was formulated such that it facilitated the applications made by TTSL (Tata Teleservices Limited) in the form prescribed for grant of BSL.

Responsible: Vinod Vaish, secretary, DoT; V. K. Sharma, AD VAS-I; A. S. Verma, director VAS—II; J.R. Gupta, senior DDG VAS; P.K Mittal, DDG (BS); and Ramachandaran, member of Parliament.

Deviation: A procedure was formulated to apply the entry fee paid by the fourth cellular operators (discovered in 2001) to new entrants under UASL regime in 2003 and also consider applications or grant of UASL on FCFS (first-come, first-served) basis. Formulation of procedure was thus contrary to the decision of the Union cabinet dated 31 October 2003. The decision to apply entry fee discovered in 2001 for the new entrants without revision was also opposed to the policy requirement of the price of spectrum being commensurate with opportunity cost.

Responsible: A.S. Verma, director VAS-II; J. R. Gupta, senior DDG

VAS; P.K. Mittal, DDG (BS); B. B. Singh, DDG(LF); the then director (LF); the then LA(T); P.P. Ramachandran, member of Parliament; N. Parthasarathy, member (F); Vinod Vaish, chairman TC; secretary (DoT); then minister.

Deviation: TRAI reiterated its said recommendation dated 27 October 2003 in its recommendation dated 4 November 2003. Without placing this recommendation before the TC, DoT decided to follow the procedure applicable to BSL for granting UASLs and to apply FCFS criteria and to collect entry fee from new UAS licensees as was paid by the fourth cellular operator in 2001, and based on such decision issued LoIs to TTSL and Bharti Cellular Ltd.

Responsible: V. K. Sharma, AD VAS-I; J.R. Gupta, senior DDG VAS; Vinod Vaish, chairman TC; secretary, DoT; the minister.

Deviation: A need having been felt for legal opinion on 26 October 2007, DoT, through the Ministry of Law and Justice, sought the opinion of the Attorney General/solicitor general on procedure to be followed for grant of new UAS licences. On 1 November 2007 the minister of law and Justice had opined that it was necessary that the whole issue is first considered by the empowered Group of Ministers and in that process legal opinion of attorney general could be obtained. However, the minister took the view that the opinion of the minister of law and justice was out of context and decided to continue following the same procedure of grant of new UASL.

Responsible: Nitin Jain, director (AS-I); A. K. Srivastava, DDG (AS); K. Sridharan, member (T); the minister.

Deviation: Procedure was formulated not to have a cap on number of UASLs on the basis of recommendation of TRAI dated 28 August 2007 without placing them before the Telecom Commission, by placing only before the full-time members of the Telecom Commission, that too without furnishing the entire recommendations of TRAI and by giving only one-day notice (as against seven days' notice).

Responsible: D.S. Mathur, secretary, DoT.
Deviation: On 7 January 2008, in deviation from the decision of DoT dated 24 November 2008, a procedure was formulated as per which an applicant who complied with LoI conditions first has to be granted UASL licence first, without the matter been placed before the TC. Decision was based on the contents of the letter of the minister dated 26 December 2007 addressed to the prime minister. Approved by the minister, the decision was taken to treat the contents of the letter of the minister as the policy of DoT.

Responsible: A.K. Srivastava, DDG (AS); M. K. Sridhara, member (T); S. Behura, secretary DoT; the minister.

Deviation: A procedure was formulated as per which applications received upto 25 September 2007 only were to be processed and also to grant priority on the basis of date of compliance with LoI. Absence of communication of the critical change in procedure contemplated by the first press release, considering that the second press release issued on the same date required applicants to collect LoIs before 3:30 p.m., was opposed to the requirement of transparency and fairness.

Responsible: A. K. Srivastava, DDG (AS).

Deviation: Review of availability of spectrum is also necessary for enabling growth of telecom sector, as envisaged under NTP 1999 and the tenth plan. However, despite significance of review of spectrum availability, the same was not done.

Responsibility: R. N. Aggarwal, P. K. Garg, R. P. Aggarwal.

Deviation: The decision dated 12 November 2001 in U.O. No. 842-350/2000-VAS formulating procedure for allotment of additional spectrum of 1.8+ 1.8 Mhz at the beginning itself subject to payment of additional 1 per cent AGR was taken in deviation of the requirement of obtaining recommendations from TRAI or placing the matter before TC. It was approved by the minister of state.

Responsible: A. K. Srivastava, director VAS-I; J. R. Gupta, DDG (VAS); the member of Parliament; Shyamal Ghosh, chairman (TC).

Deviation: Formulating the procedure for allotment of additional spectrum beyond 6.2 + 6.2 MHz up to 10 + 10 MHz for 1 per cent AGR only, on the basis of SLC, though had financial bearing, was taken without there being recommendations of TRAI and without consideration by TC. The additional allotment of spectrum used to be made on the basis of unilateral claim made by applicant without any verification.

Responsible: J. R. Gupta, DDG (VAS); Shyamal Ghosh, chairman (TC); the minister.

Deviation: A procedure was formulated on 18 July 2003 for allotment of spectrum beyond 8 MHz + 8 MHz, by accepting the report of the Committee on Efficient use of Spectrum (Lalwani Committee), though recommendation of the said aspect was beyond its terms of reference. This took place without placing the matter before TC and/or without any recommendations from TRAI.

Responsible: R. J. S. Kushwaha, JWA (T); K. H. Khan, member (T); Vinod Vaish, chairman (TC).

Deviation: Failure on the part of WPC wing. Though WPC wing was not involved in the decision-making process, it chose to comply with such procedures formulated when access licensees approached it for allotment of spectrum.

Responsible: R. N. Aggarwal, P. K. Garg, R. P. Aggarwal.

It appears from the report that everyone in the DoT was responsible for one lapse or another.

In the additional spectrum allocation case, the CBI had alleged irregularities on the part of the accused on various grounds that included non-approval from TRAI and the Telecom Commission, which had caused loss to exchequer. On 16 October 2015, the special court dismissed these claims and gave out detailed reasons as to why the accused cannot be put on trial based on the allegations.

Allegation: DoT was required to obtain recommendations of TRAI regarding the quantum of additional spectrum to existing operators.

What the court said: TRAI recommendations dated 26 June 2000, and 24 October 2000 were already there and the DoT was not required to ask for fresh recommendations. It further said that these recommendations cover both 'inadequacy of existing spectrum' to the existing operators and also 'need for additional spectrum'.

Allegation: Additional spectrum was allocated to three companies in the most efficient band of 900 MHz, though as per the order dated 1 February 2002, the spectrum was to be allocated in 1800 MHz band.

What the court said: Witnesses have stated that additional spectrum was to be allocated to the existing operators in 1800 MHz band, but ultimately it was allocated in 900 MHz band on 'account of technical constraints'. The court further added that there is no document on record to prove that band was 'wrongly changed'.

Allegation: Shyamal Ghosh, former telecom secretary, in conspiracy with accused telecom companies allocated spectrum beyond 6.6 MHz and up to 10 MHz to the firms by charging 1 per cent of AGR, whereas on past analogy it should have been 2 per cent that is 1 per cent each for two tranches of 1.8 MHz.

What the court said: Limiting of AGR to 4 per cent for 10MHz of spectrum is 'compatible with the circumstances prevailing in the industry at that time, more so, when the concept of rate of percentage of AGR to be charged itself was not fully firmed up and everybody was suggesting his own rate of percentage charges'.

Allegation: Ghosh was appointed as chairman of Universal Obligation Fund on the recommendation of the former telecom minister Pramod Mahajan.

What the court said: All the 'substantive allegations' in the charge sheet are 'either distorted ones or contrary to record'.

The court's conclusion stated:

> The conclusion of aforesaid analysis of the events, evidence, documents and other material on record is that the charge sheet is a distorted and fabricated document, based on deliberately redacted and garbled facts. It has been so drafted as to create an impression of a grave crime, where there is none. An attempt has been made to create an impression in the charge sheet that everything was done on a single day in the dark hours of evening of 31.01.2002. There is no doubt that the charge sheet has been filed for extraneous reasons. In the end, I find that there is no incriminating material on record against the accused and the accused deserve to be discharged. Accordingly, the accused stand

discharged. To the best of my understanding, when action is taken against CBI officials for a fraudulent charge sheet, Justice Patil and Kapil Sibal's name should also be added.

The CWG Case

I will only deal with the observations of the Shunglu Committee to illustrate the scandalous handling of the Games in the UPA period. The report found that the Games were awarded in 2003 and were to be in 2010, giving the CWG authority enough preparatory time. Without due consideration, the government committed to underwrite the Games on the false promise of revenue neutrality. Several other obligations compromised our best interests. The level of authority enjoyed by the president and CEO of the CGF (Commonwealth Games Federation) was not conducive to good management. A period of seven years was available to prepare for the Games. The first three years were squandered in peripheral activity thus reducing the available time to a mere four years. The much delayed preparations reached a feverish pitch so near the Games that most actions became 'emergency' decisions compromising cost and quality. Someone was responsible for the enormous waste of money, and in a multi-ministry scenario, only the PMO could be liable to allow things to deteriorate to that level.

Another startling fact reported by the *Hindu* on 5 March 2012 on the Commonwealth Games scam: 'There are many documents related to the projects which are untraceable. A number of documents were missing from the Organising Committee office,' and later in Paragraph 1.3 of its report, the Shunglu Committee also recorded, 'The High Level Committee also undertook 'digital imaging' of computers and information obtained from the same has also been used.' Removing important files has been a central theme across scams during the UPA regime.

The Coal Scam

P.C. Parakh, the former coal secretary, has discussed this case in detail in his book *Crusader or Conspirator*. I'd like to discuss the Foreword to this book to highlight, yet again, how scams cannot happen without the knowledge of the PMO. This Foreword, written by a former cabinet secretary who knew the functioning of various government organs, states:

> To Parakh's credit he had clearly proposed the auction method, which indeed was approved by the Prime Minister of the day; however, the interests of the politicians involved managed to subvert this sound decision, filibuster its implementation for a decade, while in the mean time ensure that the 'treasury is looted'. The matter is in [the] highest court.
>
> Suffice it to say that the Prime Minister comes out as a mute, ineffective spectator. Note that the same Prime Minister was able to take a firm stand on the nuclear deal and in FDI in retail issue; however he was wimp in implementing a decision taken by himself, in the face of corrupt forces surrounding him.

It is clear that even in this case the scam was centrally planned. Later in another case, the then law minister tried to edit a CBI note. He lost his job, but as per central policy, the prime minister was kept clear of the responsibility for the scams so that his influence could be used to direct the CBI's investigations.

Later, *Business Standard* on 25 August 2014 reported, 'In mid-August last year (2013), the coal scam took a twist after Coal Minister Sriprakash Jaiswal admitted that some crucial files relating to the investigation between 1993 and 2004 had gone missing. The admission came after a Supreme Court directive to the government to co-operate with the CBI's inquiry.'

Now that almost all inquiries have reached their natural death,

I am publishing this book on the 2G saga and the reform process, covering both the high and the low points. It is to show that reforms can only be implemented through resolve and determination, but also to give caution to someone potentially undertaking reforms. Caution that those who are benefitting from the inefficient status quo may pursue inquiries against those who reform, and may also adopt other means to prevent further changes, since reforms always harm the inefficient incumbents and their monopolistic rents. The present system discourages officials from taking bold decisions prescribed in the policy. The country needs to understand and encourage reform and change in governance systems.[2]

5

The Value of Judicial Guidance

Liberalized economies give a lot of importance to private investment and competition. The competing player only invests when he is sure that the polity will treat him equally with other operators, and in accordance with the published rules. Thus, there is need of regulators, particularly in network sectors. So a new player is born—a regulator. Investors want to be sure that the regulator is just, plays by the rules, is able to issue fair regulations and orders in a consultative mode, and also has the capacity to get his regulations, orders and directions implemented in the network, and get them approved in appellate forums and in the Supreme Court. The Supreme Court of India has devoted a lot of time to these aspects in the telecom sector, and has interpreted new law in a manner which gives stability to the sector. The Court has also given wide powers to TRAI through these judicial interpretations. The sector has therefore performed very well.

Regulators in India, as they started, were a part of neither the executive nor legislature, and nor even the judiciary. Yet they were a part of all, as was TRAI under the 1997 Act. This led to endless controversies, and gradually the judicial functions were separated in all legislations by creating bodies like the TDSAT. Yet the regulators walk a razor's edge with regard to their powers, especially when the government does not want them to exercise their powers on a case-to-case basis, as had happened in the telecom sector. Fortunately, the Supreme Court spent enormous time in defining the work and jurisdiction of regulators when TRAI took appeals to the Supreme Court against the TDSAT orders restricting its powers clearly defined in the Act. To be able to do their job well, the regulator has to understand the law, particularly the one defining its sector, and has to make sure that no one hijacks any of the functions.

The foundation of a strong legal cell in the TRAI was laid by the first chairman, Justice S.S. Sondhi, a former chief justice of the Allahabad High Court. He was so aggressive about his legal powers that he upset many in the executive, and sometimes even in the judiciary. His book *Other Side of Justice* on the Supreme Court led to a case of contempt of court against him. Incidentally, Arun Shourie's book on Supreme Court cases—*Courts and Their Judgments*—would also have led to contempt of court against any lesser mortal writing such a book.

The second regulatory authority worked with diluted powers of the TRAI Amendment Act of 2000, when most of the dispute resolution and legal powers were transferred to the newly created appellate tribunal, and tried to settle down to another working arrangement. Our permanent counsel-cum-legal advisor was Meet Malhotra, a young lawyer then. He is now a senior lawyer in the Supreme Court. Malhotra, totally committed to reforms and the TRAI law, helped us in dealing with the various stages of interpretation of telecom law in TRAI, and in issuing regulations/orders/directions which could stand scrutiny of governments, Parliament, our appellate body, the high courts and the Supreme Court.

When the third authority headed by me came into existence, we realized that the sector was in a crisis. Despite seven years of mobiles and private players, and six years of regulation, the sector was not growing adequately. Tariffs were too high, only fit for the elite, and the tele-density very low even when compared to the apologetic Government of India targets; and the operators were only indulging in litigation. They were also incurring huge losses.

I remember meeting Sunil Mittal at a dinner hosted for me by the chairman of British Telecom in London. The chairman emphasized that most telecom operators in India were incurring losses and there was enormous litigation. He said that I must take action to improve the situation. We also had realized that there was enormous judicial and executive review of our decisions, and if we wanted to move forward, we had to understand the law well, and after understanding the law, we had to make sure that our regulations and orders/directions were implemented, and were also declared legal.

TRAI was also an implementing body, and it implemented various measures through its regulations and orders. Before issuing these orders, it had to be sure that they would stand the scrutiny of law before the appellate authority the TDSAT and the SC. One single adverse order could compromise or delay the entire scheme or integrated vision of the Authority to bring growth. A growth surge was required when one looks at the abysmal performance of the sector in about fifty-five years of independent India, with everyone keen on expanding communications, and government spending huge amounts of money in an erstwhile monopoly environment, yet practically achieving nothing.

In 2003, the investment in telecom was still mainly from the government. Implementation of reforms changed the position to enormous growth in telecom network and the main players becoming that of the private sector, leading to massive investments. India, with its huge infrastructural gaps, cannot afford another model in any sector. Aggressively implemented reforms, public and private investment, and Indian and foreign investment, level playing field, and clearly written regulations/orders have to be the cornerstone of

India's growth model. Wherever India has tried another model of individual agreements for different projects, it has failed.

The telecom model evolved in 2003 also had to be maintained in future years, and therefore had to protect itself against the increasing number of incumbents. The operators were big corporates and, with huge legal assistance, could get our orders reversed from the TDSAT, higher judiciary or even the government if these did not suit them. It was therefore very important that our orders, etc., were passed after transparent and due consultations, and were speaking orders, so that we could get them approved at all levels.

Our regulations were subordinate legislation which could only be upset, according to our understanding, and also as per Supreme Court orders in an earlier electricity regulation case, by the Parliament. Yet, Parliament was the only body which interfered the least, and did not upset any of our regulations, within the one month period that they had for taking such a decision.

The first blow to the Authority came when the TDSAT set aside one of our regulations. We examined the TDSAT decision and wondered how two bodies, the Parliament and the appellate body, tinker with the same regulation, and what would happen if the regulations were differently amended by the two bodies? We decided to go to the Supreme Court.

In another case, the TDSAT decided that we had no powers to pass/implement a tariff order. If we had no powers on tariff, why were we created? This issue had been decided once and for all, especially when an amendment to the original Act had specifically given us this power. Again, we had no choice but to approach the Supreme Court.

TRAI was created to let the telecom sector work in a multi-operator environment, with public and private companies having competition in a level playing field. This could only be enforced if TRAI's regulations/orders on interconnection were sound. The TDSAT ruled that we had very limited powers on interconnection, and we had to go to the Supreme Court again.

The TDSAT decisions on some of TRAI's orders benefitted a few operators. Some of the operators were strong vis-à-vis the government too, and the government was keen that we should not appeal, as was indirectly communicated to me also. Yet we decided to appeal, since we thought it was important that the law got clearly defined by the Supreme Court. Perhaps the government was upset at our decision to appeal, and with the approval of the prime minister censured me that we approached the Supreme Court too often. It is another matter that later TRAI appeals against the TDSAT orders were accepted by the Supreme Court in each case.

In my forty years in the government, I had gone to the Supreme Court repeatedly when we had big problems with the Central or a state government, and I always found that the Supreme Court delivered justice and gave relief if our orders/arguments were sound.

I am proud of the fact that the diligence shown by us before issuing orders, and in preparing for arguments before the SC, led to the rulings in TRAI's favour. Perhaps the judges had at the back of their minds the same argument that we had, namely, that the interpretations of law had to be consistent with the entire telecom law or scheme, and not an isolated section of it.

I have always wondered what would have become of the telecom sector if the TDSAT's orders had not been challenged by us, or set aside by the Supreme Court. We would then not have had many powers to regulate the sector, and would have been drawing our salaries without any work, and the sector would not have been vibrant and flourishing in India. There are not many sectors in India where the regulators have received such favourable orders from the Supreme Court.

Again, when huge distortions started in 2G after 2006, it was only the Supreme Court which gave justice to the sector and punishment to the errants.

Let us examine these cases and some other earlier cases on

telecom regulation, and the impact of these judgments on the sector, both before and after my term as chairman. Without these judgments, we could not have grown as rapidly as we did.

Delhi Science Forum and connected matters

Though this was a pre-TRAI case, it was a landmark decision for the telecom sector where the Supreme Court held that the Central government had powers under the first proviso of Section 4(1) of the Indian Telegraph Act to grant licence in the terms and conditions mentioned therein. The discretion granted to the Central government implies a fiduciary duty to act with due restraints and applying the principle of reasonableness. The writ petitions (Central) were first filed questioning the power of the Central government to grant permission to different non-government companies to establish and maintain telecommunication system in the country and the validity of the procedure adopted by the Central government for the said grant. The judgments thus validated the first effort at liberalizing the telecommunication system and enabled the Central government to bring in private companies into the network.

COAI and Others Vs *UOI and Others*: Supreme Court

The petitioner challenged the decision of the government, dated 25 January 2001, permitting fixed service provider to offer WLL with limited mobility on the ground that the said permission was arbitrary, unreasonable and unjust. The TDSAT accepted the petition but later disallowed it on the grounds that it involved policy matters and was hence beyond its purview.

The order of the TDSAT was set aside by the Supreme Court and the case was remitted to the TDSAT for consideration of the matter afresh. After getting TRAI's recommendations, the scheme was approved, and that led to full mobility and growth in the sector.

BPL Mobile Cellular Ltd Vs *TRAI*

The service provider filed an appeal challenging TRAI's decision to file a complaint before the magistrate for violation of the provision of Telecom Tariff Order (TTO) inter alia on the ground that violation of the direction is punishable under Section 29 of the TRAI Act and not the Tariff Order. Appealing against the TDSAT order before the Supreme Court, TRAI counsel Vivek Tankha and Sanjay Kapur argued that the ruling would render the regulatory authority toothless as the service providers could not be punished for bringing about schemes to lure the public and then abandoning them as and when they pleased. Agreeing with the contention, a bench comprising Justices Ruma Pal, B. N. Srikrishna and Dalveer Bhandari said what limiting TRAI's powers to enforcing TTO would mean: 'Consequently, the entire scheme of the TRAI Act would become unworkable.' Rejecting the view expressed by the TDSAT, the bench quoted a 1965 judgment to say: 'The argument is not only new but is also utterly wrong.'

BSNL Vs *TRAI and Others*

In 2007, before the TDSAT, BSNL inter alia contended that TRAI had, vide its regulation, namely, The Telecommunication Interconnection (Port Charges) Amendment Regulation 2007, dated 2 July 2007, overridden its agreement with private service providers. Vide its judgment dated 28 May 2010, the TDSAT partially allowed the appeal of BSNL inter alia holding that it had the jurisdiction to hear appeal on regulation keeping in view the fact that it had, in a large number of cases, opined that regulations made by TRAI under section 11(1)(b) were inter alia in the nature of directions. It further held that the TRAI required maintaining high level of transparency. BSNL filed an appeal against the TDSAT's decision. The Supreme Court, vide its judgment dated 6 December

2013, held that the TDSAT did not have the jurisdiction to decide vires of the regulations and the powers of TRAI to make regulations were not restricted to the items mentioned under Section 36(2) of the TRAI Act, but were very wide as provided under Section 36(1).

Star India Vs *TRAI*, and the Appeal in the Supreme Court

The petitioner had prayed for quashing of proviso to Section 2(1) (K) of the TRAI Act and the TTO and regulations of TRAI, being violation of Articles14 and 19(1) (a) and (g) and also Articles 301 to 307 of the Constitution of India. The powers of TRAI to fix tariff for broadcasters under Section 11(1) (2) of the TRAI Act were also challenged. The petition was dismissed by the High Court upholding the power of TRAI to fix tariff for broadcasters. The court further held that after amendment in the TRAI Act in 2000, TRAI has the power to fix the terms and conditions of interconnectivity between service providers, and rejected the argument that the law does not empower TRAI to fix the terms of interconnection. The SLP (Special leave petition) filed by the petitioner was dismissed by the Supreme Court, and paved the way for effective intervention of TRAI in broadcasting network, and tremendous growth later.

Videsh Sanchar Nigam (Tata) Vs *TRAI*

The TDSAT upset the first order of TRAI saying that TRAI needed to do more transparent calculations. TRAI went back after doing some work and the TDSAT ruled:[1]

> Whether Costing Methodology for IPLC adopted by TRAI was defective and lacked transparency: In the totality of circumstances we do not find any reason to hold that the costing methodology for IPLC (International Private Leased Circuit)

> was defective or lacked in transparency. (ii) Whether certain erroneous assumptions in calculation of costs that were pointed out by VSNL to TRAI were not dealt with in the impugned order: There is considerable difference between two allocation methods and would give totally different results. Therefore, TRAI was not convinced about VSNL's submissions relating to cost apportionment and allocation of satellite related expenses to the IPLC Segment. As detailed inquiry on this would have delayed the tariff fixation, TRAI allowed claims on account of satellite related expenses on this accounting head also as per the contention of VSNL. In the end we would state that fixation of tariff in any Sector is no doubt a complicated exercise and this has been amply proved in the matter presently before us. We are of the opinion that if the pricing methodology adopted has given due regard to the relevant issues and has been reasonably transparent and does not suffer from any perversity, the Tribunal should ordinarily not interfere with the pricing decision of the Regulator. We find that the Respondent in the present case has answered satisfactorily all the points raised by the appellant and we are satisfied that all the relevant points have been taken into account while determining the ceiling prices for IPLC in the impugned order. For the reasons stated above, we find no merit in this appeal and find no reason to interfere with the impugned notification. Hence, we dismiss this appeal and direct that the notification in question be brought into effect immediately by TRAI so that the benefit of the notification to the consumer is not delayed further. Appeal dismissed with cost computed at Rs 50,000/- against TATAs.

The order prevented operators from filing irresponsible appeals later.

The six cases cited above would show that the Supreme Court and TDSAT in one case, settled many legal issues in the interpretation of a new law, and set the turf for its effective implementation. Had these powers of TRAI/government not been settled, TRAI would have been a lame duck and would not have been able to settle telecom regulatory law as a vehicle for growth and restructuring.

According to us, the interpretation of law by the Supreme Court was based on many earlier rulings. We had based our appeals on these rulings, and used the InfoDev's regulatory manual intensively, which explained the best regulatory practices around the world. Besides, our orders were always passed in a consultative environment with the correct prescribed procedure, in a multi-member environment. We were very aggressive in filing appeals after a lot of due diligence, if we did not agree with any high court or TDSAT orders. We also tried to employ the best lawyers. We were also very particular that our appeal memos were prepared by the senior officers of TRAI with active involvement of the chairman. The lawyers too were briefed personally by the chairman and other senior officers. Obviously, the sector gained by TRAI's activism but the government, at the direction of the 'reformist' prime minister, chose to censure me because I refused to agree with the illegal dictates of the minister.

A lot of preparation is required before we go to the Supreme Court. Unfortunately, this is mostly left to junior officers. It is extremely important that the head of the organization takes up this work personally and briefs the lawyers, and also follows up the case in the court. This normally pays huge dividends.

While the SC judgments had beneficial impact on the telecom and the broadcasting sector, their impact goes beyond these sectors. They have laid down principles that can be used by other sectors also, and thus have helped to strengthen regulation in all sectors of economy, particularly the network sectors.

We pass laws in the government after great effort, and have to appear before the cabinet and its committees and often before the parliamentary committees. But these laws can be annulled by one single judgment of high court or the Supreme Court and the cases must be given extreme importance by senior-most functionaries in the government. Yet these jobs are often left to undersecretaries and law officers.

I remember winning a prestigious Madhya Pradesh distillery case before a three-judge bench in the Supreme Court. We had the entire Supreme Court bar against us; we were only represented by one lawyer, the late G.L. Sanghi, whom we could get with great difficulty after he returned the other side's brief. I owe a lot of my training and advocacy in law to the long briefing and preparation meetings I used to have with him. He was a great lawyer, a kind person and also a great strategist.

I had used the same practice in other litigations that I handled for different departments of the state and the Central governments. The Government of Madhya Pradesh, in order to increase income, had in 1982 levied a cess over royalty on major minerals, but the cess was stayed by the Indore High Court. We fought the case in the high court but lost in 1988. Our case was that, while the states in the erstwhile Bengal Presidency (West Bengal, Bihar and Orissa), levied the cess with an enabling provision in the Coal Cess Act 1880, we could not, leading to injustice to other states outside the erstwhile Bengal Presidency not being able to raise an equivalent income from the same mineral. We also lost the appeal in the Supreme Court. Being absolutely convinced that we were right, we later intervened in the India Cement case in the Supreme Court, saying that even the Coal Cess Act 1880, ceased when the MMDR Act 1957, was passed by the Parliament and even the Coal Cess Act could not be used to levy this cess in the so-called eligible states. The SC agreed with our intervention plea, leading to Bihar and Orissa also not being able to levy the coal cess of Rs 600 and 300 crore per year. All states therefore approached the Central government to raise royalty rates, and when this got delayed, and the Bihar treasury came close to getting bankrupt, Lalu Yadav threatened a dharna on Rajpath! The revised royalty rates were soon approved and we got an additional Rs 350 crore per year in Madhya Pradesh, more than the cess we were fighting for, through the revision.

I have always believed, as clearly enunciated earlier, that senior bureaucrats' attention to HC and SC cases can bring huge dividends. As a joint secretary in the power ministry, I faced a number of cases in the high courts and the Supreme Court regarding individual Power Purchase Agreements (PPAs) the government had entered into with private power producers. This was in an era when there was no regulator and individual agreements with each private producer was the order of the day. Since the procedure for finalizing these agreements in government was correct, and all experts had examined these agreements and tariffs in a consultative environment, all PPAs were approved in courts when challenged.

There was massive litigation against the privatizations we completed. Since we were very careful regarding procedure in each case, and all decisions were taken after due diligence by experts and in a transparent manner in a prescribed hierarchy of multi-ministry framework and up to the cabinet level, the government won in all cases. Of course, the attorney general, the solicitor general and the other lawyers were of great help in our winning all the cases.

In some privatization cases, the CAG passed some observations for the future. Those too were noted in ministries and the next finance minister found that the procedures followed were in fact correct. I thought that was the end of the matter. In disinvestment, most cases were taken to a high court or the Supreme Court, and cleared. Yet some cases went to the CBI due to huge noise in the Parliament in 2006; but these were quickly cleared in UPA-I.

Serious problems started when similar decisions were challenged in 2014, twelve years after the event, by the CBI in preliminary inquiries started after anonymous complaints, obviously at the instance of some interested parties. It also registered some FIRs hurriedly without questioning anyone in government, sometimes even on cooked-up grounds. Nothing could be more perverse. I found it personally very humiliating and demoralizing to explain complex issues of valuation, privatization and telecom reforms, to the people who had no experience of dealing with such complex issues, and were mostly partisan. Even more unfortunately, many in the government watched silently, and sometimes enjoyed what was going on. I have dealt with such cases later in the book.

6

Legislation Not Always Necessary

> In 2004, the government was facing problems with set-top boxes in cable TV and there was enormous litigation. TRAI had done well as telecom regulator. So the government used a small proviso in the TRAI Act and appointed TRAI as broadcasting regulator to sort out these issues. The process was questioned, and I could never believe that this would have smooth progress in the High Court and the Supreme Court. It had, perhaps because we were perceived as efficient regulators by everyone in the polity, including courts. Also, the courts were uncomfortable looking at these highly complex issues of cable TV, without there being sectoral regulations under the supervision of a regulator.

When I joined TRAI, a significant technical development was under way. Telephony, broadband and TV were becoming more digital, and this required a convergence law. Many countries like the USA, the UK and Malaysia implemented such laws, but the extremely progressive Convergence Bill 2001, got stuck in India, perhaps to facilitate the incumbent's business case. TRAI came back with the UASL/USL scheme, but it was not as brilliant as the converged licence. UASL was approved immediately by the government leading to huge growth. Had the Convergence

Bill 2001, been approved, we would have been world leaders in broadband. In 2014, we were at number 122, despite initiation of laying fibres to 2.5 lakh villages (NOFN project). The position will not improve till regulations change.

However, the lawmakers of that time deserve kudos for using an innocent provision in the TRAI Act—proviso to Section 2(k)—that any service could be declared a telecom service, including broadcasting service, by a notification. This was despite an earlier provision in the same section that broadcasting service could not be included. It seemed like they had anticipated that the Convergence Act 2001, which was then on the drawing board, might not be passed due to turf issues.

The broadcasting ministry started facing huge problems regarding conditional access system in cable TV, and the matter repeatedly went to the high court. The court recommended that a regulator should be appointed for the sector.

Meanwhile, the government had recognized that TRAI had made a sea change in the telecom network sector. The government encashed the prevailing euphoria and the high court's recommendation by using the proviso and notified TRAI as the broadcasting regulator in January 2004. The government had by this time realized that like in other network sectors, broadcasting was a mess without a network regulator.

Information and Broadcasting Minister Ravi Shankar Prasad and the law minister, Arun Jaitley, showed immense maturity by giving some powers of the I&B ministry to the regulator, and hoped that the telecom regulator would be able to replicate for the broadcasting sector, what they did for telecom. The team within TRAI looking at media did not let down the minister and was able to clear the mess in network broadcasting, and the cable system grew immensely.

The FM (frequency-regulated) radio business was in difficulty at this time and was not growing, as the operators had bid high amounts as licence fee which they could not pay. Channel after channel was closing down. TRAI was asked to look into these issues and give recommendations after Amit Mitra, the Secretary General of FICCI (Federation of Indian Chambers of Commerce and Industry) and presently the finance and industry minister of West Bengal, had made some recommendations. TRAI's recommendations were accepted and the sector grew.

We began regulating without TRAI having any domain knowledge of the I&B sector, staff, space or resources. These resources came gradually. For the advisor's job, I selected Rakesh Kacker, a Tamil Nadu cadre IAS (Indian Administrative Service) officer who had worked with me in the power sector, doing initial work on power regulation, law and private power cases. Tamil Nadu had a vibrant cable sector and I thought proximity to that environment would help. He had earlier worked in the Prime Minister's Office and had thus dealt with all ministries. He had just gone back to Tamil Nadu after a stint in The Energy and Resources Institute (TERI) on deputation. According to him, he was entitled to come back to the Government of India as per rules but the Department of Personnel and Training (DOPT) had not agreed to put him on the offer list though his state government had agreed. DOPT suggested he could come on deputation again. However, this would have meant he was not entitled to a government house in TRAI, and the rent allowance admissible was not good enough to get him even a very small house. Moreover, coming on deputation again could have affected his further chances of coming back to the Government of India. He was therefore ready to join in only directly and not on deputation.

I met Cabinet Secretary Kamal Pande twice and explained that I had accepted the broadcasting assignment without any preconditions. The sector was in a mess, and my experience said that Rakesh would be able to deal with the problem without collapsing under pressure. He accepted that he would recommend to the prime minister, but when the file reached the PMO the cabinet secretary recommended that since the rules did not permit, the case should be rejected.

I had to work overtime to get the secretary's advice overruled in the PMO. Fortunately, by this time, I had the blessings of everyone in the PMO, perhaps due to TRAI doing outstanding work. Rakesh came immediately from Chennai on receiving the posting orders. Meanwhile, we had got more space allotted near our office to house the broadcasting division and had got some people from the broadcasting sector.

During the first half of 2004, we were mainly in the consultation mode as no one in the country had any experience of broadcasting regulation. The first set of recommendations we gave were in August 2004 on FM radio. These were accepted with some modification by the government. This led to the revival of the radio stations that opened in Phase I. It also led to a massive expansion of FM radio in Phase II with about 300 stations becoming operational as against only twenty in Phase I.

The important lesson learned from this experience was that if the bidding design was good, it need not lead to high bids that stunt growth. And with high volumes government revenues also increased, although the revenue per radio station came down in Phase II as compared to Phase I. Unfortunately, despite the success of this model of bidding, the government did not open bidding for Phase III for a long time. It was opened in 2015.

The next set of recommendations were on cable TV, including DTH (Direct to Home). We came out in support of CAS (Central Authentication Service). Later, after I left, CAS was mandated by the Delhi High Court in the four metros originally included in the 2003 notification. Now this is being spread to other cities and also to the free-to-air channels which were left out in the 2003 notification.

The cable TV recommendations also covered DTH. In 2004, there was only one DTH operator, Dish TV, who was not able to get content of rival broadcasting companies like Star, Sony, Sun and others. Their subscriber base was a modest one million with hardly any growth. Tata Sky's application was still under examination. No one else seemed interested. Consumers had no choice but to depend on the cable operator which overwhelmingly was a local monopoly.

We mandated through a regulation in December 2004 that all broadcasters must provide their content to all platforms on a non-discriminatory basis. This was backed by the government incorporating this in the licence conditions, and later clearing the applications of Tata Sky and Sun TV. This led to a massive expansion of DTH, with over forty million subscribers today. Consumers now have an alternative to the cable TV operator.

There were other regulations introduced to protect smaller cable TV operators who were at the mercy of large broadcasters.

The courts were also very pleased because there being earlier no regulator of this network, the I&B ministry, without any knowledge of regulation and of specific powers of regulation, could not solve the numerous and complex problems of the network sector and all disputes earlier landed in the high courts and the Supreme Court. With the regulator now applying its mind in an open, transparent and consultative manner, issues were sorted out through speaking orders and new regulations, and the courts' jobs became simpler.

Some judges that I spoke to in this period were fed up with litigations on the cable TV work. The high courts and the Supreme Court in India mostly do appellate work, and these disputes came to them without regulator's application of mind on the issues, and that had perhaps led to an order of a particular high court to appoint a sectoral regulator. It is very interesting to note that similar problems between telecom operators, both public and private, who were inducted in 1995 by the government, led the Delhi High Court to give an ultimatum to the Government of India to appoint a regulator before 31 July 1997, and that is how the TRAI came into existence.

The broadcasting regulation was so successful that this measure, having no legal backing of a specific Act with clear procedures and having a subsection only as its legal backing, was able to put the sector on an even keel towards growth and manageable tariffs.

Telecom and broadcasting are litigious sectors. Our regulations helped everyone move towards growth. Even then, there were petitions in the Delhi High Court against TRAI being appointed regulator without specific legal backing and only on the basis of a notification. There were long arguments from both sides. Perhaps we won, because the judiciary was not keen on taking over these complex disputes, without a regulator issuing regulations and intervening first. Most of our regulations were also challenged in the TDSAT and here also we won all the cases as our approach was transparent and fair. Extensive consultations were held at every stage, even at the drafting stage which was a regulatory innovation in India at that point of time and is now widely used.

Another important recommendation was on community radio. During the process of consultation on FM radio, many NGOs suggested that we do a similar exercise for community radio too as this segment was languishing. The Act permitted Suo Moto recommendations and so, even though the government had not asked for any recommendations, we sent these. These were largely accepted by the government, and like FM radio the policy of the government was a huge success. At the time of sending the recommendations there was only one community radio. The government has now given permission to 450 community radio stations of which about 170 are operational.

There were two other areas where we sent recommendations but the government did not move on them. One was Satellite Radio. There was only one operator, World Space. As our recommendations were not acted upon, the problems remained and ultimately this service collapsed. The other was opening up terrestrial TV to the private sector. This still remains Doordarshan's monopoly. Consequently the cable TV space is still congested with high carriage charges. And a large amount of this spectrum is lying unused.

India has one of the world's most efficient cable TV systems, with eighty-eight million connections and a daily cable audience estimated at over 100 million people. An average rental of Rs 150 per month provides around forty channels, through over 60,000 independent cable TV operators. This is from a standing start point in 1991; India had one TV channel, the state-owned Doordarshan. Large number of competing channels and increasing numbers of DTH consumers have changed the politics of the country.

Ten years from the notification, TRAI is still the broadcasting regulator, and is involved with all initiatives of the I&B ministry, including mandatory digitization of the sector, a very progressive move. The I&B ministry does not control any aspect of running the broadcasting regulatory set-up. Yet the arrangement works very efficiently, showing that the regulatory set-up in India has matured immensely from the days of wars between the Regulator and the Ministry of Telecommunication.

A lot of improvement can be brought out in government functioning even without new laws being passed. It is typical of many bureaucrats to run for new legislation to change systems. I have shown in a later chapter how T.N. Seshan changed the entire election system in the country without asking for new election laws. Courts in India normally support improvements in the system even if it can be done with marginal/progressive interpretation of law. Getting a new legislation passed is a tedious process, and should be avoided if improvements can be made with progressive interpretations of law. My experience with disinvestment process was also similar, when many were recommending change in law for disinvestment, particularly privatization. Attempts for new legislation could have opened unnecessary Pandora's boxes, delaying privatization efforts.

PART II

REFORMS IN OTHER SECTORS

7

Reforms in a Hurry: Power Sector Reforms in Post-1991 India

Power reforms were initiated in 1991 without adequate preparation. They began soon after liberalization and the country had to pay a heavy price. Many projects finalized in consultation with prospective operators could not be converted into agreements, leading to huge slippages in meeting generation targets. Ideally, regulators should have been appointed and network elements unbundled into generation, transmission and distribution to set up institutional arrangements to deal with complicated issues of inducting private capital in the power network. This was not done till 1998, when the Electricity Supply (Amendment) Act and the Electricity Regulatory Commissions Act were passed, and electricity boards unbundled into generation, transmission and distribution companies. It was later realized that this amendment could not deal with all the issues and hence the new Electricity Act was passed in 2003. This Act has also not been implemented in its entirety and problems creating a competitive electricity market across states continue. Reforms in all sectors, particularly the network sectors, require a lot of preparation. For instance, reforms in the telecom sector were preceded by issuing the NTP 1994, followed by NTP 1999. The regulator also started issuing orders and making recommendations to deal with the break-up of the sector. In the 'competition' sector, the regulator was asked to do a five-year advocacy to familiarize the country with the implementation of the new law and to prepare regulations. The government's failure to perform due diligence before introducing power reforms led to problems and cost the country dearly. An equilibrium leading to growth is yet to be found.

Evolution of the New Economic Policy

In 1991, the government beset with a severe balance of payments crisis made an opportunity out of an adversity and set forth a bold reformist agenda. The initiatives announced signalled a systemic change from the post-colonial development strategy based on import substitution, public sector dominance and pervasive government control over the private sector. Private investment, deregulation and delicensing were the new buzzwords. For the first time, the government was forthright in its initiatives and announced it was reforming the Indian economy by bringing a series of measures aimed at achieving higher growth and increasing investment. It brought the private sector into the economy as an engine of growth, liberalized foreign direct investment, drastically reduced the number of industries exclusively reserved for the public sector, and most importantly, introduced delicensing.

Evolution of the New Power Policy

One of the sectors which embarked on the reforms path soon after 1991 was the power sector. In most other countries, this network sector was touched last due to its vicious monopoly characteristic. However, we tried to reform the sector by bringing private investment into generation, without having studied the sector or the implications of this move. We had not even done any preliminary work on power network reforms.

The same was repeated in the telecom sector. But things were remedied in this case between 1995, when private sector players were invited, and 1997, when a new Act was passed. Unfortunately, in the power sector it took seven years, 1991–98, to set up a regulatory system and break the sector into network elements. It was only after the Electricity Supply Act was amended, and a new Electricity Regulatory Commissions Act passed in 1998, that the network was broken. Till then the sector continued to negotiate with the private sector players, and allowed entry on negotiated prices, tariffs and interconnection conditions. At this stage, everyone realized that a new comprehensive law needed to be passed for smooth transition to the new power network, and the Electricity Act 2003 was passed. It was amended in 2004 and then again in 2007.

It was not without reason that both in the USA and in the UK, reforms in the electricity sector came after other sectors had been dealt with and the country had enough experience of implementation. In the UK, power reforms started when the Central Electricity Generating Board (CEGB) was broken up by an enabling law in 1989, though reforms in other sectors had started in the 1970s. In the USA, the power reforms came in the mid-1990s. Till then the sector continued as Investor Owned Utilities (IOUs) and Rural Electricity Cooperatives (RECs) for rural areas, controlling all network elements in each state. Sometimes the state governments controlled/owned these IOUs. There are different models in other countries.

We had a very aggressive power secretary, R. Rajgopalan, and power minister, Kalpnath Rai, at the time of liberalization. They decided to privatize only the new generating stations on negotiated tariffs on the basis of the capital cost approved by the Central Electricity Authority (CEA), without initiating scientific reforms and were sure this model could work. Later, the power secretary became the cabinet secretary, and no one questioned the policy evolved by him. The cost of the project, the conditions for interconnection to the grid, and the tariff to the private operators were to be decided by negotiations with no regulations being issued. When it was felt that the bankrupt State Electricity Boards (SEBs) would not be able to pay high tariffs of the private generating stations, a counter-guarantee procedure was evolved. The Government of India counter-guaranteed the payment liabilities of the SEBs and state governments. This negotiation process was to be decided between big corporates and multinationals and the Electricity Boards, with the Ministry of Power and Finance actively involved in counter-guarantee cases. The active involvement of the government and the state governments/ Electricity Boards in a negotiation process involving thousands of crores of rupees was an inefficient model. It could never lead to a viable agreement. This model was expensive but could not be given up early as negotiations had started on many projects involving large multinationals and other companies. Let us see the consequences of the cost-plus dispensation.

High Capital Costs

The price of a thermal power plant was Rs 1 crore per megawatt (MW) in the early 1980s. Power reforms of 1991 only privatized generation, leaving the SEBs to buy power from these private power plants. The cost-plus dispensation, cost inflation, perceived risks and the guarantee regime led to the certified costs going up to as much as Rs 5 crore per MW in the early 1990s. Such huge price distortions are natural when the government buys or sells any commodity at a negotiated price. This has been seen in defence, civil aviation, coal and licence/spectrum sectors in India. Unsurprisingly, the collapse of this impractical dispensation led to a reduction of the power plant costs to Rs 1.75 crore per MW in the late 1990s. The system led to operators getting approval on heavily padded costs during negotiations. Fortunately, not many projects got approved and the few projects in which counter-guarantees were approved soon collapsed due to structural infirmities.

One of the consequences of our private power policy was that, both in India and in the USA, senior politicians in the government acquired personal interests in such projects and started taking unusual initiative in their clearance. During discussions for these clearances, some of the international companies' representatives refused to come to logical terms, aware of the political support they enjoyed in India and abroad. Consequently, many felt that the resultant high tariffs were unviable for these projects, and would ultimately lead to encashment of the counter-guarantee given by the Centre. This would have been hugely embarrassing.

The key person deciding any issue in the government is the joint secretary. Since Enron's Power Purchase Agreement (PPA) and counter-guarantees were already cleared when I started dealing with private power, there was immense pressure in going forward with the other projects and to clear them. I found limited support in the Ministry of Power and the Ministry of Finance to look at projects and the clearance process afresh, since all senior functionaries were under severe pressure to expedite clearances. During meetings for such projects, I found a junior joint secretary in the Ministry of Finance standing up to these issues, blocking clearances and bringing the evolved private power policy to its logical future of breaking up the sector into network elements and appointment of regulators, etc. I owe immense gratitude to this intellectual, honest and brilliant officer, Gajendra Haldea. Everyone criticized him for raising objections, but no one had the courage to challenge or shift him, since everyone perhaps supported his objections but were not prepared to admit it. This difficult assignment and my inability to issue clearances after obtaining the concurrence of the promoters and the finance ministry for different projects resulted in a delay in my promotion by a few months. No one accepted my position; I could do nothing if the promoter and the Ministry of Finance did not reach an agreement. One project did get cleared during this period as the project promoters gave up all demands and fell in line with the ministry's position decided by Haldea. Being unhappy with me, the government decided to check my credentials again with all the state and central agencies to delay my promotion.

Fortunately, these agencies repeated the integrity certificates they had given a few months earlier. I was promoted to additional secretary in the Ministry of Power, followed by special secretary and then even appointed as secretary on the file twice. The secretary's orders were never issued. That I kept getting promoted was perhaps due to the quiet realization at senior levels in the government that I was trying to manage changes which, though leading to complaints, would bring the power sector reforms on an even keel.

Change in Power Policy

When all our efforts to start private generating stations failed, the existing Acts were changed in 1998 and 2003. By this time the country was beset with power shortages and a large number of companies lost a lot of money on failed projects. To put things in perspective, from 1991 to 1997, the country could achieve only 50 per cent of all its generation targets, mostly through the public sector. The targets were conservative to begin with. Sadly, this poor performance continues even today, with very mild improvement last year, since the provisions of the new Act have not been implemented in their true spirit. Additionally, there have also been enormous problems in getting environmental clearances for these projects and making fuel available because of trouble in the coal and petroleum sectors.

This was not so in the telecom sector, where if at all, TRAI was always overenthusiastic about exercising powers. This led to a much better network with huge growth and much lower tariffs. The regulators displeased many and paid for it.

The same Gajendra Haldea, who was accused of blocking progress by not clearing our PPAs, negotiated projects in 1993 and later, was appointed to write the new 2003 Act. He did an extremely good job. The draft law was examined in detail by the Parliament, underwent the scrutiny of a parliamentary select committee, and was then passed. The Act has already been amended twice, in 2004 and 2007, to bring in a more competitive regime. Later, Haldea was asked to write the agreements in many sectors even by the state and continues to do so. Many, including ministers in the UPA-II, criticized him but were not able to touch him.

The negotiation and cost-plus process initiated in 1991 had led to disastrous results with the capital costs rose. This was due to a perceived high demand for equipment being negotiated by different companies with manufacturers and also due to the heavy padding by operators. This was changed to a bidding process early in the year 2000. The perceived huge shortage in generation capacity and coal availability also led to the approval for setting up pithead mega power projects of 4,000 MW capacity. Such large projects essentially have to be interstate projects. Thus, for all mega projects, the Central Electricity Regulatory Commission (CERC) has much more powers than for small single-state projects.

Typically, the size and the location of power plants is determined on many economic criteria and most large plants sell power across states which require sorting out issues of dispatch, sale, shortages, frequency of the grid, etc. In the government, these issues were settled continuously through discussions between the electricity boards, the state and the Central governments and the central generating stations. Private plants require long-term arrangements, and these can only be settled in an unbundled scenario by the Act, the regulators prescribing the rules of the game and enforcing them. Reforming the sector without putting in such arrangements and then not enforcing the spirit of the 2003 Act by the CERC has only delayed the finalization of long-term arrangements and unfinished projects.

It is fully accepted that for a liberalized public–private system to work there are two primary requirements. First, the project developers need to be selected after competitive price bidding; this was initiated for almost all future projects. Second, the largest possible power market needs to be created with operators working on a level playing field. This is done to encash efficiencies of a large market and to reduce costs through increased competition. This required effective provisions in the Act, which were introduced by prescribing open access between the generators and defined consumers (and not the boundaries of distribution companies), thus creating a market. This market was to gradually expand by reducing the 1 MW consumer definitions for open access. But even the first stage did not happen in the prescribed time, and since then, the Ministry of Power, the Planning Commission (now known as the Niti Aayog), the Ministry of Law, the Ministry of Finance, the Attorney General and others have been trying to find a solution for enforcing open access which is clearly provided in the Act. Let us read the definition of open access:[1]

> Section 2 (47): Open access means the non-discriminatory provision for the use of transmission lines or distribution system or associated facilities with these lines or system by any licensee or a consumer or a person engaged in generation in accordance with the regulations specified by the appropriate commissions.

With so many people trying to find solutions to the numerous problems of the sector, I wonder whether the government should have established the CERC to manage the interconnected all-India network at all, and given it so many absolute powers, with total security of tenure, to be effective. Instead, the CERC had become a meek spectator of the problems of the sector by its own inaction. It was expected in the Act that the regulator will manage the network.

Regulators are appointed in different sectors by the Parliament when it is felt that political governments, owing to their political compulsions, cannot manage networks. It is expected that when regulators start acting, there would be huge confrontations with the multiple operators and even the government. It is for this reason that it is clearly specified that governments can only give policy directions within the Act to the regulator, and the regulators have to work in a transparent, consultative mode. They have also been provided total security of tenure to ensure effectiveness. The Act provided that open access to the defined consumer would be enforced within a prescribed period after 2004 and the government would notify an 'open access subsidy'. The government has completed all its requirements under the Act. Yet open access has not been enforced.

Problems in open access arise when state governments/state commissions/distribution companies create hurdles in non-discriminatory open access and use their emergency powers illogically. At these times, the CERC must use its powers of grid management and issue guidance/orders to the state regulator to stop such practices and take action. It should also take up these cases in the appellate bodies. There are many provisions in Sections 42, 49, 61, 62 and 86 of the Electricity Act 2003, which can be used by the CERC to discipline the open access regime between generators and consumers. It is the only way to create confidence amongst investors that they are operating without discrimination in a large market.

The advantages of a large market have been seen in the telecom sector, where, as the market expanded, the tariffs fell drastically. Advantages of a large market were also seen in Europe when this was established across nation states in Europe, both in terms of an overall market, and also in the power sector, so that they achieved a big market and could be more competitive. The argument that we cannot achieve this between states in a concurrent sector (as per the Constitution of India), in an interconnected grid with enabling provisions in the Act, with Central government agencies and the regulator controlling the dispatch, baffles me. We could have taken a similar view in TRAI after the TDSAT's judgments, or nudges from the government, and relaxed as a 'regulator'.

As a result of this inaction, the CERC has become ineffective, and the Central government and other agencies keep appointing committees to find solutions to regulatory problems. In the last decade, when three grid collapses happened, the government appointed several committees to find solutions. No one asked the CERC, even though it was responsible for grid discipline under the Act to explain its inaction. The CERC too waited for the inane recommendations of such committees. This situation is ideal for the mutual comfort of the government and the regulator. The government still controls the sector as in pre-reform days, against the intentions of the 2003 Act, and the regulator faces no problems due to its inaction. On the other hand, TRAI had faced huge problems due to their overaction. But no one denies that this overaction hugely benefitted the sector and the subscribers. The Supreme Court too, in Ruma Pal's judgment cited in Chapter 5, justified the regulator's actions. But the Supreme Court could not examine any action in the power sector as the regulator had not exercised any power.

In the power sector, the Central regulator perhaps thought that distribution was totally within the state regulator's ambit because power passed through state distribution lines. These were outside the purview of the CERC, whether or not power reached the specified consumers in a non-discriminatory manner, as prescribed in the Act. They could not see the clear definition that 'open access' was between the generator and the consumer, and was not up to the state's or the distributor's boundaries. The CERC had to enforce the provisions of the Act.

The matter, then, was left to committees which never resolved it. Had the CERC enforced in favour of an integrated market and open access till the consumer—at least for the Central and interstate private power which it controls—and implemented it through numerous grid controls, I am quite positive, it would have got the Supreme

Court's nod. Even if it had not, the Central government would have been forced to find a solution that it had not found even twelve years after the Act came into force. After all, the Central government had prescribed open access and notifications between generators and consumers under the Act, and it had to get these implemented once a crisis situation was created by the CERC. But the regulator killed the implementation of the scheme/Act by not overruling and acting against the hindrances created by the state governments. Had the CERC exercised its powers of prescribing the grid code and then enforcing it, we would not have had three total grid collapses in the last decade putting the nation to shame.

It is simple for the CERC to issue regulations with default provisions if the states do not follow open access rules and the cross-subsidies for open access notified by the Central government, prescribed up to the consumer level, under the Act. This is particularly so for Central and private sector power where most of the projects are interstate, giving clear jurisdiction to the CERC. The CERC can enforce the regulations by controlling dispatch of 40 per cent generation and numerous other means.

The regulator cannot keep waiting for a signal from the government. If the Parliament had desired an arrangement like the present one, with no open access across states, it would not have appointed a regulator.

The telecom and power sectors are both natural monopolies and the government has passed similar laws for regulating them. Network regulation has certain common features and these apply equally to these sectors. Yet the power sector has not seen the kind of growth that the telecom sector has, perhaps due to the Central and state governments taking divergent views on the issue of creating open access. If a common market has to be created for an integrated power network, this issue has to be tackled effectively by the government and the regulators. The fundamental objective of any regulation is to promote competition in the market. This is made possible through regulatory environment or rules which must ensure the following objectives:

a. Ease of entry for the players on level playing conditions in both sectors through efficient and minimum cost interconnection, carriage and termination costs, etc., sufficient capacities and easily understood rules for all producers, transmitters and consumers.
b. Environment created by shortage of power may disrupt a power market but, if honestly implemented, open access, as defined in Section 2(47) in the Electricity Act of 2003, has the strength to quickly redress shortage situations by facilitating new generating stations. Shortage environment cannot lead to a market which enables rationed supply.
c. Rules of the game should not change to commercially favour any class of players whether government or private.
d. Minimum network subsidies to increase competition in other unbundled elements.
e. Independence of the regulator through transparent consultation and issuance of speaking orders/recommendations.

Open access was to be non-discriminatory as prescribed by the regulator, who has been given the power and jurisdiction over all intervening networks of the state entities to ensure flow of power from region to region or within the same region. However, sometimes the law in this regard is not clear. So, was the law not clear in the telecom sector also, leading to different interpretations in the TDSAT and the Supreme Court? Enforcing the spirit of the Act by TRAI helped the sector enormously and led to positive final interpretations by the Supreme Court.

The CERC has moved very haltingly. In 2008, some comprehensive open access regulations came into effect. Yet the objective of ensuring non-discriminatory interconnection to Central transmission networks, intervening state transmission networks and distribution companies for all types of customers has not been fully established.

People have asked me how the CERC could enforce this. The doubters should read the powers given to the CERC regarding ensuring grid discipline. They can invoke those powers, but not acting in the name of federal polity and ignoring the specific provisions of the Act, to my mind, is incorrect. Some experts have also argued that these powers are not specifically prescribed in the Act. My conviction is that the power is inherent in reference to the Central/interstate power. I do recall the doubters arguing with me about TRAI's powers vis-à-vis ADC, carriage/termination charges, etc., being fixed by TRAI. We enforced these directives despite the adverse findings of our appellate body, and the Supreme Court ruled in our favour, stating that we had the powers. I do not know the power sector well, but even if the SC rules otherwise for the power sector, the government would be forced to find a remedy for open access as prescribed by law. Today, due to lack of open access, there is no power market and competition, and I wonder whether the entire scheme of the 2003 Act has brought any benefits. It would perhaps be advisable to scrap the 2003 Act, and go back to the government's control of the sector if the regulator is not able to find a remedy.

The government must also intervene effectively in the fuel supply agreements. It is illogical to leave it to the bidders when there is no coal supply market for such huge projects, either internationally or in the country. Consequently, many such projects are waiting for government or the Supreme Court's solutions. Improper allocations of risks, as in many such projects, have led to an illogical position that the projects are complete but yet the states and consumers are buying power from far more expensive alternatives. All this chaos in the power sector has also led to huge non-performing assets of the banking sector, and if not remedied soon, can lead to collapse of the Indian economy.

The argument against open access to large urban consumers is perhaps that this cannot be done for rural consumers. We had similar reasons for rural areas in telecom and all those were tackled by progressive regulations and subsequent reforms. Rural telecom density went up to 50 per cent today from 2 per cent in 2007. Incidentally, 2 per cent was achieved after sixty years of the monopoly phase. There are other examples of dealing with rural areas like the Rural Electrification Corporation (REC) arrangement in the USA. But open access has to be facilitated first, to create a power market, before any other reform.

Since no efforts have been made by the CERC to create a power market, no one recognizes its presence. It suits both the Central government and the CERC, and reminds me of the time when the Central government did not want me to act on Unified Service Licensing despite the cabinet's directive. I would have had a gala time if I had agreed with the minister's oral instructions. Despite its powers, the inaction of the CERC vis-à-vis its powers of issuing and implementing a comprehensive grid code leaves all initiative of controlling the grid to Central and state government agencies.

Today, we are exploring options to 'Make in India'. The rates at which the power prices will stabilize after the current auctions in comparison to competing economies would be critical to the success of the 'Make in India' campaign. Unless supply in the grid increases with more viable generation, captive generation will keep growing, leading to more expensive power for consumers and more pollution. Further, in an environment of scarcity, open access will be difficult to implement. Some experts today believe that captive power, which is produced for own use, in India exceeds grid power. This has led to great distortions. The official figures do not reflect this situation, as they only count big captive units, and that too, not entirely, as of now. These issues can only be dealt with through effective implementation of the 2003 Act. Only open access will lead to a situation where private producers will start generating only when demand is identified. It was this phenomenon in the telecom sector that targets were overachieved by 500 per cent of the Government of India's projections.

Initiating reforms in any sector requires intense research on the problems of the sector and due diligence to identify the solutions. There are no short cuts. In the network sectors, the most important reform is to create the largest possible market for the final product in which a very large number of players can enter and compete in a level playing field, assured to them by a sector regulator through transparent regulations and orders. Regulators should also ensure that external players do not disturb these conditions. Only if the regulator can assure that these regulations are implemented, the operators, particularly the new ones, will have the confidence to invest in the network to improve their services, and consequently the performance of the network. In the power sector, honest reforms can lead to a situation where both users and producers of power can decide on the advisability of new generating stations and their locations.

The government cannot be the main player in a liberalized economy.

8

DISINVESTMENT: NEW LEARNINGS

I accepted the posting offered to me as secretary (disinvestment) and the political brief to begin strategic disinvestments, commonly termed as privatization. The speed at which we completed these extremely difficult deals, with no complaints, perhaps led to my subsequent appointment as the chairman, TRAI. The enormous growth in the telecom sector due to the reforms we implemented led to the establishment of my consulting company. There was not a whiff of a complaint even eight to ten years after these events transpired. When inquiries started, they were to achieve a political purpose and were therefore accompanied with huge publicity; it almost looked like paid publicity. The inquiries were against me and not the former minister. His decision to jump into the inquiries cost him dearly in terms of perpetual harassment for a long period. I ponder whether I took the right decision in 2000, accepting a reluctant offer by the government to join as secretary (disinvestment).

My posting as secretary in the Ministry of Disinvestment in 2000 had an interesting background. I was first told that I was being posted as secretary (power), from the post of special secretary. But when the incumbent secretary, V.K. Pandit, did not want to join as member of the Minority Commission, a post being created for Kashmiris, I continued as special secretary. Later, I was told I would be posted as secretary (telecom). When the orders did not come, I questioned Principal Secretary Brijesh Misra, who reluctantly asked me whether I would like to join the newly created post of secretary (disinvestment). He was surprised at my positive response as he was doubtful that anyone in their senses would want to join a non-existent department with no clear mandate, trained staff or infrastructure, and a clear possibility of facing inquisitions later, as had happened in many countries. The privatizations completed by me early in my career, even before the evolution of a privatization policy, had faced no inquiries. This gave me confidence and I thought that there would be no inquiries here as well if we were able to develop transparent procedures which required committee approvals rather than individual approvals.

Another reason I joined this post was the obligation I felt towards the government as, in 1987, they had funded a one-year course on reforms and privatization at the Oxford University. During the training, I learnt the benefits of privatization and the boost it provided to the United Kingdom, and was eager to replicate the same in India. What I didn't know was the illogical provision in the Prevention of Corruption Act which could lead to conviction without a charge of corruption. In a nutshell, I was foolish to take up this job, especially when the government agencies could allow registration of cases in deals cleared by an HC or the SC even twelve years after the event.

I joined the Ministry of Disinvestment in January 2000 as secretary. I had neither a room nor any staff. While in the Ministry of Power, the World Bank had asked me to conduct a course on reforms for the power officials of Vietnam in February 2000. I was keen to go since the World Bank paid well, but the Parliament session was on during that period, and there was only skeletal staff in the ministry. Yet the usually overconfident minister, Arun Jaitley, allowed me to go, on the condition that I would review/edit the Parliament questions sitting on a fax machine in our embassy in Vietnam. Both Arun Jaitley and the new secretary did a reasonable job in answering for the government regarding the questions that were raised. Perhaps this was a beginning of the future shape of things for me, when issues could be resolved long-distance with the help of technology.

I was told by the cabinet secretary, and perhaps rightly, that I had to organize everything myself. So I started at home, asking my wife to work as my personal assistant. After all, no bureaucrat or minister's PA would take me seriously if I rang up directly and called myself a secretary. The cabinet secretary had also told me that there was no government space, and I would have to look at private accommodation. I was not excited at this prospect since I knew that the Ministry of Disinvestment's files would become sensitive after some time and it would be unsafe to keep them in private buildings.

I initially occupied the room of the chairman, Disinvestment Commission, and ultimately got limited space allotted in the Central Government Office (CGO) complex. We expanded as the adjoining Office of Police Reforms shifted to another building. We had decided to limit our staff to forty-nine and work through an army of consultants and investment bankers who were experts in the field of mergers and acquisitions. Initially, we knew little. Looking back, I am happy that we did not add any non-experts in the department, something we often do in government. The consultants did brilliant work and whenever the CAG, any HC or the SC looked at the privatization deals, we got the approvals barring some minor observations from the CAG in a few cases. Things deteriorated when non-experts started examining the deals on anonymous complaints—twelve years after the cases were closed. Nothing could be more perverse.

Privatization frees scarce resources, which are otherwise inefficiently utilized in running public industries, for more important needs of the country. Privatization and reforms have significant similarities. Reforms bring in private capital and increase competition in new industries and sectors of the economy facilitating huge growth; privatization does the same with the public sector industries. However, a significant difference between the two is that in reforms one does not have to deal with powerful groups existing within the public sector or the government which have a vested interest in maintaining status quo. In privatization, on the other hand, one not only needs to deal with the groups wanting to retain the current command economy model but also with groups in the public sector, who have to be convinced that their interests will not be harmed if the company is privatized.

My experience and disappointments in the Ministry of Power between 1994 and 2000 had convinced me that it was imperative to have the rules and structures of the proposed privatizations in place before embarking on the journey. My initiation into the area was eased by the discovery that though the Ministry of Disinvestment was new, there had earlier existed a Disinvestment Commission which had done remarkable work in laying down the procedures and the policies to be followed for the process.

Unfortunately, before the Disinvestment Commission could start its work in earnest it was disbanded since it was without a statutory backing, without which it was felt that it could not implement policies of the government and execute disinvestments. It was clarified that only ministries could be answerable to the Parliament and not non-statutory commissions. G.V. Ramakrishna, who had been the chairman of the Disinvestment Commission, had to wind up his office and have his work transferred to different administrative ministries which owned the Central Public Sector Units (CPSUs) chosen for privatization.

Later, all such privatization cases came back to the Ministry of Disinvestment and most were privatized. These ministries were already administering the PSUs and had a vested interest in letting the industries continue in their public sector form since the staff of such ministries enjoyed a number of perks and a lot of power. The privatization of these industries would have meant an end to this cosy relationship of between the ministry staff and the PSUs under their control. I remember how, when I joined the Ministry of Steel, I was congratulated by many that I was joining a ministry with the maximum number of CPSUs in the Government of India and would therefore have a gala time. How could one change these equations so convenient to politicians, bureaucrats and many other groups, at the expense of the taxpayer?

On joining the Ministry of Disinvestment, I got the privatization files transferred from all such ministries to my department after getting an order issued by the cabinet secretary. The resistance in different ministries to privatization was so great that sometimes senior civil servants of the rank of secretaries would resist even my physical entry to their ministries as my entry signified that their power in the form of CPSUs would soon end. In order to overcome the stonewalling, I got an order issued by the government with the help of an extremely progressive and bright cabinet secretary, Prabhat Kumar. The order stated that I would write the confidential reports (CRs) of the joint secretaries dealing with disinvestment cases in different ministries. Despite being armed with this power, there was still a lot of resistance in the ministries. Such was the degree of vested interest! Finally, at my recommendation some officers blocking disinvestments in the ministries were transferred out. Only then did work proceed smoothly but it also led to bad blood with some of my colleagues.

All the rules of disinvestment were streamlined and were issued in the form of manuals so that there could be no deviation from the rules. The manuals duly approved by the government came in very handy when the CBI, under political pressure, initiated a number of irresponsible inquiries against me, including questioning the procedures. I will discuss those cases later in the book.

In my three-year stint in the Ministry of Disinvestment, we privatized almost one unit every month—a record of sorts. The privatization process led to huge revenues. The total proceeds from privatization in India were higher than those from privatization of a large number of public sector units in China or Russia. The experience of privatization in China and Russia provides an interesting contrast with the experience in India. The Chinese and Russian governments could not privatize efficiently as they did not have private entrepreneurs who could take over the industries. Moreover, they did not have instruments such as a developed stock market which could disperse ownership widely. They tried to sell to multinationals (MNCs) but there were not too many takers as the MNCs were apprehensive about the lack of clear-cut rules to run private industries. Left with no option, the government in Russia sold the units to its employees at throwaway prices. The scheme became hugely unpopular because the public sector managers were not entrepreneurs and they led the industries to closure. This resulted in massive unemployment. Moreover, the employees who had purchased the shares of these companies at low prices anticipating enormous profits were left with huge losses when the units shut shop. In China, when they could not sell, they followed another strategy. They simply allowed a number of units to die and then replaced them with new private sector units. The strategy was flawed as they earned 'nil' income from several such units. The Indian privatization effort on the other hand was highly successful. The success was undoubtedly facilitated by our mixed economy and the presence of a developed stock market and a big and vibrant private sector which could efficiently buy and turn around public companies.

The success is well borne out by numbers. The privatization of 0.14 million companies employing 120 million people in the public sector in China led to revenues of US $8 billion. In Russia, the privatization of 1.4 million companies employing eighty million people led to revenues of US $8 billion. Compared to this, the sale of less than 5 per cent equity in 250-odd companies and privatization of about thirty companies employing about two million people led to revenues exceeding US $12 billion in India (till 2003).

After I retired from the government in 2006, I wrote a book,

Disinvestment in India: I Lose and You Gain, published by Pearson in 2008. This book lists all the details of the programme and its benefits. I would recommend this book to those interested in understanding the benefits of privatization as it explains the very high price for the privatizing units that we got for the taxpayer who owned these units. I have also explained in the book how the performance of the company led to much higher turnover, profits and taxes from the company, and its expansion leading to more employment. The inquisitions against privatization launched by the UPA government were against low valuation. When we showed the CBI team an SC ruling in 2008 that valuation did not matter if the sale was through competitive bidding, the case was closed. Fortunately for us, all cases of implementing privatizations landed in different courts in the country including, the high courts and the Supreme Court and we did not get any adverse findings. Later, in early 2014, the inquiries were perhaps a part of the grand conspiracy hatched during the period when UPA-II was in power. Had it not been so, the present finance minister would not have at that time written long articles in newspapers supporting privatization. In any case, the Supreme Court had approved most cases.

When the process started, foreign companies, except for a few, showed no keenness to enter these uncharted waters. The bids were mostly won by Indian companies. I believe once the rules of mergers and acquisitions in India become clearer, there will be global interest in Indian privatizations. In today's competitive industrial environment, all underperforming companies are acquired by other companies and the fear of this keeps all managers and owners on their toes. I would dare say that the privatization of the public sector in India has led to the maturing of the entire mergers and acquisitions sector, with more and more foreign companies also acquiring Indian companies. The economic polity today is a testament to the success of these efforts.

Earlier, objections were raised against cross-country acquisitions of both public and private companies in various countries. However, with increasing globalization, a lot of such objections have been cleared paving the path for acquisitions by foreign companies if another round of privatization takes place. Today, no country can afford to be an inefficient producer of goods and services, and the public sector is inefficient, especially in India, privatizations will soon be the order of the day. Let me deal with some of the issues in private sector mergers in the last decade.

The successful bid by Mittal Steel for control of Arcelor is a vivid reminder for all companies that unless the existing management can deliver the best results for their shareholders, empty rhetoric and tactical takeover defence mechanisms will not prevent the eventual change of ownership. As in the case of Arcelor, transfer of ownership is always contentious because it threatens the status quo and the position of the incumbent management. This phenomenon is even stronger during the sale of PSUs.

Existing managements are often merely rent seekers, trying to protect their turf. They turn to meaningless debate in an attempt to deflect attention from the key business issues. Jingoistic appeals to nationalistic sentiment have often been employed when the takeover is by a foreign entity. 'How can an Indian buy a great European firm' was a common refrain in the Mittal–Arcelor episode. 'How can the Americans buy a British company' was the battle cry when the American firm, Southern Utilities, attempted the takeover of the British National Power Co. The sentiment was so strong that Queen Elizabeth II had to use the golden share option (a mechanism created by the UK government to block transfer of control if the golden share was with the queen) to stop the sale. Even in the US, the supposed bastion of globalization, one saw the sale of a 51 per cent stake in the Rockefeller Group in Waldorf Astoria Hotel in New York to the Chinese come under severe criticism. But with performance becoming key, such arguments are fast losing ground.

An Australian official report in 2003 said: 'Most economic

commentators agree that privatization is beneficial when it results in private firms operating in competitive markets. However, the public is sceptical of the benefits of privatization.' The reason for this divergence of opinion between the experts and the public is the 'informal tactics' of the rent seekers and the inability of the experts to educate the public about the real economic issues. The public sector disinvestment debate in India is no exception.

It is perhaps for this reason that Margaret Thatcher, who, despite being the first Conservative prime minister to have assured five terms for her party in Britain, never mentioned 'disinvestment' or 'privatization' in her manifestos, though she pursued privatization with greater vigour in each term and was able to give tax cuts to boost the economy. She was unlike other prime ministers who sometimes did not last even a term due to the deteriorating UK economy. She turned the economy around and was popular (as per a survey conducted after her ouster) even when her own party members threw her out.

Times have now changed. No one was bothered about the Tatas taking over Corus and Jaguar–Land Rover and many other such cross-border acquisitions. With increasing forces of globalization, this is happening in the Indian private sector also. The Indian public is no longer sympathetic to public sector undertakings incurring huge losses and then using taxpayers' and private money to stay afloat.

Before privatization started in India, the returns on capital invested in government companies were abysmally low, making their ownership a drain on the exchequer. An educated public opinion did not accept that 107 out of 227 Central Public Sector Enterprises (CPSEs) in 2002–03 incurred a loss of Rs 10,944 crore. This was despite government support of Rs 2,700 crore. If the companies operating in monopoly environments were excluded, the remaining public sector companies only made a profit of about Rs 400 crore. The drain on the coffers of the country is obvious when one considers that this was the return on about Rs 1 lakh crore of taxpayers' money invested in equity, and almost double the amount in loans. This is something India can ill afford. Moreover, out of a total labour force of 3.5 crore in the late 1990's, less than two crore people were employed in the government-controlled industrial and service-oriented entities. Despite this abysmal record, it is the strong constituency of CPSU workers and managers which continues to stonewall privatization efforts and successfully drown out the silent majority of taxpayers who subsidize the public sector. In the process it is the consumer who continues to suffer from poor service, high prices and limited competition. Yashwant Sinha's first budget spoke of privatization. Neither the Narendra Modi government's first budget nor its manifesto have spoken of privatization. The continued disastrous performance of companies such as Air India and many others justify their privatization.

The strong performance of privatized companies, the lack of any adverse political repercussion to such privatizations, and the globalization of the Indian economy are strong factors to turn political opinion in favour of privatization in future. Besides, the huge demand for revenues to meet the expenditures of the 2014 NDA government's expenditures will force larger privatizations soon. This effort will especially be successful if an aggressive campaign is launched to prove how big a drain on taxpayers' money the public sector really is, and how the money can be better utilized. It is my belief that workers will surely back privatization.

Noted economists Jagdish Bhagwati and Arvind Panagariya in their book *Reforms and Economic Transformation in India* said:[1]

> Privatization in India has encountered numerous roadblocks over the last two decades. Opposition argues that it would lead to widespread lay-offs and a redistribution of wealth in favour of the politically connected. It has also been argued that selling profitable firms to raise revenues for general government expenditure does not make economic sense. However, our

> results suggest that selling both partial and majority equity stakes is associated with significant improvements in profitability and efficiency of PSUs. We find the sale of majority equity stakes accompanied by the transfer of management control from the government to private ownership has an economically significant impact on performance. This result suggests that full privatization may have a greater impact on profitability of firms, without requiring lay-offs or a decline in worker compensation.

The companies privatized from 2003 made far more money for the taxpayer in comparison to the minority disinvestment sale from 1995 to 2002. The shift in strategy was a conscious decision based on the fact that privatization gave us three to thirty times more money per share on a comparative basis and also ensured a sea change in the working of the company resulting in increased profit, higher taxes, growth and investment in the same company. It is true that most of the privatization in the west, particularly in the UK, was carried out by selling majority shares in the market and not a complete or direct sale to a strategic investor, but then their markets were deeper and more efficient. This ensured a quick changeover in the management. Whenever the government became a minority investor, private management controlled by private shareholders took over. In India, we have not yet reached that stage and therefore selling shares to strategic investors is necessary for some time.

Dr Manmohan Singh was the chairman of the Parliamentary Subcommittee on Disinvestment. He cross-examined me once in 2002 and was very negative regarding the privatizations which had been completed. After the meeting, I asked him why he was unhappy with me; after all I was only pursuing the liberalization policies laid down by him as finance minister after 1991 and he had then approved the privatization of ABB-ABL on negotiated price even before the launch of the privatization policy. He replied he was unhappy with the strategic privatization in favour of an industrial group because such disinvestment could lead to charges of favouritism against the secretary/minister. I answered that I was pursuing this route because the government had given permission. I argued that the strategic sale route had resulted in much higher income per share than the minority sale of shares besides making the privatized companies more efficient, which had led to huge benefits for the economy. I also pointed out that we were doing these privatizations with total transparency.

His reply was that the strategic sale route would only lead to inquiries and problems for me later. He proved himself right when his government in the second term, despite a lapse of twelve years of the privatization, started bogus inquiries against me. This was especially surprising since in the years immediately after the privatization there were no complaints or inquiries. The two inquiries which were instituted in 2008 were totally fraudulent as his own finance minister had cleared some of these transactions after CAG's minor observations. The inquiries of 2013 were far more fraudulent as I will show later.

Fortunately the CAG, which later demolished many actions of the UPA-II government, did not find anything wrong in any case of disinvestment. Arun Shourie, who was the minister for disinvestment during the NDA regime, was a great asset during the inquiries. He had not allowed any oversight while we were disinvesting and the government agencies, mindful of his spotless reputation, were not courageous enough to raise spurious objections. He was also known to mercilessly go after anyone who committed any wrongdoing until the matter was taken to its logical conclusion.

I was happy that till 2013, except for one resale in Mumbai, there were no complaints regarding disinvestments done during 2000–03. We were armed with the Supreme Court's orders stating that valuation meant nothing if the company was competitively bid and even if one company had reached the final stage of bidding, it was competitive bidding. After I retired in 2006, officers in the Department of Disinvestment explained the rationale of the valuations to the then finance minister, P. Chidambaram. The minister was satisfied enough with the explanations to overrule the CAG objections on file. The politics of the post-UPA-II scams days changed everything.

I must point out here that the political parties with leftist ideology lose heavily due to strategic disinvestment as the labour unions in public sector undertakings are one of their political tools to mobilise public sentiments. There was a furore in Parliament when the CAG's report and the government's reply were placed in 2006. Despite having defended disinvestment earlier, the finance minister decided to send the disinvestment files to the CBI for further inquisition. I personally feel this was the beginning of the 'coming' end, when the government subordinated its own judgment to that of untrained investigators. The government felt that the CBI could henceforth be used as an agent against those who had worked in the earlier NDA government; to make them talk against the NDA ministers. The UPA's attitude changed after the NDA used the many scams which came to light during their reign to attack the government. The CAG also turned against the UPA-II government due to the indefensible scams and got the complete support of the courts and of the entire polity. UPA-II's strategy to transfer some of the blame to the previous government also did not gain any success as the strategy was ill-prepared and was chalked out without any diligence.

As far as the privatized companies were concerned, their performance was improving every day and the conventional criticism of selling family silver without any benefits was proving to be baseless. I have written about the improved performance in detail in my earlier book but since the case of Hindustan Zinc Limited (HZL) has been raked up again by those who do not understand economic issues,

I am giving below (Table 8.1) some figures about the performance of privatized companies, including HZL, between 2002–03 and 2012–13:

Table 8.1: Performance of Hindustan Zinc Limited

	2002–03 (Rs in Cr.)	2012–13 (Rs in Cr.)
Turnover	1,609	13,658
Profit after Tax (PAT)	142	1,899
Earnings per Share	3.4	16.3 × 5*

Note: (*) Shares were split into five
Source: Company Annual Reports for 2002–03 and 2012–13

The position of other privatized companies also improved and I have dealt with them in my earlier book on disinvestment. It can easily be inferred that the opportunity cost to the economy of not privatizing this company would have been huge. I feel sorry that I did not gather courage to privatize some companies like Air India on valuation issues. As per the report of the CAG, the company later looted the exchequer.

Given below are some figures about the performance of Bharat Aluminium Company (BALCO) before and after privatization between 2000–01 and 2013–14 (Table 8.2):

Table 8.2: Performance of BALCO

	2000–01	2013–14
Turnover in million tone	89,164	252,035
EBIDTA (Rs in Cr.)	97	1,724
Earnings per Share (Rs)	1.95	4.22*

Note: (*) Earnings per share is of 2010–1
Source: Company Annual Reports for 2000–01 and 2013–14

Some figures about Computer Management Corporation's (CMC) performance before and after privatization between 2000–01 and 2013–14 are presented in Table 8.3 below:

Table 8.3: Performance of Computer Management Corporation (CMC)

	2000–01 (Rs in Cr.)	**2013–14 (Rs in Cr.)**
Turnover	537.68	1,338.96
Profit before Tax (PBT)	39.58	385.81
Profit after Tax (PAT)	25.09	323.61
Payment to Exchequer	14.75	62.2
Dividend	35	68.18

Source: Company Annual Reports for 2000–01 and 2013–14

Statistics about performance of Maruti Udyog Limited (MUL) before and after privatization between 2000–01 and 2013–14 are presented in Table 8.4 below:

Table 8.4: Performance of Maruti Udyog Limited

	2000–01	**2013–14**
Production (Units)	350,376	1,153,645
Permanent Employee	5,770	12,547
Outsourced Employee	3,172	6,578
Apprentices		1,099

Source: Company Annual Reports for 2000–01and 2013–14

Some comparative figures about Paradeep Phosphate Limited's (PPL's) performance, before and after privatization between 2000–01 and 2013–14 are presented in Table 8.5 below:

Table 8.5: Performance of Paradeep Phosphate Limited

	2000–01	2013–14
Diammonium Phosphate (DAP) Production (Mt)	528,460	1,008,000
Capacity Utilization in DAP Production (per cent)	73	140
Turnover (Rs in Cr.)	691.9	4,289.27
Profit (Rs in Cr.)	–141	103.59*
Tax to Exchequer (Rs in Cr.)		65.18**

Note: (*) Profit figure is of 2012–13; (**) Tax to exchequer figure is of 2013
Source: Company Annual Reports 2000–01 and 2013–14

We are trying to transform into a developed nation, and cannot continue to suffer the inefficiencies of the public sector and of monopoly companies, which is not on account of the incompetence of employees but because of the inappropriate governance structure and the absence of any competition.

To truly understand the importance of privatization, I must narrate a story about Air India. The case for Air India's privatization was going on in full swing but I was not sure whether we would be able to complete the deal due to complex valuation issues especially in a company with huge losses on its balance sheet. Singapore Airlines had shown some interest in the deal. One day Manjit Singh, a Singapore Airlines officer posted in Delhi to handle the case, brought me a letter from Mme Ho Ching, chairperson, Singapore Airlines and Temasek Holdings. The chairperson wrote that though the case was being pursued in a professional manner by the Department of Disinvestment, Singapore Airlines was withdrawing from the process since it had suffered losses in the acquisition of an Australian and a New Zealand airline. Citing the case of a Middle East airline also having lost huge monies in an acquisition in Sri Lanka and similar cases having taken place in Europe, the letter said that the general climate was not conducive to such acquisitions. I felt sorry that we could not complete the deal. We would have saved thousands of crores of the taxpayers' money in later years.

Much later, when I was chairman, TRAI, the managing director of Temasek (India), Manish Kejriwal, rang me up to request a three-hour meeting with Mme Ho Ching. Though I did not understand the rationale for a three-hour meeting, I agreed. When she came, she utilized the three hours to cross-examine me on the Indian telecom sector and its operators. Then at around 1 p.m. she hurriedly left. Later, Manish told me that Temasek had finalized a two-billion-dollar investment in Airtel and wanted to do due diligence with the regulator of the sector and the company before signing the cheque. He also told me that Mme Ho Ching was the daughter-in-law of the Singaporean prime minister (she is the present prime minister's wife) and was in a hurry because of a luncheon engagement with Prime Minister Atal Bihari Vajpayee. She was full of humility when she met me and I could not guess her VIP status. I was impressed with her and the professionalism of her country in dealing with commercial issues. Incidentally, this investment gave her a good profit.

At the end of this section, I feel I must deal with the comparison between privatization and minority disinvestment. One indicator of disinvestment's efficiency is the price at which shares are sold and the only barometer can be the price of the share divided by its earning. The higher the price to earning (PE) ratio, the more gains there are for the taxpayer who owns the shares. And later if the company does well, the shareholder does well too, earning more from the company, as has been shown many times in privatization deals.

Some figures of PE ratios before 2000 (only disinvestment of minority shares), and after 2000 (privatization of companies, except in the case of Indian Oil Corporation [IOC], Oil and Natural Gas Corporation [ONGC], Gas Authority of India Limited [GAIL] and National Thermal Power Corporation [NTPC]) are presented in Table 8.6 below. The figures speak for themselves. The figures for minority disinvestments after 2000 were higher as the share-buying public felt that these companies might be privatized later. Despite these figures, selling public shares today in minority disinvestments is something that our poor shareholders cannot afford.

Table 8.6: Share Price Performance before and after Disinvestment (1999–2000)

P/E of Sale of Shares 1991–99 (Mostly profit-making companies)	P/E of Disinvestment 2000 onwards (Both profit-and-loss-making CPSUs)
IOC = 4.9, BPCL = 5.7	IBP = 63, IBP IPO = 8.5, BALCO = 19, CMC = 12
HPCL = 5.9, GAIL = 4.4	CMC = 46.2, DCIL = 8.9, MFIL = Very High
VSNL = 6	LJMC = Very High, PPL = Very High, Jessop = Very High
	VSNL = 11 (without sale of land, which will give huge incomes once lands are sold, and will lead to a record P/E), HZL = 26, Maruti = 89, Maruti IPO = 28.5
	ONGC = 9.5, GAIL = 10.1, NTPC = 12.4, IPCL = 58, IPCL IPO = 30

Note: BPCL (Bharat Petroleum Corporation Limited); DCIL (Dredging Corporation of India Limited); HPCL (Hindustan Petroleum Corporation Limited); IBP (Indo-Burmah Petroleum); IPCL (Indian Petrochemicals Corporation Limited); LJMC (Lagan Jute Machinery Company); MFIL (Modern Foods India Limited). PE for loss-making companies cannot be evaluated, hence shown as very high.

The government is in a huge need of resources for its very ambitious rural development projects and for meeting Mahatma Gandhi National Rural Employment Guarantee Act (MGNREGA), Food Security Act, etc. It cannot allow any class of industries to perform suboptimally with the government picking up the bill for lacklustre performances. Further, thanks to reforms and delicensing initiated in 1991, a large number of private companies are already in operation, and public industries can now also be privatized for maximum gain to the economy.

Before I end this chapter on disinvestments, I must narrate the story of a chance meeting I had with the Indonesian minister of industries at a dinner hosted by K.K. Nohria, the chief executive of Crompton Greaves, in Mumbai in 1992. I was then the principal secretary of Madhya Pradesh. The Indonesian minister mistakenly thought that I was his Indian counterpart. He kept pleading for a zero import tariff in India to make the developing country competitive. I did not fully understand the implications of such a request back then, but do so now, especially after the launch of the 'Make in India' campaign.

PART III

A GOVERNMENT OF INQUISITIONS

9

The CBI Falters

The CBI was set up with the intention of containing the increase in incidents of corruption and manipulation. The organization had, and still has, some outstanding officers giving their best. However, over time a number of aberrations crept into the functioning of the organization, and the institution deteriorated into an instrument of state power. The agency has been used to harass upright civil servants and political opponents of the government in power. Successive governments have not curtailed this power, perhaps because the status quo suits every government. This unbridled power has allowed corruption to seep into the organization. The UPA-II government gave unrestrained powers to the CBI to deal with their political opponents, hoping to cover up their own sins by forcing CBI directors to make choices in their favour. I too suffered in many cases. I am a civil servant, I did what my instincts told me: cooperate with the CBI to the fullest, and not object either in the media or in the courts to the filing of baseless cases which had little or no relation to facts. I believed that the officers would honestly hear my defence and close the cases. This did happen in the first two cases based on CAG's observations in 2007. It was naive of me to think that this would always be the case.

I had defied the establishment and had refused to cooperate with the minister who wanted to initiate the 2G scam. They could not fix me in the fraudulent 2G case. But I had to be taught a lesson by the overconfident players in the Congress–DMK establishment, and for this a number of illogical CBI inquiries had to be started against me. The CBI with its tainted directors fully cooperated. These cases also gave them a hope that they could sidestep the real 2G scam of 2006 and 2008 if they could pin the blame on the Tatas and on me for actions taken during 2003–04.

Once they were not successful in the telecom case, egos were hurt. They still wanted my head on a platter to send a message to other bureaucrats: cooperate in the different scams and their inquiries, or else meet the same fate. Shyamal Ghosh's discharge in October 2015 is a grim reminder of the period when the CBI could get away with any irresponsible charge and the CBI judge's order explains why everyone in India respects the judiciary.

The PNGRB Case

There was a story in *The Indian Express*[1] on 9 August 2013 that the Supreme Court had passed observations on my appointment as an advisor to the Petroleum and Natural Gas Regulatory Board (PNGRB). A journalist rang up to tell me that mine was one amongst the seventeen cases that the CBI and the Supreme Court wanted further inquiry into, based on their investigation of the Radia tapes. There were four cases related to Ratan Tata. As it usually happens in such high-profile cases, there was a publicity blitz and news appeared in all media channels and newspapers. The case against me, as explained in one of the dailies, was as follows:

> Pradeep Baijal: Former Chief of TRAI Baijal joined Noesis, a Nira Radia lobbying company. Phone taps reveal he was then appointed Chairman of the Pipeline Advisory Committee of the

Petroleum and Natural Gas Regulatory Board by the government. Radia lobbied for RIL suggesting that this could be case of some conflict of interest.

And the content of these phone taps? I told Nira Radia I attended the introductory meeting of the Regulatory Board and felt that there might be a conflict of interest in the future, and hence resigned. There could be nothing more honourable. The chairman of PNGRB, who had appointed me on the Board with well-known experts, tried to convince me that I should not resign as there was no conflict, but I insisted. Later he appointed Hasmukh Shah, a well-known expert on natural gas. Conflict of interest issue was raised and the chairman ruled that there could be no conflict of interest in taking advice from experts. There could never be a proposal for inquiry, but the proposal was made to defame me with the news of the inquiry, the proposal having been approved by the SC. The SC could not turn down a proposal of inquiry since it did not know the facts, but the CBI knew.

It should be noted that neither were there any criminal charges being investigated, nor was any specific recommendation or decision taken by me under scrutiny. The CBI had no concrete reason to believe that I had misused my position. Should merely 'conflict of interest', which is present in the appointment of any retired government officer, become the centre piece of a publicized CBI inquiry? The fact that there wasn't any decision or recommendation or criminality that the CBI was investigating made the situation strange. Was CBI the custodian of 'conflict of interest' issues?

Timelines and Facts

The inquiry into the non-issue was intentionally dragged for a long time by the CBI and a number of people were examined. I need to explain more details of the case and request my reader to bear with me. The facts are as follow:

a. I was invited by the chairman, PNGRB, on 12 May 2009 to head an advisory committee to the Board. This was perhaps in view of my experience and work as telecom regulator and my experience in power regulation, where I had formulated the entire scheme of reforms/regulation, and my known training in the subject. The following were the terms of reference:

- To recommend most suitable economic route taking into consideration broad geographical and economic constraints.
- To recommend optimum capacity keeping in view the medium- and long-term supply projections of natural gas.
- To recommend maximum consumer outreach which will include piped natural gas (PNG) to City Gas Distribution (CGD) networks, compressed natural gas (CNG) for transportation, and natural gas to Small and Medium Enterprises (SME) sector.

He informed me that M.A. Pathan, former chairman, Indian Oil Corporation (IOC); C.R. Prasad, former Chairman, GAIL; and Hari Shankaran, managing director, Infrastructure Leasing & Financial Services (ILFS), all eminent professionals in the gas field had agreed to become members and asked if I could suggest any more name for members.

b. I consulted friends in the petroleum and regulatory sectors, including my senior Vijay Kelkar, and on 14 May 2009 suggested three names: Claire Spottiswoode, former director general of Ofgas; Ajit Kapadia, chairman, Centre of Fuel Studies and Research (CFSR), Baroda, and Ligia Noronha, senior fellow in TERI. I further stated that if Claire could not be persuaded, the appointment of Hemant Joshi, former CEO of CRISIL, could be considered. I gave the curriculum vitae of all these people and stated that there could be no conflict of interest since Noesis

Strategic Consultants, where I was a director, had not consulted so far with any petroleum or natural gas company and would not consult with any while the report was being prepared.

c. The chairman, PNGRB, informed me on 20 May 2009 that he had constituted the committee and called the first meeting on 28 May 2009. The committee included Ajit Kapadia and Hemant Joshi. All the members of the committee appointed by the chairman were eminent professionals.

d. I attended the first introductory meeting of the committee where the chairman and his staff introduced all the members and explained the work. They also gave some information about the offers received for pipelines. I found that in addition to the general principles and the objectives told to me at the time of appointment, the role of the advisory committee would be to make some specific recommendations as well. Fearing a conflict of interests in the future, I resigned from the Board on 24 June 2009.

e. Shortly after resigning, I gave interviews to *Forbes* (India) and the PTI (Press Trust of India). I stated to PTI: 'Initially, I thought the work was like that of the power or telecom regulator. But when I found that the work was enormous, I could not have done justice as I was doing something of my own.'

Thus, I did no work in the committee, and the question of even non-existent conflict does not arise. Yet the CBI wanted to do a 'thorough' inquiry, perhaps at the insistence of someone powerful. I was given no opportunity to explain my position before these well-publicized observations were made against me. Why was there a need to push the story in the media and get all newspapers and channels to declare me guilty before a fair investigation? Was there a mechanism in the government or with the bureaucracy to prevent this witch-hunt? These questions troubled me immensely.

I considered filing an affidavit in the SC but didn't as I was advised by my lawyers not to do so. The needless inquiries tarnished my image and caused huge financial loss in the form of the lawyers' fee.

The Laxmi Vilas Case

Laxmi Vilas Hotel in Udaipur owned by the India Tourism Development Corporation (ITDC) was privatized by the Ministry of Disinvestment in 2002. The hotel is located on the banks of the Fateh Sagar Lake in Udaipur and was purchased by the Lalit Group after an auction process conducted by the ministry with the help of the merchant banking team of the Lazard Company.

The CBI filed an FIR on 20 August 2014 against me and others regarding this sale. I later found out that a preliminary inquiry in this case was registered in April 2014, just prior to the general elections and the change in government. Normally, an FIR is registered after the CBI examines the witnesses and the accused. This was the practice in all cases that I had previously faced. In this case, the CBI should have spoken to the joint or deputy secretaries of the various ministries involved (disinvestment, tourism and finance), and of course the minister, Arun Shourie, and me. In the past also, the CBI chose not to include the minister's name in the preliminary inquiry reports. They feared him due to his public image and his reputation for exposing fraud. The fact that no one was examined before the FIR was lodged shows mala fide. No one from the department was questioned until four months after the FIR. And the FIR contained some blatantly incorrect statements. Some people, including me, were questioned only after January 2015.

The CBI Allegations

What did the FIR allege and what was the CBI trying to investigate twelve years after the sale process? The FIR, an excerpt of which was shown to me by one of the lawyers, had the following major allegations:

- Criminal conspiracy and collusion between Lazard, the asset valuers Karamsey and officials of the Ministry of Disinvestment (with only me being named) to sell the hotel for a price of Rs 7 crore versus a value of Rs 150 crore as determined by the CBI based on the then available land rates (as used for stamp duty calculation) in Udaipur.
- Wrongful appointment of Karamsey as asset valuers. They were not approved by the government.
- Wrongful removal of the previously appointed asset valuer, Saxena and Associates, and keeping ITDC officials out of the process.

When I was called for questioning, I asked for a copy of the FIR. I was told I should approach the court in Jodhpur. I asked for the files and papers from twelve years ago and I was again told that I should approach the court or the Department of Disinvestment. Surely, that is not how justice should work. Does a senior retired government official deserve to be treated like this? How can any person be expected to answer questions without knowing the specific allegations or having access to documents from a case years ago? I was shown the FIR later by a lawyer.

The FIR and the CBI case were baseless. The CBI did not see that the usual disinvestment procedure was to take all decisions in committee format and no decision was taken by me alone. Let me address each of the issues and questions raised by the CBI in the FIR.

Allegation 1: The Asset Was Undervalued

The fundamental argument the FIR makes is about the collusion amongst the accused to depress the asset valuation for the property; thereby causing a wrongful gain of Rs 143.48 crore. This is a flawed argument and it ignores the basic valuation tenets which guided the approach of the Ministry of Disinvestment.

The CBI did not understand the following issues and thus reached several wrongful conclusions.

a. **Discounted cash flow (DCF) methodology versus asset valuation:** The entire FIR misses the key point that as a going concern, the key to determining valuation of the hotel is the economic cash flows of the business and the economic benefit the buyer would derive from the acquisition. The entire ministry understood this. Even the Disinvestment Commission and our ministry manual had clearly stated that the discounted cash flow method was more relevant than asset valuation when selling a business as a going concern. The other valuation methodologies—DCF valuation/book value assessment and comparable analysis—undertaken for determining the reserve price were done in the manner laid out and considered by all the relevant authorities and committees. In his inaugural address at the Conference on Disinvestment in 1997, C. Rangarajan, former governor of the RBI, said, 'The discounted flow method is the most comprehensive and holds the greatest relevance.' The Disinvestment Commission too had recommended the same principle. The Lazard report on the Laxmi Vilas disinvestment also stated: DCF value is the most relevant value since as per the transaction structure the property is offered for use as a hotel. This was accepted and confirmed by the Evaluation Committee. Why was it then that the CBI chose to ignore the Disinvestment Commission, the Ministry of Disinvestment manual, Mr Rangarajan's advice and every expert on valuation across the globe?

b. **Asset valuation does not set the price:** The CBI officials also failed to understand that the asset valuation exercise was not the price-setting mechanism for the hotel. The auction and the price bid by the bidder was what determined the price and not the asset valuation conducted by the advisors. Any wrongdoing or process errors in the asset valuation did not impact the price set for the asset and the eventual selling price for Laxmi Vilas.

i. The auction process was globally advertised and several parties expressed interest.
ii. Five of the interested parties conducted due diligence on the asset
iii. Bharat Hotels' decision to bid what it did was not a function of the valuation done by the ministry but their own assessment of value and their desire to win the auction.
iv. The bidder at the time of furnishing their bids did not know what will be the reserve price which had to be fixed. It is only after the receipt of the bids that the reserve price was made known.
v. As per the process; Bharat Hotels did not know if they would be the only bidders and had to arrive at a price which would factor in any of the other five bidders.
vi. The Supreme Court had held in the BALCO case, and later reiterated in the ITDC case, that for competitive bid cases reserve price (by any methodology) did not matter: Whether the reserve price should have been Rs 514.4 crore or more appears to be immaterial when the best price which has been offered for sale of 51 per cent stake in BALCO after global advertisement was only Rs 551.5 crore.

The Disinvestment Commission also stated, 'To get best value through strategic sales, it would be necessary to have a transparent and competitive procedure and encourage enough competition among viable parties.'

i. The system which was evolved was completely transparent. It is by global advertisement that the global adviser and the strategic partner were chosen. At every stage, the matter was overseen by the Inter-ministerial Group and ultimately by the Cabinet Committee on Disinvestment.

ii. The World Bank privatization guidelines also state, 'Ideally, let the market set the price, and sell for cash.'

iii. This is consistent with the deliberations of the Evaluation Committee in the case of the BALCO disinvestment. The Evaluation Committee then deliberated on the various methodologies and concluded, as per the affidavit of the Union of India, that the most appropriate methodology for valuing the shares of the running business of BALCO would be the Discounted Cash Flow method. 'The committee further observed that the fixed asset valuation method was only a good indicator of the value that could be realized if the business was to be liquidated, rather than for valuing the business as a going concern.'

c. **Asset valuation of the CBI ignored key restrictions on land use:** The crux of the CBI case was that the actual value of the property was Rs 151 crore but the government sold it for Rs 7.5 crore. To substantiate the Rs 151 crore figure, the CBI stated that the Rajasthan government itself had asked Bharat Hotels—the company that won the bid—to pay Rs 15 crore as stamp duty. However, the CBI conveniently did not mention the fact that this demand, made by the local officer, had been stayed by the courts. The claim that the hotel had 29 acres of land which could be valued on a per acre rate as per the then prevailing circle rates totally neglected the fact that this land, being adjacent to the lake, fell within the Coastal Regulation Zone (CRZ), which meant that nothing could be built on it.

The valuation done by the asset valuers appointed by the ministry was done taking into account the restrictions on the sale of the land, the nature of the land and other associated problems.

The use of government rates or District-Level Committee (DLC) rate to arrive at a valuation is a completely mistaken approach, even if one were to follow the asset valuation approach. One must take into account that the land continues to remain in the CRZ which puts a lot of restrictions on the owner of the land (the Share Purchase Agreement clearly stated that this land was under the Red Zone). The following points make this clear:

i. There are several government notifications, including those of 1997, 1999 and 2000, which classified this area as a No Development Zone; something which has been upheld in 2007 Rajasthan High Court in the petition filed by JSS (Janathipathya Samrakshana Samithi) in 1997.
ii. The Lazard valuation report explicitly stated: The entire land is within 500 metres of the surrounding lake, and hence the Red Zone restrictions on any further construction or change in land use apply. The Karamsey valuation report stated: The Municipal Hotel Licence is cancelled by the state as the hotel is facing the Fateh Sagar Lake and coming within 500 metres of the lake. Hence, the government has declared it a Red Zone or No Development Zone, and no construction is allowed without prior permission of the state government. The state government has cancelled the licence of all hotels in this particular area.
iii. Outstanding employee litigations and other issues (including the transfer of title from the President of India to ITDC) were yet to be sorted out, and the completion plan was not available for the unit.
iv. Existence of HZL staff quarters on part of the land.

Allegation 2: Appointment of Non-Government-Approved Asset Valuers by Baijal and Others

The final choice of the asset valuer was made after a transparent process thorough a technical and financial bid. The appointment of the asset valuer was done by a Selection Committee on 14 June 2001. The Selection Committee included the additional and the joint secretaries from the Department of Disinvestment, the joint secretary from the Department of Tourism and the chief managing director of the ITDC. In addition, the joint secretaries from the Department of Economic Affairs and Urban Development were also present. The CBI in its wisdom made me an accused even though I was not present on the day the decision was made. One of the allegations made by the CBI was that the ITDC officials were kept out of the process. However, it was interesting to note that on 11 June 2001, K. Rawal from the Department of Tourism made a request to include R.C. Gupta from ITDC in the Selection Committee and he was included.

Karamsey Kantilal was one of the eighty-one government-approved valuers invited for the disinvestment process. Of the eighty-one, twenty-nine submitted the Request for Quotation (RFQ) and twenty-three were selected based on the criteria set forth by the ITDC, Department of Disinvestment (DoD) and the advisors. Karamsey received the second highest marks in the technical assessment of the Evaluation Committee and were the lowest bidders (L-1). As secretary of the DoD, I was not involved in the evaluation or the opening of the bids. Yet the CBI alleged that I entered into a conspiracy in appointing Karamsey—somehow circumventing a comprehensive bidding process conducted by a multi-ministry committee.

On 28 August, CBI officials gave an interview to *Mint* and claimed that the appointed valuer was 'not government approved'. However, a few hours of work would reveal that Karamsey was indeed a government-approved valuer. They were qualified as per the prescribed 'measurable' criteria and had also been appointed by Air India for the HCI (Hotel Corporation of India) disinvestment prior to their appointment for the ITDC hotels. There was no deception, nor was there any opportunity for the secretary to make a decision in their favour.

Allegation 3: Wrongful Removal of the Originally Appointed Valuers

The third allegation by the CBI was also factually incorrect. The original valuers, Saxena and Associates, were in fact disqualified by the ITDC. The ITDC process had concluded with the selection of S.S.K. Bhagat at a cost of Rs 23 lakhs. However, the ITDC had delayed the issuance of appointment letters. This was often the case with associated ministries as they tried to delay the sale of their properties. It was this delay which had led to the DoD taking over the process. This entire process was reviewed by Arun Jaitley, the then law minister, and redone. Only then was Karamsey appointed.

Why did the CBI register an FIR based on wrong information? Were the officials sloppy in their reading of the documents? Were the allegations in the FIR based on 'anonymous tips' alone? Were the investigative officers gullible enough to believe any source? Why did they not check the files before alleging that the ministry officials, led by me, had removed a said asset valuer? The CBI needs to answer these questions.

Before filing an FIR the CBI invariably conducts a preliminary inquiry. Surprisingly, in the Laxmi Vilas case, an FIR was filed directly without conducting any preliminary inquiry. Only the investment banker and valuers involved were briefly examined before the filing. They were examined in detail after the FIR had been filed but none of the officers were examined till about five months after the FIR. I was not examined. Perhaps the CBI officials feared that they would not be able to file the FIR if they examined me as I would have explained, like in other cases, the rationale behind all actions. In the 2G case, they told me that there was an open-and-shut case against me and I would be arrested. They could not do so as I was able to explain the fraudulent nature of the charge based on 'removed' files. The CBI officers were trying to treat their bruised egos at the insistence of their old masters. They had warned me in each case that I would be harmed if I did not cooperate. Incidentally, this was exactly what the eminent economist prime minister had warned me about if I did not cooperate. Has our CBI become an organization where its officials threatened a person without any evidence with them?

When the CBI officials came to me, I asked them about the basis of the investigation. They said that there was no complaint in writing. Just an oral complaint! Is this the manner in which our top investigative agency should function?

The facts in this case are clear. The Laxmi Vilas Hotel was disposed of in 2002. Of the twenty hotels of the ITDC, this one had distinguished itself by incurring the highest loss—a loss margin of 51 per cent. The occupancy rate of the hotel had fallen to 26 per cent. Far from being a luxury palace, the place was in a shambles. The plant and machinery were defunct and the furniture too lay derelict. Eleven parties expressed an initial interest in bidding for the hotel. Five of them investigated the property. Such was the condition that four of the five dropped out at the bidding stage. I am informed that Bharat Hotels—the winning bidder—had to spend Rs 25–30 crore in renovating the place and getting its plant and machinery in working order. Furthermore, the quality of the staff was such that Bharat Hotels had to spend up to Rs 5 crore on voluntary retirement schemes. It is also noteworthy that in many of the disinvestment exercises, like in the Laxmi Vilas case, the loss-making PSUs carry a lot of debt and bank loans. A company when sold at Rs 100 crore may have a liability of Rs 300 crore. Thus, the buyer actually pays Rs 400 crore since all the loans and liability have to be paid by the buyer. There are a number of cases in which huge PSUs with infrastructure and land had accumulated loans which were higher than the total value of the assets. In this case, immediately after disinvestment, the successors of the Maharaja of Udaipur filed a case that the property could not be sold as it belonged to them. All these points are value deflators.

Continuing the operation of such companies was a huge drain on the budget of the Government of India. These companies would have been closed long ago had they been in the private sector. Considering these points was the price paid for the hotel actually Rs 7 crore? Should the liabilities of renovating the hotel and giving voluntary retirement scheme (VRS) to employees, paid by the buyer, not be included? Why did the CBI not consider these factors?

Support in the Press

Unlike in the 2G case, other eminent professionals and politicians expressed their concern on the filing of the FIR.

In an interview to *Economic Times* on 1 September 2014,[2] Finance Minister Arun Jaitley was sharply critical of the Central Bureau of Investigation (CBI) for resurrecting a decade-old disinvestment case.

> The move by CBI risks reviving concerns amongst bureaucrats about past actions coming back to haunt them, a fear that had just begun to lift—a point Arun Jaitley conceded. 'It hurts governance because it lowers the confidence of the civil servants to take decisions.' Such actions sap morale and also worsen the business climate. 'If we are to ease the doing of business in India, if we are to enhance investor confidence, we have to free them of the risks,' Jaitley said. 'And, transactions being questioned after twelve years either by investigators or by courts is a risk. It is a huge risk, which will hurt the investment environment in the country. There is no reason at a belated stage to rake up these issues unless there is established evidence of corruption, which I believe does not exist.'
>
> Arun Jaitley urged all the judiciary, executive and legislature to respect their constitutional mandate, making it clear that lines need to be drawn. 'If judicial review and judicial independence are a part of the basic structure of the Constitution, parliamentary democracy, elected government, jurisdiction of Parliament and the government are also a very important part of the basic structure,' the finance minister said.

Mid-day on 6 September 2014 in an article by Kanchan Gupta titled 'Make CBI liable for malicious charges'[3] said:

> The CBI, that crime and fraud busting agency whose director, it is now revealed, is believed to have met those accused of committing serious offences at his home on more than one occasion, has filed an FIR against former Disinvestment Secretary Pradeep Baijal. The FIR says Baijal bungled on the sale of ITDC's Laxmi Vilas Hotel in Udaipur in 2002; that property, worth Rs. 151 crore, was gifted away for a mere Rs. 7.5 crore.
>
> In brief, Baijal, who retired from service a decade ago[sic], stands accused of corruption. He will now have to appear in court, possibly face arrest, spend his savings on lawyer's fees, deal with endless harassment, be subjected to a demeaning media trial and suffer irreparable loss of reputation. His twilight years will become a living hell.
>
> A caveat is called for. I happened to know Baijal when I was working for the Government of India. He had a formidable reputation for his honesty, and his integrity was as unimpeachable as that of his boss Arun Shourie. He retired with an unblemished record, which few bureaucrats can boast of.
>
> It is unthinkable that Baijal would have short circuited the laid down procedure for disinvestment or hopped, skipped and jumped over the checks and balances that had been built into the system.

I am grateful to Kanchan Gupta. He analysed the pain borne by me from one false case. I have been waiting for a respite for about a year. No one has yet questioned the agency or its officers.

In an article in *The Indian Express* on 5 September 2014,[4] Arun Shourie strongly defended the disinvestment. He said:

> Contrary to what the CBI has insinuated, the asset valuer was jointly chosen by the financial advisors (Lazard) and the ITDC from among the list of government-approved valuers. Five or more valuers from the government-approved list were invited to make presentations. Their qualifications and experience were jointly examined, and then alone was the particular firm chosen for the task. That care marked every other step also. As in every case of disinvestment, every single one of the prescribed procedures was meticulously followed. Every step of the process, including the setting of the reserve price and the acceptance of the final bid price, was taken with the explicit approval of the Cabinet Committee on Disinvestment. In particular, the shareholders agreement was cleared by the law ministry thrice over—at the draft stage, at the stage when it was frozen and finally when the bids were to be accepted. The then law minister is the one link between that cabinet committee and the present government: he was law minister then and a member of the Cabinet Committee on Disinvestment, and is in-charge of the disinvestment department in the present government. He has stated in an interview that he is well acquainted with every aspect of the disinvestment and that everything about the transaction was in order.

Arun Shourie told *Economic Times* on 1 September 2014 that both Arun Jaitley and he along with the Cabinet Committee on Disinvestment headed by the prime minister had closely supervised and cleared the deal. He further said: 'I am absolutely certain that every procedure was followed. There was a vigilant Law Minister, and his ministry cleared the file three times.'

On 5 September 2014, in an article titled 'Is This the Way to Energise Civil Servants?' in *The Indian Express*, he said:

> I can go on adding to the list. But the point will be obvious: we can be fairly certain that the CBI officials in Jodhpur would be

> innocent of such comparisons. There is a real problem here, and it holds a lesson. Even if one sets aside conspiracy theories, the problem is that the CBI staff, especially at the lower level, just does not understand valuation and other aspects of such transactions. I have had personal exposure to this innocence—when the CBI officials came to ask me about the disinvestment of Hindustan Zinc, for instance. At the least, that holds one lesson for all who are today trying to get the bureaucracy going: among the reforms that are urgently required is to upgrade the domain knowledge of officials working in our investigating agencies. Otherwise, goaded by pep-talks, honest officers will take decisions on complex matters, only to be hauled up 10–12 years later by persons innocent, at least of considerations that bear on those decisions.

Several junior officers have called me since this case was filed and expressed their displeasure on what is happening. They are scared to take any decisions. I empathize with them. Given what has happened to me after my retirement and the witch-hunt I have been subjected to, I should perhaps look back on my achievements with as much regret as pride. I believe that unless the government and the current leadership review the process by which policy decisions are questioned years into the future, government officials will generally opt for the safer route of taking no decisions and stalling any progress in the economy.

HZL Privatization of 2002

After the contentious privatization of BALCO in early 2001, the disinvestment of Hindustan Zinc's equity (26 per cent) in 2002 to the same buyer was a subdued affair. There were no strikes and no attempts to stop the new management from entering the factory premises. Perhaps the workers understood the merits of privatization better than many in the polity today. The fear of meritocracy and of losing their jobs had given way to optimism that private management would drive efficiencies in the fast-globalizing sector. This was not the first time when existing management and labour had been supportive of a privatization process. In 1995, all the unions of the ABL (ACC Babcock Limited) plants in West Bengal and Karnataka had supported the privatization to ABB (ASEA Brown Boveri). Were they right to support a change in ownership? Let us examine the facts.

Hindustan Zinc Limited was incorporated in January 1966 as a public sector company and produced 75 per cent of India's zinc. The decision to privatize HZL was taken after considering that there was no chance of a private monopoly being created since zinc could be freely imported with low duty rates. With the lowering of import duties, it had become evident that for an Indian company to survive in a cyclical commodity market, it needed to ensure that technology and costs were in line with global peers. Thus, it was an appropriate time for the government to sell the company into private hands and a good time for the buyers to buy as they could restructure the asset, and use it as a platform for further investments in zinc and lead (both of which were consolidating and becoming more of 'volume' plays).

The privatization brought huge benefits to the government, economy and the taxpayer. This is evident from Table 9.1.

Table 9.1: Performance of Hindustan Zinc Limited

	2002–03 (Rs in Cr.)	**2012–13 (Rs in Cr.)**
Turnover	1,609	13,658
Earning	300	8,496
Profit after Tax (PAT)	142	1,899
Earnings per Share	3.4	16.3×5*
Sales	1411	12,700
Income and Dividend Tax	144	1,845

	2002–03 (Rs in Cr.)	2012–13 (Rs in Cr.)
Royalty	86	941
Excise and Customs	174	786
Sales Tax	57	344

Note: (*) Shares were split into five
Source: Company Annual Reports for 2002–03 and 2012–13

In the immediate aftermath of the sale there were no adverse comments or complaints on by anyone. The courts were supportive. The CAG audited the disinvestment of HZL and submitted a report in 2006 with some suggestions for the future, mainly on valuation.

Twelve years after the sale, a preliminary inquiry was initiated in Jodhpur about the disinvestment of HZL. This was around the same time the Laxmi Vilas case was registered. The officers investigating both the cases were the same. In fact, during one of the interrogations in the Laxmi Vilas case, an officer told one of the government officials, 'Just wait and watch; we will open up Hindustan Zinc next.' The preliminary inquiry had not yet been converted to an FIR.

Arun Shourie was disturbed enough by the adverse publicity from both the cases to write articles in the newspapers. Arun Jaitley too did the same. Shourie even went to the director, CBI, after the FIR was filed in the Laxmi Vilas case and gave him all the facts on both cases. This included the clearance the HZL case got from a three-judge bench of the Supreme Court headed by the chief justice.

Though the CBI did not register any FIR, from the questioning it was clear that the thrust of its inquiries was about the process of valuation and bidding.

The media reported aggressively on the HZL inquiry, and the possibility of another FIR by the CBI is still alive. Let us understand the issues.

In 2012, a writ petition no. 513/2012- *Mines Mazdoor Sangh & Others* vs *Union of India & Others* was filed before the Supreme Court regarding the disinvestment of HZL. A three-judge bench of the SC headed by the CJI and comprising the CJI, Justice Nijjar and Justice Chelameshwar heard the arguments and disposed the writ petition thus specifically approving the disinvestment. Despite the SC clearing the sale, the CBI initiated a preliminary inquiry.

Valuation is a complex exercise. Valuation or the reserve price loses relevance if the company is sold by an open competitive bidding. This clearly determines the price the market is willing to pay. The government determines reserve price for almost all tenders. Often it receives a much higher price. That is the bidders' perception of the price. This principle has been clearly endorsed in the landmark BALCO judgment. In this case, the company was sold at a price higher than valuation. Regarding valuation, the Supreme Court, after detailed examination, has recorded in its judgment dated 10 December 2001 as follows: 'Whether the reserve price should have been Rs 514.4 crore or more appears to be immaterial when the best price which has been offered for sale of 51 per cent stake in BALCO after global advertisement was only Rs 551.5 crore.'

The news item came to the notice of Arun Shourie, minister at the time of this disinvestment, who gave an interview to *Mail Today* on 26 December 2013 and stated: 'There is no substance in the charges. They were rejected by the Attorney General in December 2012 and August 2013.'

Ruined Reputations

I believe that the investigative agencies should take dishonest politicians and officials to task. There needs to be a fair process and due respect given to the individuals being investigated. The CBI has an obligation to minimize leaks to the media at least till an FIR is lodged. The lodging of the FIR itself needs to be done only after due process and approval from the government—particularly when it comes to cases regarding the application of a policy or which are being investigated after a certain period of time. The CBI must give the accused and the associated ministry an opportunity to be heard before lodging an FIR. Only someone who has gone through the ordeal can comprehend the strain and distress a person and his family are subjected to by such inquisitions and 'raids'. What about the irreparable damage to the person's reputation? Now that the cases against them are closed, should the CBI not be held accountable for the slander it hurled at C.B. Bhave?

But I do feel that in this regard others too are at fault.

Has the CBI not somersaulted enough number of times for the press to realize that it must not swallow and propagate what the agency feeds them? And the civil servants—haven't they seen sufficient number of times how they have behaved in the wake of investigations against their colleagues? The moment the CBI says it has commenced an inquiry against X, his erstwhile colleagues treat him as a leper. Till yesterday, he was your colleague and friend, and now you avoid him. Shame on such colleagues and friends! That is no way to be; on the contrary, we must be the fortresses around the honest, and all the more so around one who has been a colleague and friend, and of whose competence and integrity we have had personal knowledge.

And the victims—they are so easily felled, most of all by the apprehension that their reputation has been ruined. Such agencies and their concocted FIRs cannot ruin our reputation. Perhaps one needs to learn to develop a thicker skin, as suggested by none other than Arun Shourie. Talking in a function, he said: 'Being calumnized by the dishonest is actually a badge of honour! I address audiences once a week or so. On these occasions, as is the custom, the hosts use superlatives to introduce me, the positions I have held, the awards that have been given me, the books I have written...When my turn comes, I always add that the organizers have left out my two main distinctions. First, I am the only editor who has been dismissed from his job, not once but twice. Second, I have what none of you have—I am the only one here who has three certificates of honesty from the CBI.' So, here is to thicker skins and contempt for the calumnies.

The VSNL Story

Despite doing a perfect privatization deal, I was surprised to receive a call one day in 2009 from Arun Shourie asking me whether I had read an *Outlook* article criticizing the VSNL deal. Apparently, no one in *Outlook* had read the VSNL chapter on this sale in my book or P.K. Basu's (former joint secretary, disinvestment) book on disinvestment, before deciding to write a damning article on this sale. The nature of this article clearly shows that the material for the article was given by someone in the DoT. It almost read like the charges in an inquisition. I immediately sent my chapter on VSNL, excerpts from Basu's book and a brief note to the former minister.

Outlook perhaps did not anticipate Arun Shourie's capacity for due diligence and speed, when they asked him for comments in a day. He replied to the editor of the publishing magazine on the same day. The magazine had to publish both the article and his reply. Interestingly, they still wrote that there were facts with them that show huge irregularities. If they had, they should have written. I would welcome if they wrote those even now.

I still say that this was the best privatization that we did and if there is any need for inquisition, we need to question the governments prior to 2000, who sold/parted with resources without due diligence and at very low returns to the poor taxpayer.

This was the best sale because we brought in the best competition—both Tata and Reliance—and sold at a much higher price than in earlier sales.

There were attempts to sabotage the sale through a petition in a high court a few days before the sale. We were able to convince the judge that we were carrying on the sale with utmost transparency. I attended the high court hearing myself, after both my minister and the then minister for law advised me to.

We were able to separate the land with VSNL from this deal, and today, when the government is able to sell this land, we will get huge additional revenues. UPA-I and II governments headed by brilliant economists were not able to complete this simple process. There was an earlier sale in 1992. Equity was sold with land, without the Congress government realizing that they were selling a very valuable resource for a song. They repeated this in 2G and Coalgate scams. Also, they did not take out the cash reserves. We did. After all these actions, we got a much higher PE ratio, and when the land is sold, perhaps this deal's PE ratio will be a world record.

There was an undertaking in the New York Stock Exchange (NYSE) when we sold equity through an initial public offer (IPO) that we would not disturb VSNL's monopoly, which was leading to usurious tariffs. We were bothered about the subscribers and took foolproof steps to legally remedy the undertaking. Later, despite this sale, telecom reforms were able to bring down international call rates. As a matter of fact, the Tatas were upset at the efficiency of the sale.

There was no CAG observation on this sale. Surprisingly, *Outlook* published many non-existent irregularities. The criticism gave an opportunity to Arun Shourie to go for the kill. I can never improve on his writing abilities, and so I present an excerpt from *Outlook*:

> All the processes involved scrutiny by Bankers, Law firms and were then vetted by Ministry for Law, the Inter-ministerial Group (including Finance Ministry representative), the Committee of Secretaries (headed by the Cabinet Secretary), which included Ministry of Finance, and finally by the Cabinet Committee on Economic Affairs.

> A bidding procedure was followed that gave equal opportunity to all bidders. Reliance was one of the bidders who lost in the price bid and one other bidder did not, I think, finally submit a price bid.
>
> VSNL was a listed company. It was listed both in Bombay and in New York. Therefore everything done was done and had to be within the regulatory framework of SEBI and the US regulator. Any unilateral or unfair decision would have immediately given ground to any and every shareholder—bidders apart—for bringing the entire process to a halt through litigation.
>
> The price we got was far above the market price. When you include the Special Dividend to which I shall refer in a moment, and which your informers seem to have kept hidden from you, the P/E ratio turned out to be 11. At 11, the P/E was excellent: it compared to the pre-disinvestment P/E ratio of just 6.

Rahul Khullar was my successor as secretary (disinvestment) and chairman, TRAI. I met him when he was secretary (disinvestment). He warned me that senior people in the government had asked him to investigate all disinvestment deals again and finds faults. He also warned me that he will have to find a few. Bibek Debroy, former director, Rajiv Gandhi Institute, and present member of Niti Aayog, had also warned me. Perhaps this led to another round of baseless disinvestment inquisitions and write-ups. The earlier round was on the basis of some CAG paras, way back in 2007, and was closed after inquiry. I was surprised at the new keenness for inquisitions because Chidambaram, the then minister for disinvestment, had publicly praised our effort when he released my book. He had also justified my actions vis-à-vis all CAG draft paras on file. Who was responsible for this change?

A huge responsibility is cast on the officers/ministers when they try to change the way things are done in government. They need to do the best in due diligence to be able to answer the mostly irresponsible and numerous commentators and also keep copies of documents at the time of leaving these assignments. Perhaps after completing the deal, the government should put all documents, notes, reports, cabinet notes, investment banker and valuer reports in the public domain, so that illogical charges are not made years after the deal. It was with this intention that both P.K. Basu and I wrote books on the various deals. But perhaps there is no remedy against those who criticize without reading the available documents and the press which publishes such charges without due diligence.

PART IV

THE COMPULSION OF REFORMS

10

REFORMS: NECESSARY FOR GROWTH

Arvind Kejriwal's landslide victory in the 2015 elections in Delhi showed that corruption at the government-level is not the primary issue; people are more concerned about roadside corruption. Kejriwal, very intelligently, concentrated only on this issue in his forty-nine day government in 2014 and encashed this performance in the 2015 elections. I am told that some halwais had reduced the price of samosas from Rs 5 to Rs 4 at the insistence of the Aam Aadmi Party. They said that they were saving one rupee as 'hafta' charges on each samosa that Kejriwal had helped them save. A major portion of India's GDP growth is stunted by corruption, both at the government-level and the roots. The intelligent voter wants both to go. Arvind Kejriwal's performance and that of those who have arisen in recent times will determine the future of Indian polity.

The Indian Economy

After Independence, India adopted a pattern of economic development best described as state-led growth. Projects requiring heavy investments by the state were added to the public sector reservation list under the Industrial Development and Regulation Act. Post-Independence, the capital requirements of most economies were so large that no entity other than the state was considered capable of harnessing the required resources. Underdeveloped international capital markets, significant trade barriers and the hangover of sovereignty issues ensured that most nations planned for economic self-sufficiency. Underdeveloped domestic capital markets did not create an environment in which this burden could be shared by the private sector or by foreign institutions, especially in capital-intensive, long-gestation projects such as in irrigation, power and transportation sectors.

Unlike other developing countries in East Asia, which transited to a liberalized framework in the 1950s, India was a slow reformer, perhaps due to the influence of the Soviet Union. Continued reliance on state intervention created a highly regulated economy. This resulted in lack of competition from both imports as well as from within the economy due to heavy reservations for the public sector in most industries. Industrial capacity restrictions, prohibitions in foreign trade, high tariff walls, prohibitions on technology transfer, inadequate patent protection, restrictive labour laws and administered interest rates severely limited the scope for the efficiency-enhancing impact of markets.

The planned and tightly regulated development till the mid-1980s resulted in positive, though moderate, levels of growth. On the other hand, growth rates in the 'early reformers' in East Asia were considerably higher as Table 10.1 illustrates:

Table 10.1: GDP Growth (average per cent per year): International Comparison

	1965–80	1980–90	2000	2000–10	2010–13
China	6.4	9.5	10.3	10.23	8.77
Korea	9.5	9.7	5.7	4.84	3.86
Malaysia	7.4	5.2	7	5.03	5.72
Thailand	7.4	7.6	4.2	4.4	4.33

	1965–80	1980–90	2000	2000–10	2010–13
Indonesia	7.9	5.5	4.2	5.21	6.19
India	3.7	5.3	6	7.2	6.66

For India, the growth rate came down to 4.7 per cent in 2013–14
Source: World Development Reports, World Bank (various issues)

Not only was economic growth lower in India from 1965 to 1980 but unlike the East Asian economies, which aggressively sought export competitiveness for domestic manufacturing, India sought self-sufficiency. The insularity of the economy can be gauged from the fact that India's share in world exports reduced from 1.85 per cent to 0.42 per cent between 1950 and 1980, and it grew to 1.6–1.7 per cent in 2013 with reforms after 1980.

How did India make the transition from an economic laggard, only registering a 3 per cent rate of growth (called the Hindu rate of growth), to one of the most rapidly growing economies in the world after the 1980s and then fall back again? Industrial modernization all over the world and the green revolution could not increase this growth rate till the mid-1970s, when many Asian economies were booming. But between 1975 and 1990, the country's economic growth accelerated at a rate higher than 5 per cent with gradual reforms and then increased to more than 6 per cent post-1992 after major reforms were initiated. With the implementation of many reforms initiated earlier, the Indian economy grew at 8.8 per cent between 2003 and 2007, transforming itself into one of the fastest growing economies in the world alongside China. It then fell to 4.7 per cent in 2013–14, after a few years of crony capitalism and absence of effective governance.

To understand the phenomenon, we have to divide the reforms into six periods.

The Legacy of Control in a Self-Reliant Economy: 1947–74

The first phase describes India's economic development between 1947 and 1974. The Nehruvian model was inspired by the Soviet Union and sustained in India till the Soviets themselves fell. The government was inept at running companies and controlling substantial parts of the country's industry through reservations for the public sector. India's mixed economy was considered a natural successor to the anti-colonial struggle; infant industries required huge financial support. Perhaps this phase lasted too long in India and started changing only when similar shifts were seen in the USSR and China. The powerful deputy prime minister Vallabhbhai Patel (1947–50) was opposed to the Nehruvian model of greater state intervention which gave birth of the industrial licensing system even in sectors open to the private sector. This later degenerated to rent-seeking activity by the instruments of the state and many cases of misallocation of scarce resources. The scarcity of funds for the industrial sector and the neglect of the agricultural sector produced a foreign exchange crisis in the late-1950s and several times later.

Post-Nehru, uncertainties and subsidized wheat shipments led to India being considered a basket case by the developed world. Lal Bahadur Shastri's emphasis on agriculture led to the Planning Commission giving it higher priority over capital-intensive industrialization. Apart from this, two hundred tonnes of high-yielding seeds taken from a Mexican strain were imported. These were successfully cultivated under Indian conditions and led to the doubling of India's wheat output between 1965 and 1970, contributing to the country's green revolution. It is relevant to mention here that at that time, this step too was severely criticized in terms of possibility of importing plant diseases, etc. Yet, this initiative prevented a crisis.

Indira Gandhi succeeded Shastri in January 1966, when India was facing external pressure from multilateral donors due to the balance of payments problem and a stagnant economy. She was compelled to make substantial changes in the country's economic policy, including devaluation of India's currency. This was done to enable export competitiveness and growth. However, that did not happen because her later economic policies—written under pressure from the Left after the 1969 break-up of the Congress party—undermined this step.

Devaluation was designed to take India towards growth-oriented policies but political realignments changed the direction. There was political opposition to devaluation and liberalization after 1966, and Prime Minister Gandhi's alliance with the Left ensured that the state curbed all private-sector activities to the greatest extent possible between 1969 and 1974, leading to diametrically opposite measures by the same party government in a short period. Monopolies and Restrictive Trade Practices Act (MRTP, 1969) and Foreign Exchange Regulation Act (FERA, 1974) were passed to regulate private companies and put restrictions on equity participation.

State control was supposed to contribute to poverty alleviation and human development but the inefficiency of such an environment ensured that the results were contrary. The Indian economy grew at a dismal average annual rate of 3.4 per cent during 1956–74. The huge failure of nationalization of grain trade announced in 1974 in a bad agriculture year led to the diminishing of the leftist influence on Indira Gandhi's policies. The biggest leftist influence on her, Mohan Kumaramangalam, also died in 1973.

Perhaps, she used Sanjay Gandhi to usher in anti-leftist policies, and also to balance movements such as Navnirman which destroyed her elected government in Gujarat. Finally, she was convinced that the state-managed economy will not be able to pull India out of the economic crisis of subsequent oil shocks. This led to the reluctant shift to growth-oriented policies.

Gradual Evolution of the Liberal Momentum: 1974–91

The second period from 1974 until 1991 was the time when India promoted its private enterprise gradually and reluctantly in the context of the closed economy. In the mid-1970s, after years of sluggish economic growth accompanied by a poor economic record of human development, there was a gradual change in policy. Asian economies such as South Korea, Taiwan and Singapore had demonstrated that private initiative and trade promotion could result in rapid economic growth and well-being. Most importantly, China's rise, powered by its export orientation since the late 1970s, was a convincing example of how integration with the world economy could benefit poor, developing countries. The need for industrial reforms was understood by the technocracy and was promoted by the Prime Minister's Office. The 1980 Industrial Policy statement, under the premiership of Indira Gandhi, had charted a new direction. Schemes for expanding production capacity and initiating investment without government permission were more generous than the ones announced in 1975 and 1976. The gradual reduction of regulations contributed to the acceleration in annual industrial growth from 4.5 per cent during 1961–74 to 5.9 per cent during 1975–90.

Factors such as a change in political leadership also contributed to the process of economic reform. For example, Rajiv Gandhi's premiership witnessed acceleration in technological development and industrial deregulation in India. Under his watch, thirty industries and eighty-two pharmaceutical products were delicensed. He raised the limit of asset worth of Rs 2 crore, which was regulated under MRTP Act, to Rs 100 crore and waived MRTP clearance for twenty-seven industries.

In 1981, the government embarked upon a successful joint venture with the Suzuki Corporation of Japan, which gave birth to the Maruti car. This was met with huge opposition from India's car manufacturers, who were producing cars with obsolete technology and selling them profitably in a monopoly environment. It took Sanjay Gandhi's (the prime minister's influential son) authority to break the policy cartel. This cartel was finally and properly broken only after 1991, leading to enormous growth in production and consumption in this sector. So powerful was the growth after delicensing that India did even better than China in this sector for a few years. This growth demolished the rationale of the earlier licensing policy which did not allow higher capacities or new players.

Furthermore, problems relating to the provision of physical infrastructure were also addressed. In the mid-1980s, the manufacturing of telephone switches and some equipment was deregulated, and cement was delicensed leading to huge growth in indigenous manufacturing.

The 1980s also witnessed the birth of comparative advantage in India's IT sector. It appears that this move was not planned, but was the product of the latest technologies not being blocked by law and regulation, as they usually are in India. Fortunately, the state did not put hurdles and usurious charges in the smooth international telecom connectivity that was required for such ventures. This later led India to be the leader in call centres, business process outsourcing (BPOs) and software businesses, truly integrating India with the rest of the world. India's intellectual capital also started getting recognized thereafter, and the sector became a huge export earner and contributor to GDP growth. Most importantly, it gave the growing middle class and the government huge confidence to move forward.

Industrial and agricultural development during the 1980s made some impact on economic well-being. India's success in the area of higher education had been accompanied with unacceptable levels of illiteracy and poverty. Realizing that education had suffered partly because it was governed exclusively by the states within the Indian Union, Indira Gandhi chose to amend the Indian Constitution in 1976 and moved education to the concurrent list.

The Consolidation and Sustenance of the Liberal Economy: 1991–96

The increase in the rate of growth during 1974–91 beyond the Hindu rate of growth gave India the confidence to launch far-reaching economic measures. Liberalization, delicensing and growth in the private sector put India on the path of a liberal economy. The foreign exchange crisis owing to trade imbalance also forced the reluctant policymakers to expedite changes. These changes from 1991 to 1996 describe the shift to rapid economic growth and inevitable globalization in the country. The political economy of growth and development after 1974 had produced a grave fiscal situation, and the consequent dependence on foreign commercial banks was financially unsustainable after May 1991. It was this economic crisis that empowered liberal statesmen and technocrats to move the Indian economy substantially in the direction of private entrepreneurship and economic globalization after 1991.

The 1980s had prepared the ground for this policy shift. The dire crisis prompted a firm resolve within the technocracy to promote India's competiveness and its private sector. Greater support for economic deregulation and trade promotion among economists and technocrats existed in 1991 than was the case in 1966.

P.V. Narasimha Rao, who became prime minister in 1991, understood that he was confronted with a unique situation in India's economic history and he continued with vigour what Yashwant Sinha had initiated in the short-term Chandrashekhar coalition government. The cold war had ended at a time when India was facing a financial crisis. Its dependence on the Soviet Union for markets and imports needed to be restructured with far-reaching changes in those economies too. India's policymakers made a virtue of a crisis to guide the economy towards greater reliance on markets and trade. The restrictions on the private sector in a very large number of areas that so far had been exclusively reserved for state investment were withdrawn. Simultaneously, the public sector undertakings (PSUs) were also allowed to enter any sector that was not earlier reserved for it. Provisions for referring sick PSUs to the Board for Industrial and Financial Reconstruction (BIFR) were made with social security mechanism for the employees who were likely to be retrenched or laid off. Provision for public participation and selling shares to financial institutions were also made for raising resources.

Reform Era: 1996–2004

This was an era of short-term coalition governments. It was a break from the past. The leftist influence had also waned with huge economic changes in Russia, China and eastern Europe. The coalition was willing to move ahead from old policies, and Chidambaram could produce a dream budget in a coalition government. Later, the NDA implemented a large number of pro-reform policies accelerating growth. Substantial tariff liberalization, especially in the intermediate goods, was accompanied with significant devaluation of the Indian rupee. Tariff liberalization reduced the cost of inputs and pressured the Indian economy to become more competitive. This was a major boon for export-oriented sectors like IT. India's merchandise exports doubled once between 1991 and 1999, and again between 2002 and 2003. FERA, which had restricted foreign equity to a maximum limit of 40 per cent, was replaced with a regime that allowed 51 per cent foreign equity in most sectors of the economy.

The government at this time had realized the inevitability of reforms and increasing private sector participation for growth. The weaknesses of the previous system were highlighted in a study by the National Council for Applied Economic Research (NCAER), published in 2000, highlighting the trends in public and private sector, as shown in Table 10.2 and 10.3 below:

Table 10.2: Profitability of Manufacturing
(PAT as per cent of net sales)

	Public Sector	Private Sector
1990–91	-4.5	5.7
1991–92	-5.3	4.9
1992–93	-5.4	4.9
1993–94	-6.9	6.6
1994–95	-2.3	9.1
1995–96	-2.4	9
1996–97	-4.3	7
1997–98	-3.9	6.2

Source: 'The lost decade', NCAER study

Table 10.3: Manufacturing Efficiency Indicators
(cost as per cent of net sales)

	Power and Fuel/ Net Sales		Wages/ Net Sales		Interest/ Net Sales		Inefficiency of public sector as per cent of Net Sales*
	PSE	Private	PSE	Private	PSE	Private	
1990–91	10.3	6.8	18.6	8.9	8.8	6	16
1993–94	13.5	6.6	17.7	8.1	11.5	5.2	22.8
1996–97	14.9	6.6	19.1	8.2	9.8	5.9	23.1
1997–98	19.5	5	23.3	6.5	11.7	4.7	38.5

Note: *Inefficiency is defined here as the difference between the ratio of cost (on account of power and fuel, wages and interest) to net sales between the public and private sector.
Source: 'The lost decade', NCAER study

It clearly showed the need for a further shift to greater private sector participation in industry. The private sector had grown post-1991 but could not effectively enter industries in the nature of monopolistic network industries.

Prime Minister Atal Bihari Vajpayee was able to nudge the system towards independent regulation at the time of the investment crisis after 1997 and 2000.

The Department of Telecom, as the regulator and service provider, had devised rules that were hurting the private sector financially. A serious crisis relating to investment for private telecommunication companies existed in 1999 after the government-owned MTNL was allowed, an entry, free of licence fee, into the cellular business in 1998. The initiatives of Prime Minister Vajpayee at this time enabled regulatory institutions to become more independent in settling disputes between private companies and government-owned telecommunication providers. Despite similar measures in some other sectors such as power, petroleum and gas, and many others; the growth was much less in those sectors.

The NDA government laid a lot of emphasis on creating independent regulators, and breaking the network industries into competing units to bring in private capital and management. It realized that a model for bringing private sector without competition would only result in crony capitalism, which was amply demonstrated in the power sector after 1991. It could only be checked after breaking the sector into competing network elements and allowing competitive bidding. The changes in sectors other than telecom have been slow.

Despite overwhelming evidence that market orientation, competition, greater participation of the private sector, and export orientation, together with freeing of the resource constraint by FDI inflows, provides a reasonable basis for higher levels of economic growth, these growth strategies were not universally accepted in India. Even today there are endless debates against privatization and there is always an apprehension that FDI will lead to control by external agents. Perhaps these fears are the residual shadows of our colonial past. However, those who subscribe to these views forget that the East India Company was never intended to invest in India. The colonial period was marked by the extraction of capital and resources from India and other colonies, to fuel growth in Europe. The process was assisted by the absence of a domestic sovereign authority, which could resist such exploitative extraction. In the globalized world, access to private foreign capital does not imply an erosion of sovereignty. Foreign companies seek investment opportunities in India to enhance their value, but in the process such investment creates jobs, adds much-needed infrastructure and provides a functional business link between the economies of the world and India. Such links and commitments are long term in nature and should be differentiated from the flows of 'hot money' or portfolio investment, which can be temporary. These are driven solely by arbitrage opportunities, and can lead to collapse of economies, if funds are withdrawn to take advantage of such opportunities or for several other reasons, as had happened in the South-East Asian crisis of the 1980s. In these crises foreign direct investment was the stable element in the external balance. Foreign institutional FII investments and foreign lending had reduced.

To take the reform process beyond just ensuring private capital in new industries, the NDA government decided for a strategic sale of shares of sick PSUs. This would bring in capital and also change the working environment of these companies. Fortunately, I was a part of this process. We privatized dozens of loss-making hotels and other companies. BALCO, HZL, VSNL and Maruti Udyog were amongst the main companies. We also tried to privatize some companies in the oil sector, but could not go beyond IBP. Later, the Supreme Court declared that we could not privatize HPCL and BPCL. The government stake of 4.5 per cent in GAIL was sold to ONGC and IOC, both of which were large and cash-rich PSUs in the petroleum sector. The privatized companies performance showed increased turnover, capacities, profits, dividends and taxes. It eliminated the PSUs' dependence on the taxpayer.

Reforms' Further Advance: 2004–09

Once the Congress government came to power along with the support of the Left parties, privatizations were limited. A committee was appointed to turn around underperforming PSUs. The committee gave voluminous reports, but as was the case in the past, nothing happened.

One such committee was the Arjun Sengupta Committee which recommended drastic changes in the governance structure of the PSUs. The powers of the Nav Ratnas to set up joint ventures or invest were to be enhanced. In addition, it recommended sector-specific supervisory bodies to review the performance of PSUs. These recommendations were mostly implemented in default. However, the after-effects of the growth during the NDA period took the country forward. The presence of the Left in the government during the period did not allow liberal policies to go forward, saving the country from scams which flourished in the non-Left 2009 coalition. Perhaps the Left had anticipated tendencies of crony capitalism, as shown during the privatizations of telecom and other sectors under UPA-I; hence they were against both disinvestment and privatization.

The Crony Capitalism Years: 2009–14

Despite the break with the communist parties in 2009 and the formation of a new Congress-led coalition government, the policy of privatization was not resumed. The government continued to sell small amounts of shares in the PSUs listed on the stock exchange with a view to raising resources to bridge the government's rising deficit. However, the sales (of fractional equity) did not result in any change of control or privatization, and the performance of these undertakings remained the same in contrast to that of the privatized companies, where performance improved under private sector management.

Crony capitalism reared up again during this period due to the evaporation of the government as an integrated institution to a confused coalition hierarchy. Everyone in the government revelled at such processes as they gave more opportunities for those in power to make money at the expense of the state. It was only later, when the unparalleled loot started in allocating resources, in award of contracts, and in government purchases by departments and organizations as in the Commonwealth Games, that opposition parties, particularly the BJP, started protesting. The majority of the UPA-II government treated these protests with contempt and did not take any action. This led to agitations by overzealous non-government organizations, movements led by the likes of Anna Hazare and Ramdev. The CAG also became overzealous and provided data supporting those who were agitating. Some individuals in the government also started protesting loudly. All this led to the high courts and the Supreme Court stepping in. Crony capitalism came to an end when the discerning Indian voter acted. The government started taking some corrective actions before the elections but it was too late. They were so overconfident earlier that they left long trails of corruption. They did try to remedy by taking the help of willing organizations like the CBI and tried to divert blame to the opposition, but the courts clipped their overzealous hands by supervising the investigations themselves.

Reforms can deliver a lot to the nation. However, possibilities of huge corruption increase in liberalized economies. Systems to check crony capitalism must evolve quickly. The electorate has already given its message in favour of these changes.

11

Early Reforms: Reforms by Stealth

During the early reforms in the late 1970s, for the first time since Independence, the Government of India reduced the importance and monopoly of the public sector to help the Indian economy grow. There were many instances. I will only deal with those I participated in. I was lucky to have implemented some changes. However, at that point, I did not understand their political implications.

Imported Fertilizers

The Ministry of Agriculture and Farmers Welfare used to deal with the allocation, distribution and import of fertilizers. I joined its fertilizer division as deputy secretary in 1982. The joint secretary of the division was one of the most outstanding officers that I have worked with—M.S. Chahal of the Punjab cadre. He gave a lot of powers to his juniors to try and improve the work of the division. While imports on behalf of the government were done by the Metals and Minerals Trading Corporation of India (MMTC), storage and distribution across the country was the responsibility of the Food Corporation of India (FCI). For potash and potassic fertilizers, storage and distribution was done by Indian Potash Limited. Both these companies had no competitors and were inefficient. Costs were reimbursed on a normative, which was almost actual, basis, giving no incentive to companies for efficient handling.

The scheme had an interesting background. The green revolution increased the demand for fertilizers in the mid-1970s. Indigenous producers were unable to meet this demand and increased amounts had to be imported. The price of indigenous production was low and the higher price of the imported fertilizers gave local producers a margin to make profits. They were inevitably allowed to sell at higher prices. A scheme was evolved to mop up the higher profits of producers into the Fertilizer Price Equalization Fund (FPEF) with the government. But as it normally happens in such cases, the price of imported fertilizers increased fast, leading to withdrawals from the fund. Ultimately, it led to subsidy of thousands of crores by the government to ensure lower prices of fertilizers for farmers.

The government also thought indigenous production should increase and the Marathe Committee recommended a normative cost-plus price to producers and uniform low prices to farmers. This subsidy on indigenous and imported fertilizer prices has distorted the fertilizer market over the years, and a number of committees thereafter have been unable to find a solution. This policy distorts the selection of inputs/processes for fertilizer production, geographical location of fertilizer plants and prices of inputs, leading to higher costs of production and distribution. It is surprising that the Government of India later adopted a similar scheme for power generation pricing, despite this experience, and distorted the power sector for years.

The period of 1982–83 was a good monsoon year and there was huge demand for fertilizers from all over the country. Though the FCI had massive stocks, fertilizers were not being handed over to state agencies for distribution efficiently as the FCI was too busy with its primary job of procuring, storing and distributing foodgrains. Food procurement too was far in excess of its capacity, and at many places there were complaints of foodgrain and fertilizer stocks getting mixed up. With difficulty, we convinced the food and finance ministries to sell old fertilizer stocks at 10 per cent discount through the distribution machinery of private and public fertilizer companies. One of the arguments for this price concession was that the fertilizer, being old, was slightly discoloured.

We were able to convince the Ministry of Finance that the government would gain if all stocks were sold fast and would also reach farmers in a year of fertilizer shortage. On the other hand, if they remained with FCI, only limited amounts would reach the farmer. Many also thought that a large chunk of the stock of nearly fourteen million tonnes would not see the light of day, having been pilfered/wasted away during the long years of storage. When we went to the fertilizer and finance ministries, they concurred at the secretarial level which comprised the secretary, the joint secretary, Shyamal Ghosh, and the additional secretary, Somaiya, who later became home secretary and then CAG. It is interesting that the file involving a possible loss of hundreds of crores of rupees never went to the finance minister. Incidentally, thanks to both decisions, the entire fertilizer stock was sold during the year, and the government saved huge amounts of money.

Much later, early in the first decade of the twentieth century, the reduction in rates on telecom companies led to huge increase in telecom volumes and income to the government. Yet, a perverse government headed by Manmohan Singh, aided and abetted by Chidambaram, Maran, Raja and Kapil Sibal, prosecuted Shyamal Ghosh and launched a preliminary inquiry against Arun Shourie and me. They kept a large contingent in the CBI and a retired judge, Justice Shivraj Patil, busy on these frivolous and fabricated inquiries. What these stalwarts missed was seen by the judge conducting Shyamal Ghosh's inquiry. I was fortunate that my case did not reach a judge and was closed by the CBI. It received a few remarks on the procedure, perhaps on directions from the director.

Let me come back to Somaiya. No one asked him about his decision. If Somaiya and Joint Secretary Gopal Tandon in the Department of Expenditure had not taken this decision in a meeting in one day, the scheme could never have been launched, as the fertilizer distribution season is short and would have come to an end before the decision could be implemented. Fortunately, at that time, no one feared that such decisions would be tested by the likes of the Shivraj Patil Committee that could give judgments without understanding the issues. Shyamal Ghosh was a part of the process, both in fertilizers and in telecom, and took quick decisions.

When we wanted to issue revised price notification for fertilizer prices, the Ministry of Law and Justice said we could not fix two prices under the Essential Commodities Act for a discoloured fertilizer; the only classification could be on the basis of chemical content, which had not changed in this case. Finally, after a number of visits to the law ministry, we were allowed to notify. Even in the ministry, people looked at the ends and not the means. Today, even with good intentions, we would have got prosecuted again for breaching the law. Maybe we still can for the 1983 decision.

When the scheme started, everyone warned us that the FCI was not interested in the quick movement of fertilizers as it gets paid for all the storage costs, and if the entire fertilizer moves, huge shortages due to pilferage would be discovered. However, we pursued at the field level with Bindra (general manager, marketing), and a vigilance officer, Tyagi (who later became a minister in UP), and the marketing director of many fertilizer companies. At the end of the year, we were pleasantly surprised that nearly all the fertilizer stock could be recovered from the FCI godowns and distributed to the farmers, as against less than 50 per cent in the previous years. Fertilizer companies also pursued vigorously since they saw new business of distributing imported fertilizers in 1983, and in future years. The scheme was implemented so well that for future years too we got the government's approval to store, move and distribute fertilizers through fertilizer companies. This helped introduce competition and enabled us to fix handling costs on normative and competitive. It also avoided fertilizers being mixed with foodgrains, and provided more storage space for foodgrains whose procurement was increasing every year. We were pleasantly surprised to see that the competition introduced enabled us to almost halve the handling costs for future years, and the fertilizer reached the farmer faster as it was in these companies' interest to distribute faster. With the saving in the handling costs, the government could also introduce a scheme to reach the fertilizers at the block level by giving a fixed margin to state marketing agencies for this movement.

As in the fertilizer distribution scheme, it is suicidal to have any cost-plus or normative scheme through a public sector or any other company, since the handling company, having no stakes in efficient handling, jacks up costs and then gets these approved through various methods. For government agencies particularly, it is difficult to prune costs—they come with the support of the administrative ministry even if the agencies are inefficient, and the paying ministry ultimately does not object, the transaction being within the government. Competitive schemes always save costs was a big learning from this scheme. We could never have evolved such a scheme if the government had taken a political stand that production, import and distribution of fertilizers would only be in the public/cooperative sector. With this scheme, and many others, the government was starting soft reforms, a prelude to the 1991 reforms.

Liberalization in the 1980s

The booming rate of growth in South-East Asian economies perhaps moved India towards reluctant liberalization in the 1980s, leading it to move towards deregulated private sector investment. One of the path-breaking changes made during this period was the delicensing of cement. I remember Brijendra Sahai, joint secretary in the Ministry of Commerce and Industry, piloted the move. Later he retired as chief secretary of Uttar Pradesh. This was justified by the huge shortage of cement and the licensing procedure being a roadblock to increased production. Within a short time of delicensing, the capacity of cement went up 2.5 times, whereas the production of steel (which was still in the public sector reservation list) only went up 1.25 times. Of course, steel rods, etc., were being produced by delicensed rolling mills/electric arc furnaces for use by those using extra cement, but these were not recorded in the production data due to the huge theft of power in these small-scale units, which did not require licensing.

Another deregulation was in the area of telecom equipment and switching which led to growth in the telecom sector. The evolution of a private IT industry in the 1980s also exhibited India's comparative advantage if the goods and services were produced in the private sector. Do recall the vastly superior keyboard telephones in comparison to the dial phones of the monopoly public sector era. Permitting handsets to be manufactured in the private sector in the mid-1980s was also visualized as a huge liberalization step—so restrictive and inward-looking was the earlier 'command economy' model. I remember being in awe of the first keyboard telephone I saw at the house of S.B. Lal, additional secretary, Ministry of Communications and Information Technology, in the early 1980s.

Firms were also allowed to produce 133 per cent of their capacity without a new licence. Many industries were excluded from the ambit of the MRTP Act, and the limit was also raised. A joint sector plant of Maruti was launched during this period and the automobile plants were allowed automatic expansion of production capacity. Deregulation of the automobile industry in the 1980s led to the realization of comparative advantage of the automobile component industry in the future. These small liberalization efforts of the 1980s gave India the confidence to launch fuller liberalization and delicensing in the1990s.

Liberalization in the Visakhapatnam Steel Plant

The developments in the construction of steel plants prior to 1990 were interesting. No one had the courage to remove integrated steel plants from the list of those industries reserved for the public sector in Schedule VI of the Industries (Development and Regulation) Act (IDR). The huge shortage of steel in the country and the refusal of the Ministry of Finance to fund new steel plants forced the Ministry of Steel to approve steel furnaces, blast furnaces, rolling mills and galvanizing lines close to each other as separate industries, as was permitted in the industrial policy, and then allowing them to work as one industry. The approval of the steel plants of Essar Group in Hazira, Gujarat, and those of the Mittal Group in Hazira in Gujarat and Raigarh in Maharashtra, was part of the same process. Ultimately, integrated steel plants and a number of industries were taken out of Schedule VI after 1991.

I remember many furores in Parliament in the 1980s whenever we took up the issue of removal of integrated steel plants from Schedule VI despite huge steel shortages. The charges were that a couple of bureaucrats in government did not understand the Nehruvian 'heights of public sector'. The environment of shortages gave huge demands and profits to the incumbents. I did see their hand in the furore generated in Parliament against new private steel plants.

The Visakhapatnam Steel Plant, under construction in the 1980s, was the last of the integrated steel plants sanctioned by the government. It was also the biggest, with a 3.2 million tonnes/year of steel capacity to be built in one phase. The other integrated steel plants were built at smaller capacities in the first phase, and later expanded. Like the Bhilai and Bokaro Steel Plants, this too was being built with Soviet collaboration and required huge financial allocations to go ahead. For the first time, this Soviet-aided steel plant allowed non-Soviet equipment and technologies. However, since allocations for the steel plant were low and were available on a year-on-year basis, we moved at a snail's pace.

The government's financial condition worsened in 1984–85, and the next year a sum of only Rs 300 crore was allocated for the construction of the Rs 17,000 crore Visakhapatnam Steel Plant. Construction was in full swing and most machinery was being supplied by the Soviets and other suppliers in a disciplined manner. However, keeping the payment schedule was becoming impossible. Both loans and equity for such projects were given in the government's annual budget then on a fifty-fifty basis. To partially deal with the payment crisis, the government permitted the project to borrow from Bank Paribas. However, we later realized that the SBI could give us better terms and we shifted to it.

We repeatedly asked the finance ministry to allot more funds but due to shortage of funds it was decided to wind up the project under construction in 1986. Natwar Singh was the minister for steel then and R.P. Khosla was the steel secretary. They were batchmates in service and both being thorough gentlemen, the minister felt embarrassed at repeatedly calling the secretary to his room. As the joint secretary, I was normally called for giving instructions. I would get these instructions complied after telling the secretary. The system was working fine and one day when I was sitting with the minister during such a meeting the Rax phone (meant for secretaries and ministers) rang. Prime Minister Rajiv Gandhi was on the line. As I started to leave, the minister asked me not to and started speaking to the prime minister. The PM told him that the finance ministry could not finance the Visakhapatnam Steel Plant and had decided to cancel further construction. The project was to be converted into a large number of private mini steel plants, which were allowed in the private sector at that point of time. Integrated steel plants were not allowed. However, these were going to be far more expensive. The PM further told Natwar Singh not to protest on the decision. Since I was the dealing joint secretary, the minister conveyed the decision and asked me to keep quiet and not to protest.

I promptly went to the secretary's room and conveyed the decision. I further informed him that this decision could never be implemented as it was unviable and would lead to huge losses for the government. The government would have to give damages to the contractors and would face severe shortage of steel. Moreover, an integrated steel plant structure could not be changed into a thousand mini steel plants, as some people were thinking in the government. Further, the project was approved by the government after huge agitations in Visakhapatnam, which would start again. We decided to talk to the minister again the next day after marshalling all economic arguments and counting on his sense of history that he would not like to be associated with an unwise decision. We convinced the minister that we would protest, particularly on economic grounds. I was directed to write a short (not more than one-and-a-half pages) letter of protest with no annexures, as the prime minister did not like long letters.

I immediately went to Visakhapatnam to prepare the letter along with the project officers. We managed to prepare a three-page draft presenting a horrifying picture of the post-closure scenario and left it to the secretary's enormous editing abilities to reduce it to the acceptable length. This was immediately dispatched by the minister to the prime minister. Rajiv Gandhi called a review meeting within a week.

It would be worthwhile here to recall the prime minister's insistence on short letters and precise presentations. Once, during a review meeting, the agriculture secretary had presented a commercial-looking presentation with background music to the PM and he almost lost his job. The secretary (steel) asked me to meet Sam Pitroda and take his advice on preparing a short, no-frills PowerPoint presentation for the steel ministry. He was a kind person and spent a long time with me in restructuring the presentation. The final product was a precise, fifteen-slide presentation.

When this issue was discussed in the meeting, the inevitable decision of accelerating the construction of the steel plant did not take long. The prime minister asked for the requirement for the year and the managing director, on my prodding, mentioned Rs 1,000 crore. Later, the managing director found he could not accelerate expenditure to Rs 1,000 crore from Rs 300 crore.

One of the critical requirements of the Visakhapatnam Steel Plant was the construction of the 150 km Elluru Canal with 158 aquaducts, at a cost of Rs 350 crore. This canal was to be constructed by the Andhra Pradesh government as per our MOU but construction had not started despite assurances from the chief minister. All the high-level meetings resulted in nothing. So I went to meet T.R. Prasad, secretary (irrigation), who had the reputation of being very professional. He said if Rs 350 crore could be given to the irrigation department from the Visakhapatnam Steel Plant funds, he would ensure the canal was completed on time. We had extra money this year and gave him the money and negotiated the loan payback from the water rate. True to his professional approach, he completed the difficult project on the appointed day. Much later, when I was the disinvestment secretary, he was the cabinet secretary, and helped me enormously in doing the almost impossible work. His predecessor, Prabhat Kumar, had also helped us with this work and had evolved a committee procedure, dispersing all decisions to multi-member inter-ministerial committees.

The Rs 350 crore loan helped us spend the allocated Rs 1,000 crore that year, assuring us higher allocations in future years, thus completing the project early.

Another commitment we made in the prime minister's meeting was that we would rationalize the project and bring down the project cost. The project team went to Russia, and in consultation with the Russians reduced the project cost by 20 per cent, by rationalizing equipment. Another remarkable reduction was in the labour strength to 13,000 from 50,000. This was on the basis of the 13,000 actual strength in the Russian plant of which the Visakhapatnam plant was a copy. When I asked the Russians the justification for higher equipment and the requirement for 50,000 labour in the plant's earlier Detailed Project Report (DPR), their simple answer was that we do not work. Despite installing the latest equipment in the plant, our labour strength continued to be the same on different machines as applicable to all old plants because of the National Joint Council of Steel (NJCS)—the common apex body for all labour unions of all steel plants in India.

Further, the Visakhapatnam Steel Plant had 23,000 displaced fishermen families which had to be given employment as per the prime minister's statement in Parliament. We had also developed a practice that the displaced children, who became adults during construction of the plant, were also employed. In the Bokaro Steel Plant, the DPR number of 35,000 had become 70,000 during the long construction period.

We, in the Ministry of Steel, took very liberal interpretation of the prime minister's statements since they involved more expenditure at the taxpayers' expense. Interestingly, the displaced persons (DPs) were allowed to sell jobs too. At that time the going rate was Rs 50,000. The only way to restrict jobs was to adopt different policies. There were also thousands of appeals pending in the high courts and the Supreme Court against land acquisition prices in Visakhapatnam. Our first decision was that the Visakhapatnam Steel Plant will not join the NJCS with the Tata Steel Plant also being a member. Thus the steel industry norms would not be applicable to the Visakhapatnam Steel Plant. It was a very difficult decision, since even the Tata Steel

Plant was also a member of the NJCS. This decision was not changed for decades.

The problem of numerous appeals for land acquisition cases was sorted out for us by Mani Shankar Aiyer, then a joint secretary in the PMO and later the petroleum minister in UPA-I. He convinced the prime minister to announce a high compensation if the DPs withdrew the appeals and gave up their right for jobs. The legal process was efficiently handled by the Lok Adalats of Justice Ranganath Misra, when the DPs were assured of immediate payment of much higher compensation if they signed a piece of paper, withdrawing their appeals and giving up the claim to jobs. The labour strength thereafter remained at around 13,000 till almost the start of the expansion process.

Rajiv Gandhi's announcement of the liberal land acquisition in a public meeting was welcomed and it changed the Visakhapatnam Steel Plant into one of the most competitive plants within a few years of completion. I must acknowledge the credit for change in the PMO's approach to Mani Shankar Aiyer.

All these changes were possible because Rajiv Gandhi had started looking at industrial policies through the mirror of economic viability and not on dogmas which determined employment and licensing policies in old instructions of the command economy.

The Election and Other Processes

Though elections and many other processes were not economic or industrial reforms, there was far greater scrutiny of processes at the cutting-edge level in the overall environment of reforms by stealth. The happenings in the election process were interesting as the process was largely reformed by the chief election commissioner (CEC) of India, T.N. Seshan. He did this without any change in law but only by interpreting the law in a more reformist manner and implementing reforms in his typical aggressive and strict manner.

During his tenure in the 1990s, he changed the election process forever by strict interpretation of the law. Chief election officers (CEOs) in states who did not comply with his instructions came to grief. The courts went along with the reforms introduced as they also interpreted the law the way he had, in the interest of badly needed reforms. This was a departure from earlier practices in the Election Commission, where reforms were not implemented owing to lack of clearly defined law and the commissioners kept running to a non-willing political government to reform. I will deal with this also later in the book.

I was appointed as the chief election officer in 1988 in Madhya Pradesh, on my return from the UK. I complained to the chief minister, Arjun Singh, that there was no work. He gave me additional charge of secretary (parliamentary affairs). Thus, I had work only when the election process was on or when the legislative assembly was in session. I complained again that there was insufficient work and was appointed secretary (finance) too.

Consignment Tax

At this time, we were struggling with the Government of India's proposal of imposing consignment tax. I thought the tax was unfair to backward states and very profitable for manufacturing and advanced states since their manufactured goods would receive tax at the manufacturing state level. Thus, for sales outside the state, this would reduce the consumer state's ability to tax, one part of tax having been imposed already by the manufacturing state, whereas sales tax was a state entry. The proposed tax also exempted raw material, thus putting states producing primary goods at a huge disadvantage. In anticipation of the consignment tax being introduced, states such as Maharashtra had budgeted for large additional receipts from this tax. The scheme also did not provide for any compensation for backward states. On our request, Chief Minister Moti Lal Vora agreed to write to Finance Minister S.B. Chavan at the Centre of our concerns. The finance minister appointed a committee comprising Narayan Dutt Tiwari, the then chief minister of UP, and Vora to examine the issue in detail.

I proposed letters from Vora, which were approved, to the finance minister and Tiwari explaining infirmities in the decision. Vora signed the letter after understanding its implications. However, later in the committee meeting Vora supported the tax along with all the finance ministry officials and the famous economist Raja Chelliah (everyone by this time knew that Prime Minister Rajiv Gandhi had approved the tax). On being the lone doubter after reading our letter, Tiwari did not know what to do. He also did not want to oppose alone, so he took out Vora's letters and said in his inimitable style, 'Vora-*ji*, there were some very relevant facts mentioned in your letter—can you explain?' Vora too did not know what to do and I quietly whispered to ask for his permission to speak. I thought he nodded and I started rattling out facts and figures against the tax. The arguments were strong and despite all the other nodding heads, the meeting did not recommend the tax and postponed the issue to a later meeting.

I came out of the meeting following the chief minister, hoping for a 'well done' remark. I did not get any. On reaching Bhopal, I explained to the chief secretary and the secretary to the chief minister of my feat saving Rs 300 crore per year (the tax could not be imposed with my arguments in the meeting) for the state, but told them that the chief minister had perhaps not approved my intervention and that they would have to transfer me. They expressed uninhibited support and said that they would fight for me if the CM decided to transfer me.

However, within two hours of the meeting, Y.N. Chaturvedi came to my room with his posting orders as finance secretary. I handed charge within minutes and started sitting in my other two offices of CEO and parliamentary affairs secretary, with no work. However, the Central government, having been given figures of losses for backward states and unable to make provisions for losses in the Central budget could never impose this tax. Later, Raja Chelliah himself opposed the logic of this tax. The Central government has to realize that there is very little flexibility in the states' incomes and they cannot take the burden of losses in any tax change imposed by the Central government. The ongoing moves for GST can also only be implemented after the Central government firmly guarantees making up of the states' income losses.

Moti Lal Vora was replaced by Shyama Charan Shukla in a few months and elections were ordered. On being briefed by the chief secretary of recent developments, he felt uneasy about my transfer and posted me as secretary (commercial taxes), in addition to the other two charges. This was a sensitive time as it was the closure of the financial year for taxation departments and the beginning of excise auctions, and required the secretary to take crucial decisions. The 1989 general elections had also been ordered and the leader of the Opposition, S.L. Patwa, cried foul about the CEO being secretary (commercial taxes), also. I went to the chief secretary and said that I would not mind being transferred owing to the controversy. He said that the question did not arise. I kept quiet and all leaders of Opposition, including Devi Lal, who gave many election speeches in Bhopal, objected at the CEO's posting as secretary.

In the Madhya Pradesh assembly elections (also held in 1989), the Congress government lost and BJP won, but it was taking time to announce the chief minister. Meanwhile, I along with M.L. Mehta, secretary, Vidhan Sabha, realized that a constitutional crisis was brewing and there was an immediate necessity of calling the budget session. We had no choice but to approach Kushabhau Thakre, the BJP president, whom I fortunately knew personally. He took us to S.L. Patwa's house (he knew who was going to be the CM), and we decided on a solution, while BJP announced the date of oath taking. Immediately after taking oath, he started calling me to finalize the dates of the budget session.

In one of the long meetings, I quietly mentioned that he may transfer me from the post of secretary (commercial taxes), in view of his speeches during the poll campaign. He smiled, but did not transfer me. Much later, he posted me as secretary (industries), till I left for Delhi on deputation in 1993. I had worked as registrar, cooperatives, when he was chairman, Mandsaur Cooperative Bank, and even though I had conducted an extraordinary audit of his bank, he knew that I was fair. Later, I had leveraged huge resources for the agriculture credit movement of the state and had started the successful project of converting Madhya Pradesh into a soybean state. He hoped that I would leverage more funds from commercial taxes. He also vaguely mentioned this in the first few days of taking over as chief minister and I did not disappoint him.

I had the support of the commercial taxes minister, Babulal Jain, in this task. We took many steps to successfully increase the state income, but without changing rates. I was also able to drastically reduce the rates at which we bought liquor distributed by the state, thus increasing state income. The rates were reduced by increasing competition and clearing some more distilleries. Whether we had the power to do so was challenged in the Supreme Court. The Supreme Court after hearing us did not give stay and the case was referred back to the high court. This allowed us to implement the policy. I understand the case was compromised later and the state policy went on.

Later, soon after I was transferred to the post of secretary (industries), the Babri Masjid demolition took place and president's rule was imposed in Madhya Pradesh. All the non-official chairmen of state corporations being BJP men were removed and I started working as chairman of nine state industry corporations too, thus holding twelve charges.

Start of the first Public–Private Road in India

Public–private projects were hardly known in India in 1988. When I was posted as secretary (finance) in Madhya Pradesh, we received a proposal from IL&FS (Infrastructure Leasing & Financial Services) that they would like to design/participate in a project for the construction of a public–private road between Indore and Peethampur, an industrial estate in Madhya Pradesh. No one in the state government and very few in IL&FS knew much about structuring such projects. Yet we started.

Looking at the traffic projections, it was clear that the project was not viable. We therefore decided that half the length of the project would be constructed by the state government and the rest by IL&FS, but toll will be charged only on the IL&FS road. It took us a long time to design the project and get it approved from the state government, but the resultant product was the first toll road in India and initiated a process which led to the setting up of the National Highway Authority of India (NHAI).

This road was hugely unpopular with the state Public Works Department (PWD) since it impinged on their monopoly. In one of the PWD review meetings, I had to plead with Chief Minister Arjun Singh to give us an opportunity to complete the public–private initiative. He agreed on the assurance that we would implement on time, which we did. This was possible because there were no multiple scrutinizing agencies asking different questions at different times. The state government and the CAG's scrutiny was all that the executing agencies in the government had to face. Today, multiple preliminary inquiries by the police/CBI, state vigilance, inspired news articles, etc., have made state agencies reluctant to take up such projects. With toll not being sufficient to construct such roads, different ways to make them viable have been found.

I must give credit to my training on reforms and privatization at Oxford University during 1987–88, which helped me start conceptualizing and implementing the project on behalf of the state government. It is quite clear that the state and the Central governments together do not have the funds to construct the required roads and infrastructure. Public–private projects are the only answer. India has a unique opportunity owing to huge infrastructural gaps that many projects can be identified for being funded by FII and FDI funds. China has used this model for enormous growth in the last few decades. None of the developed countries offer such opportunities. However, some of the brilliantly conceptualized and implemented projects like Delhi–Agra Expressway have hugely suffered due to state not giving them proper. This must change.

Initiating Privatization in Madhya Pradesh

In 1993, the Madhya Pradesh government privatized NITEL (National Information Technologies Limited), a joint sector project of the state government with the Press Trust of India (PTI), by selling it to R.P. Goenka. NITEL had the indomitable P.N. Haksar, who had been secretary to Indira Gandhi, as its chairman. R.P. Goenka agreed to my request to retain Haksar as chairman and I did not incur his wrath for having privatized his company in a BJP-ruled state.

Later, we also privatized half of a joint sector project between the Madhya Pradesh government and Fujitsu and Furukawa, namely, Optel Telecommunications Ltd, the first optical fibre/telecom systems plant in the country, to Fujitsu (the telecom systems plant) and named it Fujitsu Optel Ltd (FOTEL). All these projects were based on price negotiation as no one understood bidding for privatization then. The Government of India had given us a model by disinvesting 50 per cent of Maruti on a negotiated price in 1991. In 2002, when we started exercises for privatizing with Kotak as our advisor, we realized that it was an atrociously low price. I have written in detail about this project in my book on disinvestment. Unlike in UPA-II, we did not start a CBI inquiry against the finance minister who did the first round of 50 per cent privatization. Perhaps no one complained at the time of earlier privatization in 1992 as no one understood the process. Again my training helped in resolving complex issues, helping us get a much higher price from Suzuki during the Maruti privatization in 2002.

In Madhya Pradesh, Optel—the first company in India to manufacture optical fibre—was a very profitable company. Since it was in the public sector, it earned most of its profits from the arbitrage between the import duty rates for the raw material and the finished product. People in the Ministry of Finance or the Department of Telecom never examined its fibre pricing proposals, since it was in the public sector, and it was able to get away with usurious prices.

The 1991 reforms led to the private sector's entry in this area. Duty rates were reduced and this affected Optel's arbitrage model. We found that the plant could not survive unless it increased capacity at least ten times. We tried but did not get the necessary approvals from the government, though we had the resources. Competition from large private sector plants made us non-competitive and the plant closed down. The unit that manufactured telecom equipment would also have closed down if we had not privatized it. All this happened in 1992, but the telecom reforms took another eleven years. The Government of Madhya Pradesh did make half-hearted attempts to sell Optel's optical fibre manufacturing plant, but could not sell because it did not have the expertise to initiate and complete a difficult exercise of privatization. I tried to help from Delhi, but none of the bureaucrats, perhaps wiser, wanted to take the risk. And the state government kept supporting the sick and closed public sector unit at taxpayers' expense till it closed and became a relic of the past. We could have sold it at very high prices in the 1990s.

Private Steel Plants in Madhya Pradesh

My work as the secretary (industries) in Madhya Pradesh from 1991 to 1993 was interesting. Post-liberalization, we started planning for large industries in the private sector, hitherto a domain of the public sector. Jagdish Khattar, a joint secretary in the Ministry of Steel and my successor on the desk of new steel projects, decided to visit MP to facilitate new steel projects. After all, this was the state with the most viable steel plant sites. We had meaningful discussions and we started planning for four new private steel plants in MP, two in Bastar and one each in Raipur and Raigarh districts. While the two in Bastar were later killed by Dr B.D. Sharma, a former collector of Bastar who had become a messiah for tribals post-retirement, and wanted tribals to live in their old glory of non-development, the plants in Raipur and Raigarh did come up. Many new sponge iron plants also came up, but Bastar kept exporting valuable iron ore without any value addition in the district. To my understanding, such policies keep the tribals backward and poor and throw them into the clutches of Naxalites. Naxalites normally do not survive in developed areas.

Later, O.P. Jindal came to me and complained that he was incurring losses in the Raigarh Steel Plant due to high power rates. I suggested that he put up a captive power plant permitted in the new Government of India policy. He did so, but still made losses due to high coal rates. I suggested he should take a captive coal mine, then permissible in policy. He was transferred some unviable mines of South Eastern Coalfields (SECL) by the Ministry of Coal and the group later found that this unviable mine was a huge profit centre for the group. Even other industrialists found out about this and there was a mad rush for captive coal mine allotment, later leading to the Coalgate scam due to improper scrutiny and approval without transparent and honest procedures.

I returned back to the Government of India in 1993, and after a brief stint in the Ministry of Consumer Affairs looking after public distribution and standardization of products, joined the Ministry of Power to look after private power projects. Again, my training in this subject was the catalyst for the unusual change.

Back in the Government of India

On joining the Ministry of Power in 1994, I found unfruitful negotiations being held with ABB to sell ABL, a sick public sector undertaking, already referred to a semi-judicial body—the Board for Industrial and Financial Reconstruction (BIFR). The company had two plants: one manufacturing boilers in West Bengal and another manufacturing cement plant equipment in Karnataka. The company was incurring huge losses and was running with the help of reservation by the Government of India that gave it fixed orders. They had eight leftist trade unions. BIFR agreed to consider our negotiated sale package with ABB, if we got them the unions' consent. To my great surprise, the eight unions gave their consent very quickly in 1994. Perhaps they had by then understood that jobs could not be saved without the company's sale to ABB, a well-known multinational. No one complained about the negotiated sale and the price. Of course, the deal was done taking the labour unions and the BIFR on board, and had the approval of the cabinet. N.K.P. Salve, the then minister for power, had to use all his argument and accounting skills to sell the case to the cabinet. I had thought that this would be a one-minute item. No one complained on the negotiated price, perhaps because we had the approval of BIFR and also no one understood the privatization exercise. Again my training and the complete trust of my secretary and minister helped. ABB turned around the company very quickly.

It was obvious that the country needed reforms since the 1980s and the government stopped showing its preference to 'heights of public sector'. Small actions needed to be taken to move forward to the 1991 reforms, and these actions facilitated the change of policy in that year.

12

Looking into the Future: Disruptive Changes

We are now moving to an age of rapid technological changes, determining growth. The new technologies can only be introduced after making changes in 'business as usual'. In our growth process now, both new technologies and reforms and regulations will play a big role. The growth story of India started with reforms in the 1970s. It accelerated with the strengthening of the impact of digital technologies, particularly in communications, and the launch of formal liberalization measures in the 1990s. Digital technologies brought disruptive changes in most countries. The impact was higher in India due to our traditional strengths in digital technologies. Yet these disruptive technologies had to be managed through reforms and regulation to be commercially useful. Bringing in new regulations has been a very difficult task, as the book has described in many chapters. It is now universally understood that future growth in the globalized interconnected world will be through digital technologies, which are now influencing all aspects of human activity. But we will gain only if we are able to create appropriate regulatory environment to introduce them, and identified programmes are implemented efficiently.

We live in a globalized world. The earlier models of closed economies and state-sponsored growth have collapsed. We are also pursuing the path of a market-oriented liberalized economy. The state is no longer the only custodian of investment in a large number of industries.

However, the country will only receive investment from private industries, both Indian and foreign, when the rules of investment and running of the industry are clear. This requires massive reforms in all sectors. The industry is more comfortable with reforms being implemented by institutions other than political governments. Moreover, these rules need to be written and implemented in a transparent environment with judicial review, with the government mainly looking after policy issues.

Reforms and regulations are new initiatives of the last few decades around the world and expertise is gradually growing. Several industrial sectors are interrelated and a large number of regulators will create chaos. The future belongs to multi-sector regulators—a trend developing around the world.

For instance, digitization has ensured that most countries today have converged communication regulators. We will also have to ensure transition which has partially started in India. Similarly, railways, airlines, shipping have many common transportation issues. A transport regulator, with the oversight of a judicial appellate body, rather than a regulator for each sector would be more appropriate and acceptable to those who make massive investments.

There are some sectors which are vicious natural monopolies, and need a lot of preparation before private investment can come in. The railways are one such sector. Most countries undergoing reforms have touched railways the last on account of the natural monopoly problems. The United Kingdom, which did very well in reforms, floundered on the railway reforms and the government lost the elections. Japan started railway reforms late and after a lot of preparation, and has benefitted.

Technology is changing very fast and reforms should be such that government notifications under sectoral reform laws, rather than new legislations lead to further reforms. Broadcasting reforms within the TRAI Act, through a notification, and giving the reform to an existing regulator with experience in reform matters is a good example. Everyone accepts that broadcasting reforms were swift.

Despite a progressive Electricity Act 2003, open access could not be implemented in India, a very essential part of network reform. The government is now bringing an amended enactment. This is perhaps being done through a PMO initiative, which is the right place for monitoring of reforms. Lack of power reforms is one single reason for India's poor growth. Of course, since there are interlinkages, non-conventional energy, coal and petroleum sectors should be a part of the same energy regulator.

We need huge investments in India in each sector, particularly the infrastructure sector. It is important that foreign and Indian investors get confidence in our reform process for more investments in the country. A sound telecom reform institution led to more investments in the telecom sector against capital-intensive power sector in one year. The telecom sector also achieved 300–400 per cent of targeted growth in a few years, while the power sector has failed to achieve even 50 per cent of the target for the last three decades. A sound reform process and intelligently structured contracts are the surest way to accelerate GDP growth in the country. The Planning Commission did a lot of work in this area and the process should go on. Other countries have also prepared similar contracts and they must be looked at. But this work cannot be left to consultants only, since that can compromise the government's interest.

The Future of Broadband Reforms

Let me now deal with the telecom sector reforms in some more detail. An ideal situation should ensure that the regulators are not left behind by the brilliant technologists. The present Act is unable to look after the changed broadband regulatory developments. Everyone knows that the new converged broadband regulation will ultimately lead to no regulation in the sector. Only a truly converged and progressive regulation can ensure this, but in stages.

Everyone today is convinced that the economic growth in a country is dependent on the growth of broadband. The telecom revolution in India has connected about 100 crore mobiles and fixed lines. Yet in broadband, which can be carried on this medium, growth is far below the government's ambitious targets.

In 2003, we were ranked 122 in terms of tele-density in the world due to our poor mobile tele-density. Thanks to reforms and growth in the telecom sector, we are today ranked very high and are the second biggest network. However, we are still ranked 125 for fixed line and 113 for mobile broadband. This must change, as it changed for mobiles in the last decade.

For growth of mobile broadband many measures need to be taken. These are vital for India's growth, particularly in villages. The prime minister recently announced that all the 2.5 lakh Gram Panchayat villages would be connected by high-speed broadband and the Government of India will soon launch a Rs 1.13 lakh crore project to be completed in five years. The network, if successfully completed with high-speed broadband connections to urban and rural subscribers in panchayat headquarters and other villages, will change India for ever. Whether this is possible requires some discussion about implementation.

I recall South Korea taking the first initiative to increase this density by connecting all households by broadband and achieving a broadband density of 35 per cent. It did so by investing US $3.5 billion. At this time there was no national network and the investment was necessary. Since these were fixed-line connections to the household computer, the population coverage was almost 100 per cent. At that stage, even the USA had less than 10 per cent coverage with the president giving a call for higher broadband coverage. China, Vietnam and many other countries increased their fixed-line telephony coverage to have higher broadband. At that stage, our broadband density was 0.04 per cent. All targets thereafter have been missed. Targets of nine million and twenty million were fixed for 2007 and 2010, respectively. We did not reach these targets. Targets for 2017 and 2020 are 175 million and 600 million, respectively. With no network configuration prescribed to reach the subscriber in all policy announcements, and the Department of Information Technology not having prescribed a comprehensive broadband road map even today, as most other countries have done, reaching the targets is a far cry.

Such a road map defines the likely subscribers in each geographical area, and the government announces upgradation plans to mobile broadband for all last-minute subscribers. It is common knowledge that those countries which announce such plans grow in broadband. Areas that do not have public or private fibre/towers can be upgraded under the NOFN scheme later, but today, we have to move on shared resources, like we did for rural mobile telephony.

With the advent and popularization of 3G, 4G and 5G wireless technologies, the configuration has changed everywhere and we are looking at wireless broadband in all countries. We in India also face a spectrum famine, and very slow speeds. For broadband, India has no choice but to tap the mobile network, our fixed-line network being only 3 per cent, and cable TV network and use of white spaces not fully enabled yet.

It may be recalled that after fifty-five years of Independence and five years of regulation, our fixed tele-density was 3 per cent and mobile tele-density 1 per cent. This was primarily a government effort. Within the next ten years, fixed tele-density remained static but mobile tele-density changed to 80 per cent, with growth rates being the highest in the world, even three times more than that of China. The interesting difference between 2003 and today is that while 2003 was a 90 per cent PSU network, it is 90 per cent private network today in numbers. With increase in private network phones, private investment in telephones also started increasing, and by 2005, it overtook the public sector. Another interesting feature is that the public sector's investment per subscriber is far in excess of the private sector's investment, both for total and incremental investment. This reflects the private sector's efficiency in a regime of public–private level playing field. Let us further examine broadband.

BSNL set up 35,000 fibre ends by 2003 (6,000 block HQ included). Most of this network is dark even today (not connected to subscribers). We need a clear broadband policy to ensure that this does not happen to the future network also. In 2010, Bharat Broadband Network Limited (BBNL), a public sector company, aimed at setting up a network providing 100 Mbps to each Gram Panchayat (2.5 lakh panchayats), at a cost of Rs 20,000 crore. The target was for 2014. Nothing was achieved and the date has now been postponed to 2017. However, the progress is not encouraging. Even if the 2.5 lakh villages are connected with fibre, the target for broadband subscribers will not reach, particularly for rural areas unless fibre ends are connected to subscribers by wireless. It naturally follows that we must first connect the existing 35,000 fibre ends to mobile broadband wireless connections. We will then also have a model for connecting the 2.5 lakh fibre ends being laid down. Perhaps out of disuse, old fibre may not be working. In addition, the information technology (IT) department has launched a National Governance Mission of Rs 70,000 crore for e-governance, software, etc. The progress is again not satisfactory. It needs evaluation if major part of this work is transferred to public–private partnership.

The performance of PSUs laying down infrastructure in a non-competitive environment will affect the present scheme of connecting all villages at a cost of Rs 1.13 lakh crore. We must include the private sector in implementing the scheme. Such a scheme was successful for voice telephony and we have today about 3.25 lakh private and 0.75 lakh public sector towers which can be used, and expanded for reaching the subscribers in a public–private sharing mode. Today, our operators have 33 per cent of the world's average spectrum, yet most spectrum was not allowed to be shared, and, till recently, further spectrum is being given at a slow speed. And also due to the slow roll-out and non-passing of the Convergence Bill 2001, a large proportion of spectrum is not being used. If we intend quicker expansion of broadband to the subscriber, we must give more spectrum, allow full spectrum sharing and implement converged licensing. The success of the voice programme was mainly due to an affordable rate. We must remember that the subscriber is the most important element of this network.

One last point. The power network is so far mostly a government transmission, distribution and generation network, and has therefore achieved only 50 per cent of government targets for nearly thirty years, as against 300–400 per cent for telecom voice network post-2003. We need to change to a public–private mode for implementing such a huge task of broadband expansion assigned to the network, and the plan should start with the subscriber, and not end at the fibre end being provided in the government scheme for 2.5 lakh villages.

Rural broadband targets can only be met if the broadband mobile signal reaches the village and the consumer at viable rates. It was such emphasis that changed mobile telephony in India for ever. The government can only ensure this if it guarantees customers in villages, and a viable rate. We must ensure this by the government identifying village-wise and sector-wise consumers. All countries have completed such identifications, and we must start. A subsidy to consumers, if required, can be given through the huge balances in Universal Service Obligation Fund (USOF).

Of course, there would be problems of indigenous content, but this should be left to the entrepreneurs, and they would translate everything, once there is a market. Money should not be wasted on government projects. We must remind ourselves that the telecom revolution in India was driven by the private sector and not the public sector.

There are many other reforms waiting to happen and efficiently implemented. I have named and discussed two sectors.

Technology, Disruptive Changes and Reforms

Reforms started in India in 1991. As I have explained in the book, they started much earlier with small initiatives taken in different sectors. However, they formally started with the reform statement in Parliament in 1991. The main features of this statement were: opening up to the private sector, delicensing of most industries, liberal FDI policy, devaluation of the rupee and movement to market-determined exchange rates, thus entrepreneurs having a much larger initiative in our development path. Reforms encouraged them to take their own decision regarding setting up new industries rather than wait for the government to set up core industries and then to go for quotas and licences to start their own industry, in the permit-licence raj. Entrepreneurs thus started finding India interesting to contribute to and started investing, and they also came from other countries in large numbers.

There was another interesting development towards liberalization around the same period and I call it the Jack Welch effect. It was this initiative which led to the ICT (Information and Communications Technologies) industry becoming a major contributor to our economy. It led to many other effects too. Jack Welch came to India first in 1989. In his own words reproduced from his book *Straight from the Gut*,[1] he said:

> I saw India as a huge market, with a rapidly growing middle class of 100 plus million people out of an 800 million population. The Indian people were highly educated, they spoke English, and the country had lots of entrepreneurs trying to break the shackles of government bureaucracy. Highly developed from an intellectual stand point, India was an underdeveloped country from an infrastructure perspective. I thought the bureaucracy would fix the infrastructure problems and loosen some of the red tape. I was dead wrong. I was also dead right. The real benefit of India turned out to be its vast intellectual capability and the enthusiasm of its people. We found terrific scientific, engineering, and administrative talent that today serves almost every business at GE.

Jack Welch used this intellect with people staying behind in India and standardized the outsourcing model. The move was criticized and caused concern even in the USA. Its sound logic survives even today and is growing. He also said: 'The symbolism of these moves shocked the system. Suddenly we heard people say: "They really mean it. Globalization is for real".' Their global sales went from $9 billion in 1987 to $53 billion. The increased profits of GE led to a win-win model of outsourcing and changed India also.

Another advantage of the start of these services was faster globalization in India and, inevitably, increased contacts between Indian entrepreneurs and their foreign counterparts, leading to rise in exports in other areas too, more foreign collaborations, import of appropriate technologies and management practices, etc., and above all the reversal of brain drain. Increased FDI had a similar effect on the Chinese economy two-and-a-half decades back. Yet when Jagdish Bhagwati praises globalization, there is very little endorsement from people in India, and the polity gets lost in uneducated debate.

It was Welch's initiative, and also of many Indian entrepreneurs, that led to Indian and the world entrepreneurs finding out that the outsourcing/insourcing model was a viable model and was permitted in the plethora of Indian and other countries, export/import regulations. Perhaps all these regulations had covered up the fact that export/import business could be carried on wire with no physical exchange of commodities. Technologists made this possible and an absence of regulations helped everyone. This started the entire BPO/call centre revolution in the 1990s, increasing the IT share in Indian GDP to 8 per cent from almost nil at the beginning of the decade. It also led to globalization, bringing tremendous benefits to developing countries and to developed countries too. Technology and intelligent regulatory changes during the period made this hugely disruptive change possible for India.

The third event was even more interesting. The Indian state had a monopoly over media, particularly TV. The Kuwait war led to Indian interest in watching CNN. There was always an interest in watching other entertainment channels. Some entrepreneurs, Subash Chandra of Zee and J.K. Jain of Jain TV, found this was possible as there was no government regulation banning this feed to be downlinked from other countries and distributed over cable; and before the government could react, we had a fully developed cable industry in India. The absence of regulation led to some very interesting developments. Today we have eighty million cable connections and only forty million fixed-line telephone connections. There is no other country where fixed line telephone connections are not far in access of cable TV/DTH connections. Everyone would recall that it took the Indian state and its monopoly incumbent's network more than sixty years to lay down most of the telephone lines to about forty million homes at enormous cost to the taxpayer. Yet our enterprising cable operators laid more lines in a few years without breaking the taxpayers' back. I shudder to think the impact of a government regulation on the laying down of these lines. The cable TV has empowered the Indian consumer in voicing his concerns through the very large private news channel network thus reducing the power of the government. Gone are the days that the government or even the judiciary could be irrational. The recent initiative of the Right to Information Act is also a step in the same direction.

Technology and Disruption

Today, the technological and disruptive changes are taking place at a frightening speed and any country that internalizes appropriate technologies can go ahead fast. Disruptive changes have impacted comparative growth parameters of many countries through centuries. The industrial revolution changed the UK and many countries in the West. Railways, road and automobile growth changed the USA. In recent years, China has shown phenomenal growth.

This growth cannot continue, particularly after the post-boom years. The yearly GDP growth of 12 per cent in 2008 has already fallen to 7.5 per cent, and is bound to fall further. The Chinese have been trying to deal with the world recession by investing hugely, leading to further overcapacity and producer price deflation, perhaps leading to increased dumping in countries like India.

Will they be able to sustain growth and what would be its impact on countries like India, now similar in potential to the Chinese economy of a few decades back? Will the Indian market—full of development gaps waiting to be bridged by investments and a huge developing market waiting to be exploited for growth of the economy—also give profit to the investors? Would investments now move to India, the country having a huge market, trained workforce and established mechanisms to accept investments and convert them to viable projects for mutual benefit of investors and the Indian economy?

We are today aware that the familiar gradually changing world has disappeared with rapidly changing, fast-moving and more efficient technologies being discovered and commercialized in shorter periods, leading to hugely disruptive forces evolving the world over. If we analyse these over the last few years, the main one have been: shifting of focus to the East, and within this region, to the cities, the huge impact of technological changes at breakneck speed and the degree to which the world is much better connected through trade and through movement of capital, people and information. The ageing population of the West has also helped the manufacturing/working arena moving East. Those countries which have been able to manage these changes, like China in past decades, have had huge growth. There is no reason to believe that these changes will slow down. Those countries would gain which can manage technological changes and new technologies better.

Is India such a country? As a matter of fact, digitization being the common thread running through the majority of technology disruptions across the world, India seems to be an ideal recipient for investments. Technology has moved to digital in all areas with India launching ambitious programmes like 'Make in India', 'Digital India', 'Smart City', etc., and the prime minister's interest in supporting the launch of an 'Indian Google' and many other such initiatives. Different chapters in the book have shown that even the best environment and announced government programmes lead to nothing unless the reforms are intelligently structured and honestly implemented. The highly ambitious and perfectly conceptualized 'Digital India' and other supporting programmes seem to be failing in structuring, legal and implementation tests.

Digitization has also slashed to nearly zero the cost of sharing, discovering and transacting information. We are lucky that Indians have shown strengths in these areas leading to changes taking place in this sector. India also has immense intellectual capital at the highest and lowest educational levels capable of encashing the zero-cost transfer of digital knowledge. And it has been able to demonstrate this capability in the era of reforms formally launched in 1991.

Without reforms, India would perhaps not have been able to take the advantage of disruptive technologies.

New technologies have always taken us forward. Yet very often regulations have disabled them. I have already described what happened in the telecom sector. There are many other examples in other sectors. For example, supercritical boilers could not get introduced in the power sector, as the investment rules did not encourage introduction of efficient technologies. Reforms as have been witnessed in these areas can thus catalyse disruptive technologies entering India and increasing their impact. And also, a network having been established to connect all Indians to 2G and TV, the growth in broadband can be hugely accelerated by intelligently upgrading the network. The present programme is not making an impact and needs structural changes to move towards the ambitious Digital India, capable of changing India in the next decade towards 10 per cent GDP growth.

The disruption process often brings totally unanticipated changes also. I will only deal with three disruptive and unpredictable changes identified by analysts in the world over the last decade. One was the shale discovery reducing oil and gas prices and America's dependence on energy imports, leading to huge drop in prices which were constantly increasing earlier. The second was not Facebook, but Facebook's purchase of WhatsApp at a huge price due to its free instant messaging application; also, Facebook's entry into the mobile market and its huge increase in advertisement share, thus demonstrating the importance of applications. The third was the Mars mission showing India's capacity of frugal innovation. Let us now look at India-specific changes in the last decade.

Indian engineers and firms also took huge advantage of international connectivity and experience during the Y2K days, when the world was checking its computers for post-2000 performance and had the maximum share of this business worldwide, and got known as 'you have a software problem, ask Indians to fix it'. This branding can bring enormous benefits in the increasing digital world.

Telecom disruption post-2003 regulations with minimal costs ensured a fifty-fold drop in tariffs, hundred-fold increase in mobile numbers and a 2–50 per cent mobile tele-density increase in rural areas after 2007. The post-2003 phenomenon of mobile growth was completed in less than a decade. The enormous growth in communications contributed to 4 per cent of India's GDP from about 1 per cent only a decade back.

The successful and very cheap Mars mission has brought India to the forefront of satellite technology and frugal technological innovation. This was achieved with the help of increasing knowledge of our engineers and the capacity to manage and coordinate production with our SMEs in manufacturing high-precision parts and managing software for complex operations. This will surely disrupt the world market in the satellite sector—a sector very important for international communications—and should encourage other technology sectors too, once we move to an aggressive agenda on R&D. The start of this process post-Mangalyaan is already visible. A common thread in Indian innovations and disruptions is that they have so far revolved around communications, and have mostly led to reducing prices. We have thus gained hugely by the innovative disruptions in the recent past, and have acquired capacity to deal with the future. What is the future like?

A McKinsey book, *No Ordinary Disruption*, has indicated that today many technologies have massive potential for bringing out disruptive changes in the next decade. Any country that places itself right vis-à-vis these technologies in an interconnected global world will come out the winner in terms of growth, and this is precisely what happened in the last decade in India. Due to rapid technology developments, these changes will have to be dealt with faster and with greater finesse in reforming the sectors than in the past. Our greatest advantage is our human resource, demographic advantage, the reformed telecommunication and IT network and our experience in implementing reforms.

But as in the last decade, there may be unexpected changes also in this fast-changing world. In India these disruptive technologies will be able to bring enormous growth if sectoral reformers/ regulators are able to get them implemented in an efficient and viable manner. Let us see where we stand vis-à-vis these identified disruptive technologies:

- Mobile Internet: Increasing inexpensive and capable mobile computing devices and Internet connectivity. With very large mobile numbers, the sector has enormous potential, yet growth has been suboptimal due to poor implementation of the New Optical Fibre Network programme.
- Automation of knowledge work: Intelligent software systems that can perform knowledge work. With India's track record in such work, India can enormously contribute to the world effort.
- Internet of things: Networks optimizing processes. With India's experience in Y2K and development of BPO's software, India can immensely contribute.
- Cloud technology: Hardware and software to be delivered on the net. Again a lot of experience in India.
- Advanced robotics: With our performance of Mangalyaan, India can be a huge source.
- Autonomous and near-autonomous vehicles: These are already being developed, and with a huge production base, can multiply multifold.
- Next-generation genomics involving fast, low-cost gene sequencing, big data analysis with the help of supercomputers and synthetic biology (writing DNA). This is the fastest-growing technology in the world to deal with diagnosis of medical conditions, and pinpointing cures. India has huge comparative advantage.

- Energy storage devices: India has a huge market which can be exploited for manufacture.
- 3D printing: Again an additive manufacturing technology which can be developed further.
- Advanced material: Advances in material science to develop materials having superior characteristics as have led to nanotechnology.
- Advanced oil and gas exploration and recovery of unconventional oil and gas.
- Non-conventional energy with reduced climate impact.

Only those countries can effectively develop these technologies for commercial usage that have a large user population, proven track record to change 'business as usual' in favour of these futuristic scenarios, enormous intellectual capital, experience in dealing with the digital world, potential of quick 'start-ups' on the Net, sound international connectivity and experience. The country also needs large corporates to accumulate such work for viable business case, and capacity to design public–private projects and contracts, and also ability to reform/regulate in many sectors. We are lucky to have accumulated experience in these areas over the last two decades.

The Government of India has taken several measures to encourage developments towards making India digital:

- One of the topmost initiatives in the form of Digital India Programme of the government which aims at transforming India into digital empowered society and knowledge economy is expected to provide the required impetus for development of the IT industry ecosystem in the country.

  The government has come out with the draft policies for all the areas mentioned above. Our successes so far have used the private sector enormously and they would require hand-holding for this enormous task, and enormous help for upgrading our R&D capacities.

- We are today concentrating on bringing out these changes by launching programmes such as Digital India, Smart City, Ease of Doing Business, increased labour productivity through change in labour legislation, etc. We have thus correctly identified the programmes for growth, and if these are implemented anywhere near the projected targets, India would be the fastest-growing large emerging market before 2020. India's projected growth model is presently also concentrating on the services sector, where we have a natural advantage, and productivity growth in these areas due to better communications will lead to higher productivity in the entire economy. However, growth does require effective and targeted implementation of identified programmes mentioned above. The present growth levels leave much to be desired.
- Thanks to the 2G revolution, today we have connected all our population to telecom networks. With mobile Internet technologies and applications developing fast, we only have to modify/upgrade this network to connect everyone to broadband, the vehicle for country's development in the next decade. Though the programmes have been identified, the structuring for growth is oriented towards monopoly public sector, and like telephony till 2003, is bound to fail. There is urgent need for restructuring.

Once effective implementation of internalizing the identified disruptive technologies starts, we should reach the GDP growth rate of more than 10 per cent.

PART V

THE PERSONAL STORY

13

The Early Years

> No bureaucrat looks for problems. As a result, many do not work for bringing in change. Yet, I repeatedly worked in such areas and, despite continuously having problems, looked forward to new reform projects. I have often wondered why I got into such areas of work and, despite problems at each stage, persisted with such work. Maybe my early years can provide some insight.

I lost my father when I was nine years old. He died in a car accident in 1953 when he was thirty-two. I became the man of the house.

He used to drive fast and the sixth accident claimed his life. My mother, an intermediate in arts, was twenty-seven. My sisters were aged eight and two. He left us penniless.

My maternal grandfather had five other children and three of them lived with him. However, he took us into his house and encouraged my mother to do intermediate in science and MBBS. She joined the Provincial Medical Service of Uttar Pradesh in 1962 and retired as medical superintendent in 1983. We had some ancestral property in Firozabad, where she opened a nursing home after retirement in 1983 and ran it profitably till 2004. The nursing home was so profitable that she faced an income tax raid, courtesy the quota raids on successful professionals in the V.P. Singh era. Of course nothing was proved against her, except some technical irregularities leading to a fine of Rs 6,000 but the case had to be fought till the tribunal.

From 1953 to 1962, the year my mother joined government service, we lived from hand to mouth. Even our admission to Hindi-medium schools and eventually college was dependent on our ability to get merit scholarships to sustain our studies, and since we wanted to study, we never disappointed.

An engineering course in the University of Roorkee (now IIT, Roorkee) from 1961 was far more expensive and required a national scholarship. I got the scholarship. Meanwhile, my mother, having joined service in 1962, could also help and she paid me handsomely to make up for our earlier life as paupers. Happy days returned after nine years.

My father was a senior superintendent of police when he died near Garhmukteshwar in Meerut. Today, there is an intermediate college in his memory which policemen built from contributions.

Despite my father's position, we could not have survived had Pandit Govind Vallabh Pant, the chief minister of UP, not got the All-India Service Pension Rules amended to give my mother a pension of Rs 125 and the children Rs 25 per month each. My father was lucky having worked with Pandit Pant earlier, who noticed my mother's plight.

Of course, there were many senior officers who helped. Y.N. Verma, A.N. Jha, Govind Narain and Satish Chandra, friends of my father from the police service, helped enormously. All the police officers of Uttar Pradesh helped. B.N. Lahiri was then the inspector general of police (IGP) in UP. Later, after I joined the Indian Administrative Service, I was trained by his son P.K. Lahiri, my collector in Khandwa. G.B. Pant's son, K.C. Pant, was my steel minister when I was joint secretary (steel) in the Government of India.

In 1961, I could have joined the Railway Service of Mechanical Engineers College in Jamalpur or Roorkee University. But Roorkee was a three-year course and I figured it made one senior to one's classmates as Jamalpur was a five-year course. I thus joined the Indian Railway Service in 1965 only after graduating from Roorkee in 1964, but not before teaching there for six months, and then working as an industrial engineer in the General Electric Company, Calcutta, for another six months.

Had it not been for the sultry weather and the beginning of gheraos on the workshop floor in Calcutta, perhaps I would have continued in the inspiring environment of Calcutta, where all mechanical engineers landed after graduation.

Later on, in Jamalpur, I found that the Indian Railways had changed the seniority rule and I was not senior to those who joined Jamalpur. A lot of my friends, particularly the brilliant Ashok Soota (former managing director, Wipro; founder of Mindtree and Happiest Minds), advised that if I wanted to join the government I should join the IAS, the best service, and not settle for the railways.

This advice, and the change of railway rules, prompted me to join the IAS in 1966. In the interview, I frankly admitted that these factors had prompted me to join the IAS and this, I believe, got me close to the highest marks in the interview. I would not have been selected otherwise. A number of engineers who cited a change in inclination after graduation as the reason to join IAS did badly in the interview. Honesty and frankness worked for me even then.

Preparing for the exam and interview while still working in Roorkee, Calcutta and Jamalpur was challenging. It was touch and go. Despite getting into the IAS, later I liked the idea of continuing in railways where the service conditions, the perks of railway passes, excellent colonies and clubs made life comfortable and rich. Further, railways shielded the young officers as it required little to no interaction with the local politicians, almost till later stages in the government. In comparison, the IAS required one to interact with the best and worst of the political class right from day one in the service, making life difficult.

Unlike the railways, one rarely worked in the comfortable hierarchy of your own service in the IAS, making you a stranger at your workplace, but mercifully at top positions. Whether in a subdivision or a district, or as a departmental head in a secretariat or in bodies like the TRAI—one had a leadership role rather than a comfortable existence of working with officers from the same service. While in the railways, and after getting into the IAS, I mentioned to my seniors that perhaps I would continue in railways and enjoy doing engineering work. Without exception, they forced me out. I still remember that the then general manager of the Eastern Railways, Mr Krishan, who used to come to visit Jamalpur periodically, checked with the deputy chief mechanical engineer (Dy CME) of Jamlpur, T. Prasad, a few times whether I had left. Some of the junior officers even forced me to do a Bharat Darshan courtesy of the unlimited railway passes and the beautiful Railway Rest Houses almost everywhere.

I left Jamalpur for Dehradun to Mussoorie with a heavy heart. I was warmly invited to the fiftieth celebrations of the Jamalpur Railway School and found prominent mention in the book released to commemorate this event. One of my similarly placed seniors, who joined the IAS after Railway Engineering Service, was the illustrious Krishan Kumar, who later became a union minister and is remembered for his unorthodox ways in Jamalpur and later in the administrative service. I still have many friends from my Jamalpur days.

After completing training in the Academy of Administration, Mussoorie, one gets out in the real India, in subdivisions, districts and the secretariat. This training is critical for any young officer, who gets to know India through this exposure; and is the ultimate preparatory ground for senior assignments in the future.

I spent eight months in Mussoorie and one doing Bharat Darshan, after which I spent time at district training in Kurnool, Andhra Pradesh. This training is not in one's home state. Kurnool had a powerful Zila Parishad, particularly with Vijay Bhaskar Reddy (who later became the chief minister of Andhra Pradesh and also a Union minister) as the Parishad chairman. He took interest in our training and used to drive us around to development projects in the district.

The one year of training in Khandwa, Madhya Pradesh, was also interesting given that I had three collectors, courtesy of the changing political governments. I also had my training along with Vinod Vaish, another officer of my batch in service. It was providential that I worked with him again at the end of my service, when I was chairman, TRAI, and he was secretary, telecommunication, and later member, TDSAT, the appellate authority of TRAI. Much later in 2010, four years after our retirement, we faced the CBI and the JPC together on charges cooked up by functionaries in the Government of India.

I was always interested in tribal areas. They were different from areas we normally lived in and gave more scope for innovative work. On completing my district training in Khandwa, I managed a posting to Dantewada in south Bastar. The inflow of Naxals had just started there from Andhra Pradesh and there was no competition in getting a posting there.

My first collector in Khandwa, P.K. Lahiri, was horrified at my choice of posting and ordered me to go to Dantewada via Indore where he was posted. It was a roundabout way, but it made little difference since I was a young bachelor driving to Dantewada in my Standard Herald car with all my belongings.

When I reached his house in Indore, he proudly announced that he had informally discussed my posting, as sub-divisional officer, Mhow, with the chief secretary, MP.

Dantewada was still a fascination and I convinced him that I still wanted to go there. He agreed on the condition that I first meet the chief secretary in Bhopal. The chief secretary asked me to go to a much more developed area in Harda, Hoshangabad, near Bhopal. It was difficult convincing him that I wanted to go to Dantewada, and I left soon after he agreed, lest he change his mind.

Dantewada, the subdivisional headquarters (HQ), was a village with a population of 400 and no electricity. Panthers would sometimes scratch their paws at the window at night. It is two districts now, Dantewada and Bijapur, in Chhattisgarh. We sometimes heard of Naxalite infiltration from Andhra Pradesh. The two districts are now full of Naxalites.

I stayed in Dantewada for eight months before being ordered to join as undersecretary in the General Administration Department immediately, filling in for a deputy secretary about to go on leave.

Working with Samar Singh, the collector of Bastar, was a memorable experience. At the start of each month, he would write about all the pending important work with me and wanted a report on implementation at the end of every month. He did so with other officers too and kept everyone on their toes. He managed to put an end to illegal felling of timber in the district, and being an erstwhile prince, he ably supervised the affairs of the Bhanjdeo family. The Bhanjdeo family meant a lot of trouble to the government after Pravir Chandra Bhanjdeo's assassination.

It was during my stay in Dantewada that the Bailadila Iron Ore project was inaugurated in 1968 by Dinesh Singh, a powerful Union minister, in the presence of Vidya Charan Shukla, another Union minister from Madhya Pradesh. Most of my stay was spent in making arrangements for the inauguration and the VIP visits, the project made enormous difference to the area with modern development touching this backward region for the first time.

Madhya Pradesh was also trying to set up a steel plant in this region based on the surplus from the iron ore project after meeting the export commitment to Japan. A negotiated amount went to Japan, who had financed the project. The proposed Visakhapatnam Steel Plant was the other contender for getting iron ore from this area. Visakhapatnam won and we lost. Visakhapatnam had a groundswell in favour of the steel plant, in contrast with the *jholawallahs* (do-gooders) who opposed a steel plant in Bastar, believing that tribals were a happier lot without any development. In the Abujhmarh area of the district, an extremely backward region, such people wanted the tribals to be left to total splendid isolation to the extent that the state government cooperated by not allowing outsiders to enter, and resisted any development. Later, the area was transformed into a Naxalite headquarters and the state government could not enter. Things have started moving towards development only now, after about fifty years of only exports of iron ore from Bastar. One steel plant near the district headquarters, Jagadalpur, is nearing completion, and another near the Chitrakoot waterfalls is near finalization.

Perhaps Bastar would not have seen enormous growth in Naxalism in the areas adjoining Dantewada had the steel project come in. This is a point of view I would intensely debate with B.D. Sharma, ten years my senior and a former collector of Bastar. His point of view was that the tribals should lead their own way of life. Unfortunately, time has shown that the 'museum and isolation' policy on tribals has not worked. I have separately narrated in the book how I had a different point of view with Chief Secretary R.C.V.P. Noronha on the same issue and almost paid a price for this different viewpoint, but for his kind, tolerant nature. It shows that unless you have the courage to differ with the 'business as usual', you cannot be a reformer. In my view, development has always been preceded by some confrontation, which must be managed for harmonious growth in the longer term, and no area should be left without the benefits of development.

The interiors and the tribal areas have their own problems which cannot be dealt with under the general principles seen in state capitals. Denying development to tribal areas which are normally remote, with unproductive soils and forests, is short-sighted and risks protest from such areas later and the eventual growth of Naxalism.

14

Encouraging a Penchant for Change

> The real experience for an IAS officer begins when he gets charge of a district. It is here that they interact with all issues of administration in different areas. I had interesting experiences; a moulding similar to the many officers before and after me.

After leaving Bastar, getting back to civilization in Bhopal was a welcome change. Very soon, in 1970, I was transferred to Jabalpur as additional collector.

Sharad Yadav, president of the Janata Dal (United) (JD[U]) , was then the president of the students' union in Jabalpur University. We in the district administration had many inevitable confrontations with him. My respect for him grew when serious leftist and political literature was found in his room during one of the raids. Till then, I had considered him only a daydreaming student agitator. He was later detained under MISA (Maintenance of Internal Security Act), fought and won the Lok Sabha elections from jail in Jabalpur and has never looked back.

Two years later, I got posted as collector, Raisen, a district near Bhopal. Life took a turn for the worse as I got viral myocarditis, a dangerous heart disease. The doctors gave me a maximum of three years to live. It was a new disease and cardiologists visiting India came to see me, treating me like a guinea pig. Like all doctors, they said I could survive longer with a strict medical regime, personal discipline and God's grace. Luckily, the treatment prescribed by Dr Sujabi Roy of AIIMS and Dr Goldberg, a famous cardiologist from the UK, took me beyond the three years. But the disease still cost me 12–15 missed heartbeats every minute for years.

Today my heart beats normally—forty-three years after getting the disease. The disease lasted ten years and I was on a heavy medication of barbiturates for the entire period. The medication caused drowsiness. This side effect had to be managed. I was able to do so by again getting a posting in the tribal districts of Betul and Bastar, with hardly any medical facilities, to deal with my disease. The advantage of these small towns/tribal districts was that all those around me were more tolerant of a young collector who had to sleep briefly every afternoon, without knowing the reason for this compulsion. And I was specifically told by all the doctors in AIIMS and the UK that the only treatment was heavy dosage of barbiturates. The lack of medical facilities did not matter.

Before moving to the districts, I spent one year as deputy secretary, Department of Home, with a kind boss, S.S. Gill, who was more careful about my health than I was.

He always took up new projects. The two projects I remember from this period were trying to legalize 'satta' in Madhya Pradesh and the of surrender of dacoits, a project led by Jayaprakash Narayan. Even after all these years, I clearly recall the long discussions we had with the satta king from Bombay, Ratan Khattri. There was a lot of excitement in the secretariat when the satta king used to visit Gill and help him prepare a bill to licence satta. The Government of India found the consequent bill unacceptable.

The project for the surrender of dacoits was more interesting. We, under the guidance of S.S. Gill, subjected the dacoits to intense pressure by declaring unusually large amounts as rewards for informers as prize money and an incentive scheme for surrendered dacoits. Consequently, dacoits found it profitable to surrender; so much so that some dacoits from Uttar Pradesh came and surrendered in Madhya Pradesh. The different environment after the surrender led to enormous growth in the area. Our chief minister, P.C. Sethi, became very popular and almost a folk hero in these areas. His resemblance to Dilip Kumar helped.

Gill made a huge difference wherever he worked. As Secretary General, Asian Games, 1982, he completed all the arrangements at less than the budget estimates one month before the start of the games. After this, he became dispensable and got shifted to the Backward Classes Commission. Before leaving the Games, he also facilitated the introduction of colour TV and a massive upgradation of the Delhi infrastructure as part of the Games requirements. Compare this with the scandals associated with the Commonwealth Games under the UPA-II government.

In the Backward Classes Commission, he prepared a report—the Mandal Commission report—which, after its acceptance by the V.P. Singh government, changed Indian politics forever. Later, as secretary, Ministry of Information and Broadcasting, he launched 100 TV stations in record time, again changing the Indian cultural scene, particularly with the launch of serials like *Mahabharat* and *Ramayan*. His main strength was his ability to visualize the future and implement progressive schemes. He was able to deliver as people feared him and know the consequences of targets not being met. However, the service did not give him what he deserved.

Senior bureaucrats must periodically take up new initiatives to improve government functioning, else they will rightly be called 'Babus'. Ultimately it is for the political executive to accept or reject such recommendations. But we must pursue improvements, so that the political government is never short of progressive ideas. And sometimes, they do get implemented.

My postings to Betul and Bastar as collector brought rich

experiences. Bastar, a district of enormous size and problems, was unique in many ways. It was in places like these that one learnt the most, as normal rules of administration did not work, and one had to continuously adapt and innovate. I was posted to Bastar in 1973 after spending one year in Betul.

Bastar was an allowance and a tribal district (meaning additional Rs 150 per month) and I reached there with my seven years of service, thirty years of age and a doubtful heart condition. It was the largest inhabited district in India, with an area larger than Kerala. It is a commissioner's division now with seven districts in the state of Chhattisgarh, but with Naxalism totally out of control. Before signing my posting order, Chief Minister Sethi asked the chief secretary about my heart condition (he was kind to remember). The chief secretary checked with me and told him that I could manage and the chief minister signed the file.

On reaching Bastar, I found the Naxalite problem more serious, and proposals pending for sending ten police battalions to control them. I immediately rushed to Raipur, where the chief minister was visiting, and requested him not to send the battalions as they, being from the dacoit areas of Madhya Pradesh, would probably rape tribal women, drink their free distilled liquor and eat their *kukkud* (poultry)—thereby fuelling anger of the local population and increasing Naxalism.

The chief minister agreed, but warned me of serious consequences of failure in controlling the Naxalites. I then realized the danger of making proposals spurred by emotions and that controlling Naxalite activity without full police cooperation and a weak police administration was an impossible task.

I then remembered my days with infamous surrendered dacoits like Tehsildar Singh, Malkhan Sigh, Moorat Singh, Pooja Babba and others. I had found them very friendly and heard the way circumstances forced them to be the dreaded dacoits they were. I decided to contact the Naxalite leaders through the usual contacts in the district. They said they would only come to see me after 11 p.m., after crossing the River Indravati flowing in front of my house, if I agreed to permanently remove armed guards at my residence. Their fear was that even if I wanted otherwise, the police chief would get to know through the guards and would get them eliminated.

They started coming once a week after the guards were removed in the name of economy. They were young men from Andhra, often highly educated, motivated and courteous. How could they be our enemies, I thought. They presented me many books on dialectical materialism, a Marxist theory. The papers of these books and their thick cardboard covers revealed their origins. They were interesting to read. So thick was the paper and the covers that I burnt them with difficulty after the Emergency was declared, fearing a raid on my house for cooperating with Naxalites. I feared that someone would misunderstand this Naxalism connection of mine, despite the commissioner and the chief minister being aware of my attempts to use this informal connection to control Naxalites and to keep them from killings. I had allowed them to do political activity and assured them that security forces would not threaten them.

Bastar with a primitive economy and exploitation of the poor tribals was not the Naxalites' area of interest. The region only served as a hiding terrain whenever Andhra Pradesh police mounted its operations against them. Bastar provided them the ideal hiding ground without roads, industry or any development, and we the non-tribals had abetted the non-development in the name of keeping tribal identity alive.

But what was this tribal identity? Let us examine the case of Abujhmarh.

Abujhmarh covers about 10 per cent of Bastar's area of 40,000 sq kms. Bastar had population density of about 10 per cent of that of the country as a whole. Abujhmarh had 10 per cent of Bastar's population density. Like, the entire south Bastar in the past, shifting cultivation continued here. In the 1930s, this was banned in south

Bastar by an enlightened diwan of the state. Abujhmarh went unnoticed because of its isolation and low population density, and thus continued the shifting cultivation. During a land survey in Bastar, someone decided that no land survey needed to be done there as the lands had no ownership and the tribals primarily depended on forest produce. Since no development took place and there was no contact with civilization, the tribals too did not wear clothes—save for a loincloth—making it a fertile ground for onlookers and mischief mongers. The state government in its wisdom banned outsiders from entering Abujhmarh without a permit from the collector. This worked well till the Naxalites came and started setting up their base camps there. The police could do nothing. In the absence of roads, no development instruments could reach there.

Collectors, however, used to undertake annual tours of the area. On one tour, I found very high child mortality and number of cases of disease. I decided to send a medical team. This was a very successful operation, as the tribals offered no biological resistance to drugs, and simple medications produced miraculous results. When I visited Abujhmarh the next year, the tribals were upset that there were no doctors in our team that only comprised the collector, his wife and the former commissioner Reinboth, who had come to visit Bastar after retirement.

By this time, the state government had delegated the powers of sanctioning roads in tribal blocks to the collectors. I sanctioned four roads to connect this area. When the news reached Bhopal, Chief Secretary R.C.V.P. Noronha was furious and I was summoned to Bhopal. He questioned me on the sanction of roads into Abujhmarh, a banned area. I argued that we had no right to keep an area as a human museum and each area deserved means of communication and development. He said that I should be suspended for breaching government orders regarding entry. I replied that on this issue, I would welcome suspension and kept arguing for roads. He was a kind man. He called me home in the evening and offered me rum. He joked that IAS officers, with their meagre salaries, could only afford rum and anyone drinking more expensive liquor was corrupt. On the main issue, he was sorry that the government delegated vital powers to youngsters, but sent me back without cancelling my order. Out of respect for him, I cancelled the road sanctions and sent the file to the state government for approval. The file got lost in state scrutiny and perhaps never reached the chief secretary. Today, with roads not being constructed, no one can enter Abujhmarh; it has been taken over by the Naxalites as their central command post. I feel sorry today for having cancelled my orders, whatever be the reason, and referring the case to the state government.

Bastar, particularly its interior, was always fascinating for the outsiders. I entertained many guests and writers who wanted to visit or write about Bastar. One such visitor used to be Tarun Bhaduri, Jaya Bhaduri's (now Jaya Bachchan) father. He used to stay in my guest suite and was always glued to his small typewriter, writing stories. One story was on Baijnath Panda, the first Indian diwan of Bastar around the 1930s, who banned shifting cultivation after seeing its detrimental effects. Tribals did not like it and this led to the famous Lohandiguda rebellion. It was so severe that troops had to be sent from Maharashtra to quell the rebellion. The Indian diwan was naturally removed, termed as undiplomatic by the British. He left Bastar a disillusioned man. But the tribals understood that there was something wrong with shifting cultivation and started settling on newly surveyed lands. A drive along the River Sabari to the south of Bastar, with Orissa on the other side (where shifting cultivation was not banned), would show Baijnath Panda's wisdom. Orissa is now implementing a large project worth crores of rupees for replanting and saving the hills in the region, whereas Bastar does not have a single barren hill. Tribals in Bastar used to compare hills with women and remark that a woman with a bald head does not look pretty.

I became curious about Baijnath Panda. From some locals I found out that he had moved as diwan to another small state and then retired in Garha, Jabalpur. By the time I reached his Garha address, he had unfortunately passed away.

In one of the reviews after the declaration of the Emergency, Chief Minister P.C. Sethi was disappointed that I had only detained three persons in such a huge district. He asked the commissioner to review my actions. I therefore had to detain many more. Some of the targets had to be the big traders from Bharatiya Jana Sangh (now BJP). I had taken help from one of them to bring rice from Andhra Pradesh to prevent acute shortages in Bastar every year as no amount of correspondence from this remote tribal district to the state government helped. The district had inadequate stocks of rice, the staple diet, which led to big riots in Dandakaranya one year and consequent police firing. I called this big trader and warned him about the impending raid on his godowns after the declaration of the Emergency. He could thus sell all his stocks before the raid. He was however detained since at that time the district magistrates did not have to record reasons for detention. Our judgment could only be overruled by the Central government.

Bastar with all its tales of the eccentric Maharaja Pravir Chandra Bhanjdeo, more than 90 per cent tribal population, the strange tribal system of administration, the free liquor and dances, the bare-breasted tribal women, the famous Dussehra festivities and the Rath Yatra and many sites was an exciting tourist location for some. At the height of the Emergency, Sanjay Gandhi decided to visit Bastar despite Chief Minister Shyama Charan Shukla's advice that he should visit Jhabua, another tribal district in the state with a developed Congress organization base. Bastar had none, and the chief minister was concerned about how the rallies—a favourite of Sanjay Gandhi—would be organized as huge attendance was a prerequisite. The chief minister consulted me and I advised him to send Youth Congress leaders from other areas and a cabinet minister from Raipur. Very soon, I found Moti Lal Vora, the then vice chairman of Madhya Pradesh Roadways, and other senior Youth Congress leaders and members of Parliament from Madhya Pradesh: Mahesh Joshi, Rameshwar Neekhra and Gufrane Azam in Jagdalpur. They made the arrangements for the rally. We coordinated these arrangements. M.L. Vora oversaw the movement of trucks and buses to Jagdalpur bringing tribals. They came in huge numbers with their dance attire, drums and musical instruments, anticipating fun in Jagdalpur, where they used to come for their Dussehra festivities organized by the state government. The tribals were told that another Dussehra was being organized for them. The district administration also organized a tribal exhibition, equally liked by the tribals and the numerous VIPs that descended on Jagdalpur.

Sanjay Gandhi came with his wife Maneka in a single-engine plane from Allahabad. He flew the plane himself without a co-pilot, after having taken a dip in the Sangam in Allahabad; this being Kumbh Mela time. We had no regular airport in Jagdalpur, only an airstrip perpendicular to the national highway (which used to be blocked whenever a plane was to land). The rest of the district was forest without any identifiable marks and Sanjay Gandhi's plane only had huge smoke fires at Jagdalpur as a guide. Naturally the plane got lost for some time.

Our anxiety mounted as the plane got delayed with limited fuel after such a long distance. Fortunately, we saw the plane after we thought it was lost and it landed smoothly. Of course, we had a tough time controlling the tribals after they saw the bird descending. The airstrip had no effective fencing and depended on home guards to enforce crowd control. The next day's rally had a huge attendance, but the tribals started dancing and playing drums soon after the speeches started. For them, the function was a variant of the Dussehra festival. We had a very tough time silencing the drums and asking the leaders to abridge their speeches—normally an impossible task.

No leaders, trucks or buses could reach Chotte Dungar, the site for another rally in the interior of Abujhmarh. Word was spread about a tribal mela and huge birds descending. This ensured that the attendance was huge. Of course, the district administration had a tough time in clearing the thick jungles for a helipad and some jeep movement for people like us. On reaching Abujhmarh, Maneka and Sanjay were moved having seen so many men and bare-breasted women, and decided to give some helicopter rides to them.

The leaders' speeches were in Hindi, followed by a translation in Abujhmaria, the local dialect. We told all the government's gurujis to give lead for claps when the leaders made inspiring comments. We knew the tribals would then take over. It went very well till we realized that the claps were on the Hindi speech and not on the translation. Everyone was impressed by their knowledge of Hindi! We claimed that there was a successful adult literacy program run by the local teachers.

We used the Emergency powers to widen roads, remove encroachments and seize a lot of illegally cut *malik-makbuja* (tribal ownership) timber from very powerful timber contractors. I thought this was a great achievement through the enormous powers the Emergency gave us. While the rallies were going on, we heard that the Government of India had ordered elections and revoked the Emergency. In the subsequent elections, Congress lost and the Janata Party government took over. The Shah Commission was appointed to look into the excesses committed during the Emergency and organizing Sanjay Gandhi's rallies in Bastar was inevitably one of them.

The change in the political government in 1977 led to a mild agitation against me and I was transferred in October 1977, after three years in Bastar. On reaching Bhopal, I was summoned by Chief Minister Kailash Joshi, who asked me how I could leave Bastar with a labour movement in Bailadila at flashpoint and the Naxalite movement also at a sensitive stage. He read about this in my exit charge report and felt I should have pointed out these conditions to the state government before moving out—the new state government having no means to find out about the conditions prevalent. Also, a decision had to be taken on a very sensitive issue for Bastar: who would sit on the chariot during the ensuing Dussehra celebrations, a practice Bastar rulers had imported from Jagannath Puri in Orissa.

V.K. Saklecha, the deputy chief minister, felt that Vedwati, the widow of Pravir Chandra Bhanjdeo, should sit. She had joined Janata Party after the parliamentary elections and had helped the party win all the assembly seats in Bastar district. I argued that the voting percentages in the assembly constituencies within the parliamentary constituency was the same in both elections and Vedwati's entry had made no difference, and this carried the day. The Danteshwari deity continued sitting on the chariot. I told the chief minister, the other ministers, the chief secretary and the home secretary present in the meeting that I had left Bastar immediately on receiving transfer orders, but could go back if the state government ordered. I also told them that I was transferred from Bastar on the Janata Party's protest and it would be embarrassing for the Janata government, if I went back. The chief minister promised to reconsider and allowed me to stay back in Bhopal. A large number of tribal labourers were killed later due to police firing on Bailadila labour agitators and the Naxalite problem increased enormously with the state sending more police battalions, leading to more bloodshed. Kailash Joshi, a very kind man and a member of Parliament from Bhopal till 2014 and my minister of industries (1991–93), still blames me for what happened in Bastar after I left. He said that if I had gone back, the police firing might not have happened. He felt that I raised unnecessary objections.

I had also told in the meeting that the transfer back to Bastar would not be convenient for me, since I was transferred after three years in Bastar, a long tenure by Bastar standards. We had recently had our first child in Bastar and there were hardly any medical facilities there. I remember, once I had a serious problem in my ear, and without an ENT doctor in Bastar I had to take treatment from an eye doctor. I also had to call a gynaecologist from Raipur, 350 km away, for checking on my wife's difficult pregnancy.

To give an idea of distances and lack of connectivity in Bastar, I was once camping in Bhopalpatnam, a sub-tehsil in Bastar on the Maharashtra border, along with the superintendent of police, when the police wireless informed us that there was firing in Dandakaranya, a Bengali refugee settlement in north Bastar. Three lives had been lost. We travelled 350 kms in the same district before reaching Dandakaranya after sixteen hours. We found that the commissioner and the DIG of police had already reached there from Raipur, the divisional HQ, and were making necessary relief arrangements. The firing had taken place due to the inadequate rice stocks in the area.

Almost forty years after I left Bastar, people still remembered the different approach I had taken to deal with the Naxalites. I was called to give the keynote address for a day-long seminar inaugurated by the chief minister. I still advised that the Naxalite problem in Bastar needed a carrot-and-stick approach.

After the 1977 elections, I had to face four inquiries in the Shah Commission. On day one, when charges regarding the massive tribal movement in trucks for Sanjay Gandhi rallies was being examined, a lawyer pointed the judge's attention to the operation 'truck movement' going on opposite the Commission office to celebrate Chaudhary Charan Singh's sixty-fifth birthday. He was embarrassed and perhaps this was one of the reasons that he later requested the Madhya Pradesh government to set up a subordinate commission to inquire cases against me. The Deoras Commission headed by District Judge Deoras was appointed. He was distantly related to the senior RSS leader, Bala Saheb Deoras, and had a holier-than-thou attitude. He found me guilty on each count, even without evidence. He often used to call his entire family to court, to demonstrate how he was grilling a former collector. The grilling continued for many days. The Shah Commission rejected the recommendation since there was insufficient evidence and asked Judge Deoras to examine more. Deoras was upset and convinced the state government to declare him independent. After the state agreed, he forwarded the original reports with some amendments. By this time, I had been appointed registrar, cooperative societies, and made significant changes in the cooperative movement. The state government did not reject the recommendations of this VIP judge but raised some questions. Later when action was to be taken against me, I protested to my minister, Laxmi Narayan Sharma. He could not get relief from the chief minister and took me to meet the doyen of the Janata Party in Madhya Pradesh, Kushabhau Thakre, in his small room at Peer Darwaza, Bhopal. He was impressed with my case and told me he would examine me further after elections before forming an opinion. He asked the CM to hold back his final decision till elections in 1979. However, the Janata Party lost, and this stage never came. The Congress government, even during president's rule, was keen to overturn the Deoras report on all counts, which they did. I however did go to Kushabhau after elections and he listened to me. My main case was that I did everything on explicit government orders, though some of them were ex post facto in the written form. Judge Deoras had held that ex-post facto orders were illegal. How could a bureaucrat reject telephonic instructions of the chief minister/commissioner? Yet such legal interpretations continue even today, like in the telecom inquiry against me in 2010.

The job of registrar, cooperatives, has a touch of politics. The office is supposed to audit and supervise all cooperative societies in the state. Some of these cooperatives, specially the apex ones, are headed by politicians of the class and seniority of chief minister. The registrar can audit, suspend, discharge and remove these politicians from the cooperatives. He is thus always walking on a razor's edge. I remained registrar for four years—from 1978 to 1982—with different political governments in the state—Congress and BJP. When I joined, our cooperative movement was financing agriculturists without borrowing concessional credit from the Reserve Bank, and used to be proud that we were self-sufficient. I found this silly as the agriculturists were deprived of adequate credit, and consequently used inadequate inputs like seeds and fertilizers. We decided to launch a credit expansion movement—higher credit to more farmers—and in three years increased Reserve Bank refinance from zero to Rs 100 crore and agriculture credit from Rs 23 crore to Rs 120 crore. Consequently, use of fertilizers, etc., increased and so did agricultural production in the state. Years later, I had to pay the price of this expansion. Chief Minister Sunder Lal Patwa waived all agriculture loans in the state, and I as finance secretary had to find the resources to fund this waiver.

Madhya Pradesh was a primitive agricultural state, not growing cash crops. On a visit to Indore in 1979, the chairman of Indore Land Development Bank, Radhey Shyam Sharma, came to see me with a delegation of soybean farmers complaining about poor price of the crop in the market. He requested that the crop be included in the support price scheme. The grains looked like black urad pulse. I pleaded ignorance about the crop.

Radhey Shyam Sharma explained that this was a miracle crop, ideal for the soil and rainfall conditions of Indore and Bhopal divisions, and could convert the entire Kharif fallows and coarse grains of the region to the highly versatile soybean. On reaching Bhopal I consulted the director, agriculture, who also pleaded ignorance, but assured me that he would send a deputy director, whom he had sent to Illinois University for training on soybean.

The information this officer gave me was impressive, and along with director agriculture, we prepared and submitted a proposal to the Government of India for including soybean in the list of crops for support price coverage. The government officers looked at us contemptuously and said that there was no soybean as claimed, but only black dal. I fortunately knew the agriculture secretary personally, his daughter having married my assistant collector in Bastar, and my argument that if there was no soybean, no purchases would be made found the sympathetic ear of the secretary and soybean was included at a price double of the market price. Hell broke loose in mandis thereafter, with very heavy arrivals and we had to organize money, storage space, etc., for NAFED (National Agricultural Cooperative Marketing Federation of India) to purchase. I still remember we procured four lakh tonnes. We did not have processing units to process the soybean and the farmers next year wanted to grow more soybean. We did not have money to finance them.

The European Union noticed and asked for a project report to finance soybean processing plants. But financing the farmers for this cash crop and its extension was a problem. We had successfully completed huge expansion of the Amul milk project in Madhya Pradesh that year and during the meetings, Dr Kurien had expressed interest in moving to oilseeds. I therefore rushed to Anand and he agreed to help. Typical of Dr Kurien, he helped us in a very big way.

In a few years, our soybean production went up from four to forty lakh tonnes, with processing plants all over the state—both in the cooperative as well as the private sector. Madhya Pradesh today produces, processes and exports 70 per cent of soybean and its products in the country. We do not have such primacy in any other crop. Much later, Digvijaya Singh (I had worked with him as registrar when he was agriculture minister in 1979) visited me in my office of chief election officer (I held additional charge from 1988 to 1993), after winning an election in Rajgarh against the BJP strongman Pyare Lal Khandelwal. He came to thank me that I was very fair during the election process, and consequently, Rajgarh had a fair election enabling him to win.

I mentioned to him that I still value the days when we were both advancing soybean cultivation in MP and now the state had become the soybean state of India. He pointed out that it would be wrong on his or my part to take complete credit since Kailash Sahara, an industrialist from MP (of Ruchi Soya fame), deserved the credit for identifying the crop as ideal for the state's conditions It was Sahara who brought the original seed from the USA. He stated that Sahara had visited him once requesting that the state government should not mess with the crop as this action will increase soybean prices in the markets and make the crop unviable for his processing plants. He also said that he had not acceded to Sahara's request. It is another matter that despite the increased prices, the great industrialist that he was, Kailash Sahara became the biggest soybean processor in the country and later also the biggest oil processor.

A similar story, many years later, was that of Sunil Mittal. He was initially unhappy with me having facilitated huge expansion in the mobile telecom market in India with reduced tariffs, consequent to intense competition in a level playing field, and he thought this would be a disadvantage for him. He ultimately emerged the biggest player in the Indian telecom and many other markets. He almost enjoyed a monopoly mobile market earlier, like Kailash Sahara's for soybean in Madhya Pradesh, proving that competition brings out the best in everyone.

The most important period over this time was my one-year training course on privatization and reforms at Oxford University. This was an unusual period with Margaret Thatcher and her finance minister, Nigel Lawson, pushing reforms and privatization to the maximum and turning around Britain's economy. Of course, they had to deal with huge opposition and strikes of very powerful labour unions in England controlling coal mines, steel plants, power distribution, etc. Often, the unions succeeded in paralysing the nation, albeit for some time.

My one year sabbatical to Oxford University on privatization and reforms during 1987–88 had an interesting background. When selected for the fellowship, I chose the subject 'Management of PSUs' as I had been in the Ministry of Steel with maximum PSUs under its control and Arjun Sengupta's proposal on French-style MOUs had raised a lot of debate. Though I was not required to, I sent the introductory paper I was required to send to Oxford to K.C. Pant, the minister for information. He called me and said that everyone studies management of PSUs, yet PSUs have not improved their performance. On the other hand, Margaret Thatcher is doing something different called privatization and justifying it too. He felt this and the reforms being currently pursued in the UK would be an interesting subject for study. I knew nothing about privatization and reforms and asked Jairam Ramesh, a colleague then in the Planning Commission, who was always ahead in studying new developments on governance issues. He gave me many research papers, which led to the final paper, and I was selected to study privatization and reforms and left for Oxford.

This one-year sabbatical changed my life. Reforms and privatization started being talked about then in the government also. All my jobs in the state and Central governments thereafter had something to do with privatization and reforms, since people in higher echelons of government knew that I had done a course in reforms. These assignments earned many kudos and also inquiries. On coming back to Madhya Pradesh, and being posted as secretary, finance, we designed and completed the first public–private road in India, the Indore–Peethampur road, along with IL&FS. We also privatized NITEL, a joint sector project.

Before joining the Ministry of Power in 1993, I was appointed as joint secretary, consumer affairs, in charge of public distribution and standardization and quality control of products-subjects acquiring a lot of importance. Things went very well till N.S. Chaudhary was secretary, but problems arose with the new secretary, N. Sundaram, joining. He treated me as the agent of the old secretary.

Another incident happened. My minister, A.K. Antony, told me not to issue orders on any important matter unless the matter was approved by him. I protested that this order should be conveyed to the secretary and not to me, but he told me that he was being cautious by also repeating the order to me. Soon, he went on a long tour of Kerala, and for containing price rise, the secretary issued an order for reducing the storage limit of oils under the Act. I knew that the

NDDB (National Dairy Development Board) kept huge stocks of edible oils, mostly as a buffer for the government, and proposed that the Ministry of Agriculture be consulted. The secretary did not agree and wanted orders to be issued immediately. I put up the draft order stating that the order should be got approved by the minister as per rules. I knew two things, having worked with Dr Kurien on Operation Flood and Operation Soybean in MP, that the secretary had a personal problem with Dr Kurien and that the minister would never approve such a step without consulting the Ministry of Agriculture. The secretary wrote on the file he had consulted the minister over the phone and orders should be issued. In view of the minister's specific orders to me, I tried to contact him over the telephone but could not. His PS told me that he was in the interiors and could not be contacted. I doubted whether the secretary could have contacted him, but in view of the secretary's clear written orders, I issued the orders. All hell broke loose since NDDB godowns were raided and the police started looking for Dr Kurien to arrest him. Kurien rang me up asking how the orders were issued without consulting the Ministry of Agriculture. I told him the facts and a few minutes later Agriculture Minister Balram Jhakar started protesting to the prime minister, even threatening resignation if Dr Kurien was arrested. A.K. Antony soon contacted me from Trivandrum airport and got the facts and soon landed in the ministry.

The order was cancelled and I became a persona non grata with the secretary, who gave me a three-page adverse CR. I was unlucky, since soon after the incident Antony resigned from the cabinet on some other issue and later became chief minister, Kerala, and could not review the secretary's report. Even after his resignation, he used to visit Delhi. I went to him and asked him to intervene and take up the matter with the prime minister. He told me that he did not intervene in administrative matters. In the meanwhile, N.K.P. Salve, the power minister, was looking for a joint secretary who could handle the numerous cases pending in the high courts and the Supreme

Court on the controversial Enron and other private power projects, when I went to him for help. I had worked briefly with him when he was an MP from Betul, and I was the collector. He had also dealt with me as secretary, finance, Madhya Pradesh when his Finance Commission gave an adverse draft report and I had successfully got it changed through legal means/representations, leading to a very favourable report. He also knew that I had one year's training in privatization and reforms in the Oxford University and used this training to justify my lateral transfer to the Ministry of Power, a near impossibility in the Government of India. I had to do a lot of work to get the secretary's adverse remarks expunged, especially at a time when my promotion as additional secretary was due. I also had to fight cases against Enron's PPA in many courts. Since they were on process and not on content (rates, PPA conditions), I won all the cases for the government.

My second Government of India term was from 1993. Before this posting, CEC T.N. Seshan wanted me to join as deputy CEC in 1992 after the elections. I had already worked as chief election officer in Madhya Pradesh for five years and did not want to work more in this field. Fortunately then, I was not on offer to the Central government and the state government's refusal to allow me to go on deputation to the Election Commission did not lead to a blacklist. Working with T.N. Seshan earlier was an experience. He did not plead for change in law, but implemented electoral reforms with whatever power he interpreted he had, and he interpreted the maximum powers. Since he was doing well, no court interfered with his assessment. He made the election process much cleaner by aggressively pursuing electoral reforms, and in doing so, substantially cleaned the system. He created an election machinery where he was feared even in the remotest corner in India during elections.

In the present situation the management style of T.N. Seshan has become quite relevant. The impasse created due to the policy paralysis can be resolved if we follow the style of Seshan, who implemented reforms with determination and resolve to correct the weakness and inconsistencies of the system. I followed his instructions and interpretations of the election machinery's powers to the last word. Naturally, some people took note in the government hierarchy.

Ten years later, in 2003, when I was being considered for chairman, TRAI, the principal secretary to PM, Brajesh Misra, called me to his office and asked me what he should do with the file lying before him. I guessed it must be my file for appointment as TRAI chief. I replied that a file reaches the principal secretary's table after an obstacle race, and he should sign it. He said he would not, since he feared I would turn into another Seshan. I was surprised at his knowledge of my connection and fondness for Seshan's style and replied that he was right, but I would only be tough when things needed to be done in the government's interest. Having worked with his father who was chief minister of Madhya Pradesh and with him in the Central government, I would always follow his instructions. After signing, he asked me to take the file to the prime minister to get his signatures, who raised his eyebrows in his inimitable style. I requested him to sign on the dotted line. He did, and I immediately started to leave the room lest he change his mind. As I was leaving the room, he asked me whether the principal secretary had spoken to me. I told him he had. He asked me to get orders issued immediately as there was a lot of opposition to my appointment.

People recognize a bureaucrat's worth only if he is able to comprehend and implement new ideas. Of course, sometimes he has to pay heavily, but the system eventually works to sort out everything in the long run.

15

Life after Retirement

I was a bureaucrat most of my working life. Due to aggressive implementation of government policies, I often faced inquisitions. But after brief checks, these were all dropped. After retirement, I worked as a consultant, but faced multiple inquiries on work done while in service. These were unusual inquiries and started twelve years after the work had been done, especially when there were no complaints in the intervening period. The inquiries were false but kept me busy.

I retired as chairman, TRAI, in March 2006. Normally life after retirement is peaceful for a bureaucrat. Also, the TRAI rules prohibited me from doing anything after retirement for one year. I visited my son and daughter working in the USA and the UK, respectively, at that time and wrote a book, *Disinvestment in India: I Lose and You Gain*, published by Pearson.

The minister for finance, P. Chidambaram, released the book enthusiastically, and praised me before a huge audience at the FICCI hall. He said he was fascinated by the book, and without my requesting to do so, he read passages from the book during the launch. I was thrilled that the finance minister of India found it worthwhile to read excerpts from my book.

In particular, he read the portion about my nomination for the privatization course in Oxford by the Government of India. He did not mention, out of humility typical of him at times, that he had nominated me for the course as minister (personnel) of the Government of India. He had also agreed to release the book in the presence of Arun Shourie, his political opponent, and the chairman, INTUC (Indian National Trade Union Congress), who could not join at the last minute due to illness, but had publicly supported privatization efforts.

Normally, ministers avoid such political consensus on the dais, and I thought that our honest efforts at privatization had brought in a political consensus on these highly desirable measures. As the minister for finance, he dismissed all minor observations of the CAG on file. Of course, when the Left orchestrated huge noises in Parliament, these cases were referred to the CBI by the government. This was the first time that the government subordinated its views on important economic and complex issues to those of CBI. The phenomenon led to dangerous consequences for the government later. The CBI looked into two Hotel Corporation of India cases, found nothing and closed them quickly.

After the book's release, I went to present the book to the prime minister. He was kind enough to remark that I should have requested him to release the book. I replied apologetically, explaining my rationale that a release by the prime minister would have meant the function being held at 7, Race Course Road, with lesser invitations being allowed. Since the book was about our achievements in the controversial area of privatization, I was keen to invite far more people. When the function was held many did not get chairs and had to sit on the stairs, even in the huge FICCI hall.

At about the same time, many at the decision-making levels in the Congress started discussions with me on my appointment as governor. I told them that I was only interested in going to Arunachal Pradesh, since it had a site for constructing a 22,000 MW hydropower plant, in comparison to the 15,000 MW of Three Gorges Project of China, and 2,400 MW of Bhakra. I was interested in being a catalyst for construction of this project. Many dams are fascinating in India, including the Tehri dam, which is the highest dam site in India, but none can remotely compare with the Arunachal project.

I remember being told by Arvind Verma, a former secretary, irrigation and power, that when Mrs Gandhi saw the Tehri dam, she remarked that only God could have created such a site which would have given power at the rate of 35 paise per MW as per the DPR. It is another matter that our rethinking on the project and enormous delays destroyed the project, but it is still a viable hydropower dam.

It may be recalled that China was noticed in the world community when it showed the skills of completing the huge Three Gorges Project that displaced 1.5 million people. The Arunachal Pradesh project would only displace 1,500 people but submerge half of Arunachal Pradesh, but these areas are only uninhabited valleys. Additionally, there is so much of water in the project that the power factor (percentage of time when the project works vis-à-vis capacity) would be 60 per cent, thus reducing transmission costs enormously. We had done some work on this project in the Ministry of Power when it was transferred to us by the Prime Minister's Office, courtesy N.K. Singh, then secretary, who understood the need of starting work on the project. Earlier, the Brahmaputra Board, which was looking after the project, only existed on paper. Arunachal was interested in the project because as per rules, it would have got 14 per cent of the revenues from this project, making it the richest state in the country based on per capita income. I was told that this dam was a contentious political issue which could not be opened and I lost interest in the opportunity.

The question of what to do after retirement bothered me. Before I retired, IBM (International Business Machines) had invited me for a two-day training seminar for its executives in India and abroad. I had sessions on both days: one day on disinvestment and the next on telecom reforms. At the end of the sessions, some executives of Indian origin came to me and asked to see me in my room. They asked me if I was prepared to start a lobbying company in India; they would then resign from IBM and join the lobbying company. They were impressed that I had handled difficult government schemes of privatization and telecom reforms extremely well and had done all the lobbying internally for these schemes. With an expanding space for the private sector in India, I would do well with a professionally run lobbying company, they felt. I told them that I could do nothing for one year as per the rules and lobbying companies were not specifically permitted in India, though not banned either, and I would not like to get into this grey area.

Normally, bureaucrats do not liaison with the press; ministers do. Both my ministers in disinvestment and in telecom, Arun Jaitley and Arun Shourie, were extremely bright people with a modern mindset. They understood that these issues were highly controversial and involved a huge change in the way business was done in India. They also understood that it was not advisable for them as politicians to do all the lobbying in favour of these controversial measures. However, to deal with massive changes in the way business is done in India, courtesy of disinvestment and network reforms, they asked me to increase my interaction with the press and other interest groups, a kind of lobbying for what we were doing in government.

That is why, perhaps, I was noticed by professionals from IBM to open a lobbying company with them after retirement. Though I did not join them, the idea remained stuck in my mind. I then contacted my rather conservative batchmate, C.M. Vasudev, to collaborate with me. He had been secretary, economic affairs, and India's executive director to the World Bank. Our desire was to help companies communicate their challenges better, understand the regulatory framework and work closely with their industry associations to put forth their views on any regulatory change they wanted for their sector. With no savings of our own to speak of, we reached out to some venture capitalists, but found their terms most inappropriate.

About the same time, Nira Radia approached me with a proposal to start a consultancy company and offered that she would help seed the company with a small investment. I did not know Nira; so I checked on her from the source everyone now uses—Google. There were just a few entries about her son having been kidnapped and then released a few years back. Other than that, she ran a public affairs company which was reported to be the biggest in India. I was unsure about the merits of opening a consulting practice with a public affairs company (often misunderstood as lobbying) as a sister organization. However, it reminded me of the proposal made by the young executives of IBM and I associated the work with that of think tanks in the West (like Aspen Institute which I joined for a short while later). Even then I did not have the courage of starting business with a relatively unknown person, and decided to consult, and join, if C. M. Vasudev agreed. He also met Nira Radia and agreed. After all, Nira Radia was the public affairs consultant to the most reputed company in India—the Tatas—and she represented all of the Tata Group companies and a number of other multinationals.

Vasudev joined the company Noesis in February 2007 and I joined in April 2007, after the mandatory cooling off period. I had also found during my term as TRAI chief that most telecom regulators were consultants after retirement. There was a lot of demand for the newly emerging discipline of network reforms around the world and I had been a telecom regulator but had also worked on power regulation and been trained in other regulations as part of the reforms courses I attended. The salaries we accepted in Noesis were nominal and less than the salary of chairman, TRAI, at that time. However, one of the terms of appointment for both of us was that we could independently work for UN organizations. We were flooded with UN work and would have also got benefits of 10 per cent sweat equity had we continued with the company.

I restructured telecom regulation in many countries on behalf of the ITU and did a lot of training work for them and the World Bank in South-East Asia and Africa. We had a number of consultancy projects for Noesis in India and abroad. Later, Nira's companies also started consulting for Reliance. But around 2010, a huge controversy broke out about taped conversations of Nira Radia, perhaps the result of investigations instigated by corporate rivals. Also, she was a British national, a divorcee, and had a high profile, an ideal target for spreading canards. I can only say even with my limited experience of working with her (given that we would be focusing on our own consulting assignments) that she was highly professional in her approach and work. Her firm was competent at public affairs and was the largest public affairs company in India and perhaps the eighth largest in the world.

As a retired government officer not wanting to work for any one business group, we all believed that an independent consulting company was the best choice. Little did I know that despite no involvement or association with anything in the telecom sector in India, except one consultancy with Tata Teleservices on spectrum, I would be dragged into the 2G scam, during 2010–11, implemented by the government players after my retirement in 2006.

When the tirade against Nira Radia started, it was directed at me too, and in my case the rumour was mostly about my work as chairman, TRAI, and when nothing was found, the tirade shifted to privatization cases some time in 2013. This led to much publicized CBI inquiries against me and I can say with confidence that the basis of these inquiries was the tampering of government documents by some in the government and flawed arguments for the purpose of initiating the inquiry.

I ran to Arun Jaitley, my former minister and one of the best legal and political brains in the country, for help. He agreed to help me pro bono along with Harish Salve. I could not have paid their fee. Of course, I had to engage junior advocates to prepare the case. While discussing all cases with Arun Jaitley, and asking him his reaction on the rumours spread against me, he opined that after the brilliant work done as secretary, disinvestment, and chairman, TRAI, I occupied a pedestal in the public's mind. I had made myself vulnerable when I decided to come down the pedestal and become a consultant. I argued that all retired telecom chairmen in the world were consultants today. The argument did not impress him and perhaps many others too.

While we received kudos internationally, back in India, both the Joint Parliamentary Committee and CBI looked at trumped-up and well-publicized charges against members of TRAI and those responsible for implementing changes in government. I hope no bureaucrat suffers such indignities again for honestly implementing reforms.

The inquiries were a tremendous strain on me both financially and emotionally, and also on my health; and it will take me long before my life comes back on rails. Changes are difficult to implement. If anyone attempts to do so, he must do it at his own risk, and must be prepared to face consequences later. The political class, at whose instance most changes are initiated, are not likely to stand by you, barring a few exceptions of course. And if the political class feels that reforms are necessary, it must evolve rules which protect bona fide action.

At present, it is easy to harass a public official by starting a case against him under the Prevention of Corruption Act (amended) even if no corruption is proved, just on the ground that his action caused loss to the government. Being prosecuted without an element of corruption under the Prevention of Corruption Act is beyond my understanding. But those pursuing crony capitalism in government merrily use this provision, along with an obliging CBI, just to force public servants to toe their line and assist them in their nefarious activities.

ANNEXURES

Annexure 1

Excerpts of Cabinet Note and its Approval

Government of India
Ministry of Communication & IT
Department of Telecommunication
F. No. 808-26/2003-VAS" Dated 31st October 2003

Note for the Cabinet

Subject: Approval of Recommendations of the Group of Ministers on Telecom matters

"......................

2.4 - 4th Term of Reference: To chart the course to a Universal License:

2.4.1 The GoM took note of the exercise that had already been initiated by Telecom Regulatory Authority of India (TRAI) in regard to authorize Licensing Regime in the Telecom Sector Chairman, TRAI and Chairman, HDFC were specifically invited made presentation before the GoM.

2.4.2 TRAI submitted its recommendations to the Government on this matter on 27.10.2003. TRAI has recommended that the present system of licensing in the Telecom Sector should be replaced by Unified Licensing/ Automatic Authorization Regime. The Unified Licensing/Automatic

Authorization Regime has been recommended to be achieved in a two-stage process with the Unified Access Regime for the basic and cellular services in the first phase to be implemented immediately. This is to be followed by a process of consultations to define the guidelines and rules for achieving a fully Unified Licensing/Authorization Regime. TRAI has recommended that it will enter into a consultation process so that the replacement of the existing Licensing regime by a Unified Licensing Regime gets initiated within 6 months. Broad rationale, key recommendations and some key policy issues that have been addressed by TRAI are listed in the Annexure-IV (Page 19-21).

2.4.3 The salient points of TRAI recommendations in regard to the Unified Access Licensing (basic and cellular mobile) are as under

i- Unification of Licenses to be done in two stages
  a- Unified access regime for basic and cellular services in the first phase immediately.
  b- Unified authorization regime encompassing all telecom services in the second phase

ii- Fee paid by fourth cellular operator to be benchmark for migration of basic players to the new access regime.

iii- Cellular operators not to pay any fee for migration to the unified access regime while basic operators to pay the difference between fourth cellular operator license fee and the BSO fee already paid by them.

iv- Reliance Infocomm required to pay Rs. 1096 crores for migration in addition to penalty of Rs. 485 crores for offering cellular type services.

v- Process of migration to the new regime to be voluntary.

vi- The existing BSOs after migration to Unified Access Licensing Regime may offer full mobility, However, WLL(M) operators after migration will be required to offer limited mobility service for such customers who so desire.

vii- No additional fee to be paid for any of the circles where there is no fourth cellular operator.

2.4.4 Enhancing the scope of current Telecom Policy (NTP-99) to provide category of Unified License and Unified License and Unified Access Service License

NTP -99 recognises access service providers as a distinct class. For the purpose of Licensing, this has been sub-divided into cellular fixed and cable service providers. NTP -99 also states that convergence of both markets and technologies is a really that is forcing realignment of the industry. This convergence now allows operators to use their facilities to deliver some servces reserved for other operators to use their facilities to deliver some services reserved for other operators necessitating a re-look at NTP-94 policy framework.

For bringing into effect the regime of Unified Access Service for basic and cellular service licenses and Unified Licensing comprising all telecom services. It would be necessary to enhance the scope of NTP-99 to include these as distinct categories of licenses as per NTP-99.

2.4.5 TRAI recommendations on entry fee for WLL (M) based on TDSAT judgment:

TRAI has also submitted its recommendations in regard to additional entry fee payable by basic services operators for providing WLL(M) services on which Government had sought its recommendations based on the judgment of TDSAT dated 08/08/2003 in the WWL(M) case. TRAI has given detailed resoning on this matter and has recommended additional entry fee for such of the Basic Service Operators who provide WLL (M) service. The salient features are in Annexure-V(Page22).

2.4.6 Based on the above the GoM has recommended the following course of action

i- The scope of NTP-99 may be enhanced to provide for licensing of Unified Access Service for basic and cellular license services and Unified Licensing comprising all telecom services. Department of Telecommunications may be authorized to issue necessary addendum of NTP-99 to this effect.

ii- The recommendations of TRAI with regard to implementation of the Unified Access Licensing Regime for basic and cellular services may be accepted.

iii- The recommendations of TRAI in regard to the course of action to be accepted subsequently in regard to the implementation of the fully Unified License Authorization Regime may be approved.

DoT may be authorized to finalize the details of implementation with the approval of the Minister of Communications & IT on the receipt recommendations of TRAI in this behalf.

iv- The recommendations of TRAI in regard to additional entry fee payable by basic service operators for providing WLL(M) service on which Government sought its recommendations based on the judgment of TDSAT dated 08/08/2003 in the WLL(M) case may be accepted.

v- While there appears to be no case for giving any compensation package to them because of the perception that the finances of the cellular operators are strained and because of the effect these may have on financial institutions. Finance Ministry would address the difficulties of the cellular operators, If any separately and appropriately.

vi- If new services are introduced as a result of technological advancements which require additional spectrum over and above the spectrum already allotted/contracted allocation of such spectrum will be considered on payment of additional fee or charges, these will be determined as per guidelines to be evolved in consultation with TRAI.

Approvals and directions being sought

In view of the above recommendations of the govt. approval of the cabinet is sought for proposals contained in

- i- Para 2.1.2 (relating to spectrum; Reference page 2-3)
- ii- Para 2.2.1 (relating to rural telephony; reference page 3-4)
- iii- Para 2.4.6 (relating to Uniform License; reference page 7-9)
- iv- Para 2.5.5 (relating to limited mobility; reference page 10)
- v- Para 2.7.2 (relating to mergers and acquisitions reference page 11)
- vi- Para 2.8.2 (relating to imposition of trade tax reference page 12)

The approval contained in R. Poornalingam, additional Secretary, Cabinet Secretariat's approval letter DC No. 30/CM/2003 dated 3 November 2003 approving DoT proposals.

Annexure 2

Ministry of Finance Note to PMO on Allocation and Pricing of Spectrum

"March 25, 2011

Facts of the case:

1. Based on the decision of the Union Cabinet dated October 31, 2003, guidelines for the Unified Access Services (UAS) were issued on November 11, 2003 which allowed for UAS license to provide basic and/or cellular license using any technology in the defined service area.

2. The Union Cabinet had authorized DoT to finalize, with the approval of the Minister-in-charge, the details of implementation of the UASL regime, including the calculation of the entry fee depending upon the date of payment based on the principles given by TRAI in its recommendations. In the context of the release of adequate spectrum needed for the growth of the telecom sector, the Union Cabinet in October 2003 had decided that the Department of Telecommunication and Ministry of Finance would discuss and finalize spectrum pricing formulae which would incentive for efficient use of spectrum as well as disincentive for sub-optimal usage.

3.The license fee for UAS license was reduced by 2%, across the board, with a further reduction by 2% of AGR for first two cellular licensees (for a period of 4 years with effect from April 01, 2004) in order to spur investment and growth, and, ultimately yield more revenue to Government.

The financial implication of the proposal was estimated at Rs. 968 Cr. for the first four years, and, Rs. 885 crore per annum thereafter. The proposal to the above effect, initiated by the then Minister of Communication and Information Technology (Shri Arun Shourie) was approved by the then Minister of Finance (Shri Jaswant Singh) on December 12, 2003, without any examination as regards financial implications.

4. TRAI, in its recommendations dated May 13, 2005, has indicated that in the existing licensing framework, entry fee includes onetime spectrum charge. TRAI recommended that as in the existing framework the spectrum charges should have two components: onetime spectrum charges and annual spectrum charges. It was recommended that there should be no one time spectrum charges for allocation of IMT-2000 spectrum to the existing service providers. As regards the new entrants, the onetime spectrum charge would be equal to UASL entry fee in that service area minus the component of the registration charge based on the entry fee paid by new BSO (entered in/after 2001), specified by TRAI in its recommendations on Unified licensing regime dated January 13, 2005. TRAI also recommended that the existing method of annual spectrum charge in terms of percentage of revenue share should continue.

5. In response to the TRAI recommendation dated May 13, 2005, DEA as per relevant notings and in letter December 21, 2005 to DoT indicated that, for allocation of additional spectrum, while price discovery through auction may not be appropriate, the hybrid option of a base fee, combined with revenue share, appears to be the most appropriate. It was also recommended by DEA that the issue should be put up for consideration and appropriate decision by the committee of Secretaries (CoS) and thereafter, by a Group of Ministers (GoM). DEA did not question the methodology suggested by TRAI on issue of one time and annual spectrum charges.

6. The thrust of the Union Cabinet decision of October 31, 2003, in regard to spectrum pricing was for MoF and DoT to "…. Discuss and finalize spectrum pricing formula, which will include incentive for efficient use of spectrum as well as dis-incentive for sub-optimal usages….". Though there was no basic disagreement between the two Departments on the basic thrust of the TRAI recommendations on pricing in 2005, DEA had advised DoT to

take up the matter in CoS and thereafter, by a GoM. This was presumably not done by DoT. The matter was also not followed up further by DEA.

7. A Group of Ministers (GoM) was constituted by Cabinet Secretariat on February 23, 2006, on the issue of vacation of Defense spectrum and raising of resources for the purpose. DEA, vide D.O. letter dated March 28, 2007 asked DoT to include issues relating to 'spectrum pricing' within the ambit of the GoM. It was, however, not specifically communicated whether 'spectrum pricing' meant only spectrum usage charges or entry fee and spectrum usage charges. The view of DoT was that the spectrum pricing is within the normal work carried out by the Ministry as indicated in their letter dated April 2, 2007. In a D.O. letter, dated April 19, 2007, to the Cabinet Secretary, Finance Secretary had indicated that since these issues would have economic and financial ramifications, they need to be discussed in the GoM. The contention of the DoT that these issues are within the normal work was not entirely correct. It was explained that a sound policy on spectrum allocation and pricing will not only result in optimal utilization of spectrum, but would also have revenue implications. Vide OM dated May 17, 2007, Cabinet Secretariat advised DEA that Finance Secretary and Secretary (DoT) may discuss for resolving the issue of inclusion of spectrum pricing on the ToR of GoM and advise the Cabinet Secretariat about the decision taken in the matter. DEA sent an OM to DoT on 18.05.2007 indicating that technology neutrality and spectrum price must be included in the ToR of the GoM. In its letter dated June 06, 2007 Finance Secretary requested Secretary, DoT to include spectrum pricing in the ToRs for the GoM. It was also said that the methodology to be followed for 'spectrum pricing' would logically follow the vacation of spectrum which is the main task of GoM. A view was taken in DEA then that the matter may be resolved through correspondence, failing which meeting with DoT could be held. In its letter dated June 15, 2007 on the subject, DoT indicated that since spectrum pricing and charges for the use of spectrum is a dynamic issue, it is to be reviewed and considered from time to time in the context of the changing technology and international best practices in consultation TRAI. Thus DoT precluded the role of MoF, if any, in finalizing spectrum pricing. This letter however does not appear to have been received and processed on the file of DEA. Thereafter, DEA did not take up the issue further, either with the DoT or with the Cabinet Secretariat.

8. DEA explicitly took up the issue of fixation of entry fee on November 22, 2007. In the context of the three crossover licenses for CDMA operators issued by DoT, DEA had argued that it is not clear how the rate of Rs. 1600 crore determined as far back as in 2001, has been applied for a license given in 2007 without any indexation, let alone current valuation. It was also said that all further action to implement the said licenses may be stayed. While the intent of DEA was to settle this issue in generic sense for all licenses, the letter itself referred only to the crossover licenses. In response, DoT vide their letter dated November 29, 2007 indicated that the decision to allot the dual technology licenses at the 2001 entry fee was justified on account of the decision taken in the Cabinet meeting held on October 31, 2003 and TRAI recommendations dated August 28, 2007. (The TRAI recommendation of August, 2007 was not placed before the Full Telecom Commission). This was also not further responded to by DEA. No follow up appears to have been done from DEA/DoT as per available records.

9. As a response to the DoT letter dated November 29, 2007, the then Director (Infra) initiated a note highlighting the need to revise the entry fee. This note, dated December 17, 2008, while it was marked to Joint Secretary (On tour/Additional Secretary (Economic Affairs [AS(EA)] does not seem to have been put up to the next level of consideration. Records also indicate that the then AS (EA) put up on 09.01.2008, in a separate file, a comprehensive concept paper on the extant telecom sector policy. The subject header of the note mentioned the references of the DEA letter of November 22, 2007 and the DoT reply of November 29, 2007. The note recommended both revision of the entry fee fixed in 2003 as well as adoption of an auction methodology for determination of the spectrum usage charges. The position paper was prefaced with a note of the then AS (EA) dated January 9, 2008, which inter alia mentioned that she had been directed to attend the meeting of the full Telecom Commission, which had been scheduled to be held on January 09, 2008 and had now been postponed to January 15, 2008. This position paper was used by the then FM as a basis of his 'secret note' to the Prime Minister on January 15, 2008 wherein, an auction based mechanism was recommended for future allocation of spectrum (beyond the "start up"spectrum), with the spectrum allocations having been made in the past to be treated as a closed chapter.

The recommendation was in the context of spectrum usage charges and not with regard to the entry fee.

10. A full Telecom Commission meeting took place on January 15, 2008. One of the agenda item was pricing of spectrum. However, it only included annual spectrum charge (revenue share) and not the entry fee. MoF representative who attended the meeting did not raise the issue of revision of entry fee.

11. The conclusions arising from the paras 9 and 10 ante can be summarized as follows: the DoT response of November 29, 2007 was brought to the notice of the then Finance Minister on 9.1.2008, along with suggestions to argue for revision of the entry fee and adoption for auction with spectrum usage charges as the bid parameter; the fact that a Telecom Commission meeting on the issue was scheduled on January 15, 2008 was also mentioned; no response, however, was sent by DEA to DoT either on the issues raised by DoT in the communication dated November 29, 2007, or with reference to the impending meeting of the Telecom Commission; no intervention on entry fee were suggested in this meeting by DEA representatives; and, finally, a note was sent by the then Finance Minister to the Prime Minister on January 15, 2008 wherein auction of spectrum was argued, but only with the reference to spectrum beyond the 'start up' spectrum. The licenses allotted in 2007 and 2008 only carried the 'start up' spectrum embedded with them. The note of the Finance Minister did not deal with the need, if any, to revise entry fee or the rate of revenue share. The issue of revision of entry fee was taken up by the MoF subsequently in November 11, 2008.

12. Subsequently, in a meeting held on January 30, 2008 between the then Ministers of Finance and Telecommunications, it was noted by the then Finance Minister that he was for now not seeking to revisit the current regimes for entry fee or revenue share.

13. Secretary DoT formally wrote to DEA on February 8, 2008 enclosing an approach paper, wherein, DoT proposed to price allocation of spectrum beyond 4.4 MHz and, enhancement of spectrum usage charges. It is indicated in the approach note that Secretary (Finance) was of opinion

that auctioning is legally possible for initial allotment of spectrum of 4.4 MHz. DoT indicated that as 4.4 MHz is a part of the license agreement, no spectrum acquisition charge is supposed to be levied. The approach paper states that even if it is priced, it will also disturb the level playing field and the present LoI holders who have already paid entry fee for license may be construed as the de-facto price of initial spectrum i.e. Rs. 1650 cr. for pan India license. Based on the DoT letter, an initial note on the subject was prepared in DEA on February 11, 2008, wherein the entire range of spectrum was proposed to be charged for both new and old operators, using the entry fee as the price of embedded spectrum and indexing it with the increase in the AGR of the telecom sector between 2003-04 and 2007-08. The note also ruled out the option of auctioning spectrum for various reasons explained therein. A note for discussion was put up by the Finance Secretary on April 07, 2008, outlining the proposals in respect of both 2G and 3G spectrum bands. After subsequent discussions with DoT, and, in response to a draft note for Cabinet of DoT, for financial approval for creation of the Air Force Network (AFNET), DoT were informed with the approval of FM on April 08, 2008 that all allotments of spectrum, beyond 4.4 MHz, may be specifically priced and charged for and the spectrum usage charges may be calibrated with regard to circle specific "scarcity value" of spectrum instead of basing it on bandwidth as has been the practice. The then Finance Minister sent a "non paper" to the then Minister of Telecommunications on April 21, 2008 conveying that an "in principle" decision may be taken to price the spectrum beyond 4.4 MHz, as had been suggested by DoT.

14. in a meeting between the then Finance Secretary and Secretary, DoT on April 24, 2008 DEA adopted the following position: spectrum usage charge may be linked to circle specific "scarcity value"; spectrum upto 6.2 MHz may not be priced; and, spectrum beyond 6.2 MHz may be priced using the base price of Rs. 375 cr. per MHz indexed to growth in Adjusted Gross Revenue (AGR) with reference to the year 2003-04. In subsequent meetings DEA presented its stand that spectrum usage charge may be revised as a percentage of AGR; spectrum upto 6.2 Mhz may not be priced; and, spectrum beyond 6.2 MHz may be priced using the base price of Rs. 266 cr. per MHz indexed to growth in Gross Domestic Product (GDP) with reference to the year 2003-04. This position was thereafter communicated to DoT vide DO letter dated June 27, 2008 of the then AS

(EA). Further meetings were held between the then Finance Minister and the Minister of Telecom on May 29, 2008and June 12, 2008 of the then AS (EA). Subsequently, in a meeting held under the Chair of the Prime Minister, on July 4, 2008 (as recorded in the note of the then Finance Secretary dated July 6, 2008), the then Finance Minister and Minister of Telecommunication agreed to the proposals on enhancement of spectrum usage charges and pricing of spectrum based on indexing the base price (Rs. 266 crore per MHz) and compounding using SBI PLR from existing allottees of spectrum beyond 6.2 MHz. However, the price of revision of entry fee was not discussed in the meeting.

15. a meeting of the Telecom Commission was convened on November 11, 2008 to discuss issues relating to one time spectrum charge and spectrum usage charges. Approval of the then FM was taken on the same lines as had been agreed to in the PMO meeting on July 4, 2008. The enhancement of the spectrum usage charges was expected to yield revenue of Rs. 4149 cr. annually, an increase of Rs. 1270 cr. over the annual revenue yield (~Rs. 3000 cr.) on the current rate structure. However, in addition, DoT were also asked vide OM dated November 11, 2008 to suggest a mechanism for updating the entry fee of Rs. 1658 cr. (fixed in 2003-04), for all allotments o licenses after January 01, 2009. Thus MoF raised the issue of updating the entry fee albeit only for the licenses allotted after January 01, 2009. Thus MoF implicitly agreed to imposition of same entry fee as that prevailing in 2001 for licenses allotted upto December 31, 2008.

16. It is, therefore, clear that there were consultations between MoF and DoT in the first half of 2008, on the formula for charging 2G spectrum based on indexation to the PLR of the SBI, which related only to the allocations beyond 6.2 Mhz. In the matter presently under consideration (i.e. allotments of 2G licenses in 2007-08) spectrum allocations were not made beyond 6.2 MHz, on the pricing of which, DoT and MoF were in agreement. On the other hand, the new licenses have only got 4.4 MHz of spectrum each.

17. Secretary (Finance) had suggested to go for auction for initial spectrum of 4.4 MHz in early February, 2008. DoT was not keen to do the same since it had said that it will disturb the level playing field and the present LoI holders who had already paid entry fee were likely to go for litigation. DoT

opined that 4.4 MHz is a part of license agreement and initial entry fee for license may be construed as the de-facto price of initial spectrum. There was a way out by invoking clause 5.1 of the UAS license, which inter alia, provide for modification at any time the terms and conditions of the license, if in the opinion of the licensor it is necessary or expedient to do so in public interest or ion the interest of the security of state or for the proper conduct of the telegraphs. DoT could have invoked this clause for cancelling licenses in case MoF had stuck to the stand of auctioning the 4.4 MHz spectrum. Perhaps some litigation would have arisen as a consequence. It may be mentioned that while the UAS licenses were signed between February 27, and March 07, 2008, spectrum allocations were done starting only in April, 2008, almost 4 months after the LoIs were issued. However, these were not charged (beyond the normal spectrum usage charges) since there was consensus, at the levels of the Ministers concerned, that spectrum beyond the 'start up' levels only should be charged.

18. Detailed replies on the issue s raised by the Members of the PAC during the oral evidence of the Finance Secretary were sent to the Lok Sabha Secretariat on July 21, 2010. Comments of the Department of Economic Affairs on the draft performance audit report on the issue of licenses and allocation of 2G spectrum were sent to the Director General of Audit on August 11, 2010. These were put up for the first time to the FM for information when copies of these were forwarded to the Cabinet Secretary under intimation to the Prime Minister's Office (PMO) on January 05, 2011.

Annexure 3

TRAI Affidavit

ANNEXURE 9
IN THE SUPREME COURT OF INDIA
(CIVIL ORIGINAL JURISDICTION)
WRIT PETITION (CIVIL)NO. 10 OF 2011

IN THE MATTER OF :

Dr. Subramanian Swamy	...	Petitioner
Versus		
Union of India & Others.	....	Respondents

WRITTEN NOTE ON BEHALF OF THE TELECOM REGULATORY AUTHORITY OF INDIA BY RAKESH DWIVEDI, SENIOR ADVOCATE.

SIGNIFICANCE OF TELECOMMUNICATION SERVICE :

1. As per Cabinet Resolution dated 11.04.1989 constituting Telecommunications :- **(Shivraj P.R-Annex. 7/P.48-50) CAS comp. P-120-122 Vol. I.**

   No. 15[1][2]87-Cab-1. Telecommunication service is an essential infrastructure for national development. It has impact on social and economic activities. Besides, business, industry and administration depend heavily on information and telecom for productivity, efficiency and their day-to-day operations. Its development, therefore, is vital for nation building.

2. As per NTP, 1999- **(CSV Comp. P. 73-85.)**
The Government of India (Government) recognises that provision of world class telecommunications infrastructure and information is the key to rapid economic and social development of the country. It is critical not only for the development of the Information Technology industry, but also has widespread ramifications on the entire economy of the country. It is also anticipated that going forward, a major part of the GDP of the country would be contributed by this sector. Accordingly, it is of vital importance to the country that there be a comprehensive and forward looking telecommunications policy which creates an enabling framework for development of this industry.
3. While inaugurating India Telecom, 2007, the Hon'ble Prime Minister stated as below: **(CAS Comp. P. 78-81/Vol. II)**
"Growth in the telecom sector is a critical component of our infrastructure plans and it plays an important catalytic role in our development process. The opening up of the telecom sector has created an impressive forward momentum in India, resulting in massive investments and expansion in supply which are signs of a vigorous, competitive and fast growing sector. I am very happy that the telecom department has ambitious targets for the future – 500 million telephone connections, 40 million Internet connections and 20 million broadband connections. Raising the investments needed for this ambitious plan would be a tremendous challenge for the industry as well as for the country.
I would like to draw your attention to a few issues concerning this booming sector. First, there is the issue of access and the large rural–urban divide in connectivity. Although the growth in the last few years has been truly impressive and our tariffs are among the lowest in the world, vast stretches of our rural population have little or no telecom penetration. Rural tele-density is still in single digits. I had heard of plans for a Phone in Every Village some twenty years ago. We have not yet reached that goal. This is why we have emphasised telecom connectivity in our Bharat Nirman programme.
There will be multiple benefits from increased rural telecom connectivity. At a narrow level, there will be a new burst of growth for the sector as a whole. On a larger plane, however, there will be multiplier effects for the entire rural economy. As better telecom

connectivity and consequently better IT connectivity – becomes a reality, our rural hinterland will become more integrated with the rapid growth processes now taking place in the rest of the economy. There will be increased economic opportunities for our rural people – through better education, through improved market access for their products, through improved employment prospects, and through greater purchasing power in their hands. The spin off benefits will be felt, not just in telecom, but right across the economy as a whole. Telecom connectivity has the potential to play a transformational role in our rural areas. I expect all key players in this vital sector to realise and fulfil this latent potential. You need to rise to the challenge by devising innovative mechanisms for achieving our collective ambitions."

4. Growth of Telecom Service also effectuates and expands the horizon of Fundamental Right to free speech, strengthens rational integrity and also bolsters free flow of trade, commerce and intercourse throughout the territory of India and even globally. It enforces the basic human freedoms. If growth happens at affordable prices the national economy as a whole grows for the benefit of all. Thus spectrum should be so distributed as best subserves the common good for it is a national resource. That is the mandate of article 39(b) of the Constitution for building a welfare state.
   1983(1) SCC-147, Sanjeev Coke Manufacturing Co.
   1995 Supp(1) SCC-596, Jilubhai Nanbhai Khachar

HISTORY :

5. 42 CMTS Licenses, 8 in 4 metros and 34 in 18 state circles had been awarded to 14 operators prior to 1999 . In metros licenses were awarded through beauty contest and in circle through a single stage bidding process. The license fee was a fixed amount predetermined in case of metros and determined through bidding in the case of circles and amount was payable over the tenure of 10 years. (See Pg. 39-40 of Recommendation 11.05.2010)
6. In the year 1999 though the number of subscribers had grown to over one million subscribers, most of the projects were facing problems and were unable to arrange finance for their projects and the targets remained unfulfilled. The private sector entry was slower than envisaged. Technological changes had blurred the difference between

wireline and wireless services and there was the phenomenon of convergence of both markets and technologies. The NTP, 1999 was framed in this background. It notes the problem and allows the operators to migrate from a fixed license fee regime to a revenue sharing arrangement. The Policy in Para 3.1.1 states as below:

> "Availability of adequate frequency Spectrum is essential not only for providing optimal bandwidth to every operator but also for entry of additional operators.
>
> It is proposed to review the spectrum utilisation from time to time keeping in view the emerging scenario of spectrum availability, optimal use of spectrum, requirements of market, competition and other interest of public. The entry of more operators in a service area shall be based on the recommendation of the TRAI who will review this as required and no later than every two years.
>
> CMSP operators would be required to pay a one time entry fee. The basis for determining the entry fee and the basis for selection of additional operators would be recommended by the TRAI. Apart from the one time entry fee, CMSP operators would also be required to pay licence fee based on a revenue share. It is proposed that the appropriate level of entry fee and percentage of revenue share arrangement for different service areas would be recommended by TRAI in a time-bound manner, keeping in view the objectives of the New Telecom Policy."

6A. On 12.07.1999 a reference was made to TRAI for determining the licence fee on revenue sharing basis. The Government by order dated 22.07.1999 decided that as per the policy the licence term would be extended to initial 20 years and will be extendable by additional periods of 10 years. The revenue sharing was provisionally fixed at 15% of AGR subject to review by TRAI. Later TRAI made its recommendation on 25.01.2001. With some changes, the Government determined the licence fee as 10, 12 and 8 per cent respectively for Metros and A, B and C Circles. On this date BSO's were permitted limited mobility. The licence fee was further reduced w.e.f. 01.04.2004 to 10%, 8% and 6% of AGR respectively for Metros and category A, B and C service areas. The changes were with respect to the definition of AGR. The operators who migrated on this basis to the licence fee regime questioned the AGR norm before the TDSAT in petition No. 7 of 2003. By judgment dated

07.07.2006. TDSAT allowed the petition and directed TRAI to submit a fresh recommendation. TRAI again submitted its recommendation to TDSAT as per its orders. The petitions were then finally allowed directing deletion of certain factors from the definition of AGR. The judgment is dated 30.08.2007. Civil Appeal No. 9646-7661 of 2010 has been filed before this Hon'ble Court by Union of India and the same is pending.

7. In the meantime the Government decided to grant a third CMTS license to MTNL for Delhi and Mumbai service areas (1997) and to BSNL for all service areas except Delhi and Mumbai (2000). They are only paying license fee on revenue sharing basis and Spectrum charge.

7A. From 01.04.2002, the Government opened the ILD (network carriage service) service for private operators on the basis of a separate ILD licence, carrying an administratively fixed entry fee of Rs. 25 crores and an annual licence fee of 15% of AGR. Later from 01.01.2006 this was reduced to a one time entry fee of Rs. 2.50 crores and an annual licence fee of 6% of AGR and this is without any roll-out obligation except from having at least one switch in India.

8. After the TRAI Act was amended in year 2000 pursuant to its recommendation a 4th CMSP was introduced in every circle through a multi stage bidding process (2001). This bidding was different from the previous single stage bidding which resulted in payment of highest bid as a fixed fee in instalments over a tenure of 10 years. Here the highest bid became the one time entry fee and thereafter Licence fee on revenue sharing basis and Spectrum charge based on AGR had to be paid.

9. Until the year 2003 the licenses were separate for BSO and GSM. The BSO had the benefit of limited mobility through CDMA technology known as WLL. NTP 1999 had noted the problem arising out of convergence of market and technologies.

YEAR 2003 :-

10. In the aforesaid backdrop consultation process for grant of unified license was initiated *suo moto* by TRAI on 16.07.2003. It was noted that enhancement of tele-density is a National Objective set by National Economic Policy and this revolves around access networks and need to make available low cost access. In March 2003, the subscriber

base was 13 Million which almost doubled in the next 7 months (Pg. 13/2003 Rejoinder) . it was expected the wireless subscription base would grow to 100 Million by the end of year 2005 (Pg. 14). This required an investment of around Rs. 50,000 crores. In this light TRAI recommended that within 6 month "unified licensing should be initiated for all service communication in all geographic areas using any technology". This regime was to be finalized once "in principle" approval was received from Government of India. Thereafter TRAI would submit its final recommendation. **(CAS Vol. II Pg. 2-45 @ Pg.18) (Pg. 17)** . It was recorded that the Unified Licensing Regime is to be achieved in a two stage process. As a first step it was recommended that unification of access service at circle level be taken up immediately. Existing operators were to have option to continue in the present licensing regime or to migrate to the new UASL regime in the existing circles **(Pg. 19 @ Pg. 20)**. Regarding entry fee 3 alternatives were noted and then TRAI recommended that entry fee of the 4th Cellular operator should be the entry fee for UASL. The BSO would pay the difference by adjustment of what was already paid by them. This was for migration to UASL at circle level. There was no extra entry fee for circles which did not have 4th Cellular operator **(Pg. 23 @ Pg. 24)**.

For issuance of new Cellular mobile licence it was felt that it would be appropriate to have more competition when unified licensing regime was initiated after period of 6 months. But in the meantime if additional players are to be introduced in the existing licensing regime (CMTS), then it may be done through a multi stage bidding process as in the case of 4th Operator. **(Pg. 30 @ Pg. 31).**

10. As noted by report of Justice S.R. Patil, at about this time a group of ministers on telecommunication was constituted on 10.09.2003**(Annex.22 Shivraj Patil Report Pg. 266-267)** to see how additional spectrum could be released and to chart a course to a universal license. TRAI's recommendation dated 27/10/03 was considered by the group of ministers and its acceptance was recommended to the Cabinet.

At para 2.1.2(3) the Cabinet note provides for finalisation of Spectrum pricing formula by DoT and MoF and at para 2.4.6. (2) the DoT was authorised to finalize the details of implementation of UASL regime including calculation of entry fee on **principles given by TRAI in its recommendation.** This Cabinet note was approved by

Cabinet on 31.10.03 **(Pg 268 of SRP CAS Comp. Vol. II Pg. 46-74/ Annex. 22 of SPR)**.(Pg 57 of 2010 Recommendation). The concept of spectrum charge and entry fee along with license fee were at that time being made applicable to CMTS licensees from year 1999, when migration from fixed fee regime was permitted. The Cabinet note is dealing with two different concepts in para 2.1.2 and 2.4.6. In para 2.1.2 the Cabinet is directing DoT and MoF to discuss and finalise the Spectrum price formulae(Spectrum charge formulae), and in para 2.4.6 it is asking DoT to implement UASL regime as per principles given by TRAI in its recommendations. That is also how the Cabinet approval was understood by DoT and TRAI and there was no note of discordance.

11. The DoT guidelines for UASL dated 11.11.03 **(CAS Comp. Vol. I Pg. 1-6/Annex-22, Pg. 298-304 SPR)** is consistent with TRAI recommendation 27.10.2003, when it refers to entry fee paid by the fourth cellular operator. On 11.11.2003 the Central Government issued an addendum to NTP-99 informing its decision to issue UASL and Unified Licence.(Copy enclosed). It emphasises that "provision of Telecom Services at the cheapest possible rates and by the most reliable mode is the sine qua non for India to consolidate its position as a leading but of communication systems".
12. In the DoT guidelines dates 11.11.03 it was stipulated that new access services license shall be given only in category of UASL. With this stipulation para 7.39 of TRAI recommendation dated 27.10.03 became redundant as it pertained to CMTS license. Thereafter, by letter dated 14.11.03**(Annex-25 SPR Pg. 203)**, 19.11.03 **(Annexure A herein)** and TRAI minutes dated 24.11.03**(Annexure B herein)** it was recommended by TRAI that the entry fee of new UASL would be entry fee of fourth cellular operator. The Minster of Telecommunication accepted this position on 24.11.03 **(Annex-26 SPR Pg. 306-310)**. He also approved First Come First Serve (FCFS) for grant of new license. (Pg 70-71 SRP). On 03.12.03. DoT decided to grant new UASL licenses on basis of entry fees of fourth operator.
13. If the backdrop of 2003 recommendation is kept in view it would be apparent that context was introduction of UASL as a first step to the introduction of completely unified licence for all Geographic Areas. Further the context was the grant of permission to existing licensees to

migrate to UASL. For migration the entry fee of 4th operator had already been adopted in the recommendation and same had been accepted by the Group of Ministers and Cabinet. By May 2003 incoming calls had become free and the tariff of outgoing calls had come down to Rs. 3.24 per minute from Rs. 16.93 for both outgoing and incoming in 1999. The subscriber base had also grown multifold and a bigger spurt was expected. The target was set at 100 Million by the end of year 2005. In this context a new entrant was also permitted to obtain a license on the same basis as a migrant to UASL.

28 licences were then granted in year 2004.22 licences were then granted in year 2006. And one licence was then granted in year 2007. With respect to the grant of these licenses there has been no complaint.

14. So far as fully unified licence is concerned, TRAI's recommendation of 13.01.2005 was rejected by Government on 12.07.2007. As regards the other recommendation May 2005 in the context of spectrum related issues, there has been no response.

CAG not right

15. (a). New entrant decision was taken by TRAI as authority on 19.11.2003.

(b). Cabinet endorsed TRAI recommendation for migration on 4th operators price:- **(CAS Comp. Vol. II, Pg.46-74)**

[Once migration to UASL at 2001 price approved, then New UASL at the same time could not be issued at a different price. Difference would give entrenched player an advantage in the same time space and would have breached Article 14].

(c). Cabinet said UASL be worked out on the principles set by TRAI in Rules. So the clarification by TRAI could be accepted.

[The other part of Cabinet decision relating to "Spectrum Pricing formula" does not relate to entry fee. It pertains to Spectrum charge].

(d). However TRAI has no role in executive decision making of Government and if it is felt that Cabinet decision was required then it was for DoT to ensure it.

16. (a). Considering the 2003 situation of nascent development, the backdrop of two migrations, introduction of UASL as a first step towards fully unified license and Cabinet approval to this, the

initiation of consultation process by TRAI for unified licence, the stage of development then, as well as the long passage of time the Legality of grant of licences in year 2004 should be accepted.

(b). There is also no challenge to licences granted in 2004 and 2006 in the Writ Petition. Even in CA there is no issue raised. Attempt to bring it in through moulding of relief without pleading or prayer should not be accepted.

(c). As per 2010 Recommendation of TRAI, there are 7.56 million subscribers in Dec. 2001 and 75.94 million subscribers in Dec. 2005. (Pg. 2 of 2010 Recommendation). In December, 2003 it was 22 million subscriber.

(d). The tele-density in 2001 and 2003 were not different and were low. The tariffs had come down steeply after entry of 3rd and 4th Operator (See Pg. 9 chart of 2007 R). Between 1999-2000 it came down from around Rs. 15/- per min. to Rs. 7/- + per min. And in year 2001 it came down to Rs. 4/- per min. In year 2002 it came further down very marginally **(2007 Recommendation @ CAS compilation Vol. I Pg. 126-136/Annex. 39 SP Report Pg. 590-630).**

17. The NTP 99 called for a 2 yearly review. So in above backdrop the TRAI while recommending decided to stick to 2001 entry fee. The decision can neither be characterised as arbitrary nor unreasonable nor contrary to the goals set by NTP, 1999, which being a policy decision is statutorily binding on TRAI under Section 25(2) TRAI Act.

    The impact of 2003 decision was that the subscriber base increased to 149.62 million subscribers by December, 2006. The urban tele-density increased to 48% in March, 2007 and the rural tele-density, grew to 6%. The Government of India's revenue from Spectrum charges increased from 10280 Cr. in 2004-05 to 20900 Cr. in 2006-07. The License fee increased to 63600 Cr. in 2006-07. (See page 42-43 2007 R). This also led to more competition, there being 6-9 operators in every service area. And the tariff began matching the fixed line tariff. In the year 2006 it fell to less than Rs. 2/- per min. (Pg. 9 of 2007 R). So there was overall growth and public interest was benefitted.

18. In granting licence there was no discrimination and whoever applied was given the start up spectrum. It was an open ended policy. The Cabinet of Government of India didn't object. No one questioned the

policy in Court of Law. The raising of issue today is highly belated.

YEAR 2005:

1. As noted above, the UASL was intended to be a first step in the two-stage process for a fully unified licensing policy. In its October, 2003 report, TRAI had expressed its proposal to examine the second stage of unified licensing after in principle approval was granted by Cabinet. From the note for the Cabinet dated 31.10.2003 and the Cabinet Approval dated 03.11.2003 (Pg. 46, 50 and 74 of Mr. Sundaram's compilation). It is evident that the two-stage process was approved by the cabinet and was thus a policy decision. An addendum was also issued to NTP-99 on 11.11.2003.
2. On 13th January 2005, after due consultation, the second phase of unified licensing was recommended. First, there was a preliminary consultation paper and then a final consultation paper and an open house discussion. However, the recommendation for unified licensing regime was not accepted by the Government of India as communicated by a 3 line letter dated 12th July, 2007. On the date when recommendations were sought on some specific issues from TRAI (April, 2007) **(Vol I of CA in WP(C) No. 10/2011 Annex R-1, Pg. 1-10)**, the said recommendation was pending. The 2005 recommendation mentioned that spectrum related issues are being dealt with separately and until the spectrum guidelines are issued by the Government of India, the existing spectrum pricing and allocation proceedings will continue (Pg. 5).

   Subsequently, on 13th May, 2005, TRAI gave its recommendations on Spectrum related issues. This recommendation dealt with Efficient Utilisation of Spectrum, Spectrum allocation and Spectrum pricing. It mentions "the revised Spectrum allocation guidelines must keep the Spectrum availability, efficiency of utilization and area coordination in mind." (Pg. 57) and further that "new operators should be allowed if Spectrum requirement of existing operators have been met and additional Spectrum is available." (Pg. 64). On Spectrum pricing "It is recommended that as in the existing framework the Spectrum charges should continue to have two components: one-time Spectrum charge and an annual Spectrum charge. (Pg. 92). It was further recommended that "existing method of annual Spectrum charge in terms of percentage of revenue share should continue." But there should be periodical review (Pg. 99-100). No decision has been taken by the Government of India on this recommendation.

One, this is a most unsatisfactory approach to TRAI's recommendation. Not to give reasons for non acceptance and not considering the recommendation are contrary to the spirit of Section 11 and also a breach of its letter. The result is that interim stage UASL licence continues to be issued.

YEAR 2007: (Vol I/Writ Petition(C) No. 10 of 2011/Pg. 11-192 CA)

1. Two issues are arising with respect to the TRAI recommendations of 28.08.2007. The first is regarding the recommendation of no cap being placed on the number of access service providers. The second is the recommendation for not holding auction in 2G band. (Para 6.7 Pg. 137).
2. It is submitted that the above said recommendations should be understood in the light of the request dated 13.04.2007 **(Vol-I CA Pg. 1)** of the Central Government to give recommendations on the issue of limiting the number of access providers and review of the terms and conditions mentioned in Para 2 of the letter. The first para of the letter mentions there are 5-8 access service providers in each service area and as per present policy any eligible Indian company can apply for UAS licence. These are increasing the demand on Spectrum in a substantial manner. The Government is contemplating review of its policy. The letter incorporates a suggestion that a limit should be placed on the number of access service providers in each service area and to ensure adequate quantity of Spectrum to them to enable expansion of their services and maintenance of quality of service. (Pg. 143 of 2007 R).
3. The TRAI was not informed about the quantum of Spectrum available and even the number of applicants was not indicated.There was no indication that new UASL was going to be issued. The issue was posed in a general manner [As is now disclosed at Page 43 of W.P. No. 423/2010 CPIL, when the request was made in April 2007, there were only 23 applications pending and most of them were with regard to B grade and C grade Circles].

NO CAP

4. Para 6.1 of the recommendation should be read and understood in

the light of the reasons given in Para 2.12 to Para 2.40. The substance of the reasoning is that there should be no placement of **artificial** cap on the number of access service providers. An artificial cap eliminates the threat of potential competition which is necessary to sustain competition. Competition had benefited the Indian market and therefore barriers to entry into the market should be reduced/removed. In para 2.28 (**W.P.(C) No. 10 of 2011**) it is stated that "the Authority believes that when such market forces are said to be the determinants of entry decision of a firm in the access market, **placing artificial entry restriction** in the form of a licensing policy may not be appropriate **at this stage.** In para 2.32 it is observed: -

> "A major implication of placing a cap on the number of access providers is that, such a policy would mean even if an access service which does not require the spectrum or a service which requires spectrum of a band whose availability is not in short supply will also be not available to the society."

In para 2.34 it was emphasized that the issue should be revisited and reviewed periodically depending upon new data on "**availability of Spectrum in the near future.**" Reference was made to the May, 2005 recommendations of TRAI, which emphasized periodic review depending upon development in the market, level of competition, development of technologies and availability of equipments. It was concluded in Para 2.36 that :-

> "It is not advisable to exogenously fix the number of access service providers in a market which is in a dynamic setting".

5. The recommendation of "No Cap" was merely a recommendation that no artificial cap should be fixed exogenously in a market which is in a dynamic setting and even this was subject to review in the light of new data on availability of Spectrum. This recommendation does not mean that licences should be granted without considering the available Spectrum. The idea was that existing operators must continue to feel the heat of potential competition and emergence of new technology.
6. Significantly, in Para 2.38, TRAI insisted that there should be predictability and transparency in Spectrum management as investors base their decisions upon the likely availability of Spectrum which is a key raw material for the wireless industry. TRAI recommended as below:-

"The Authority recommends that it is necessary, to ensure that allocations of spectrum are made in accordance with the laid down policy and the information on such allocations and pending requests for allocation of spectrum, the reasons for pendency, the duration of pending requests, etc. is available in public domain. Above all, the likely availability of spectrum in different bands in all the circles, the time period by which it will be available for allocation, the criteria to be adopted for setting up a 'q system' needs to be made public."

7. Further, in Para 2.40 it was observed as below:-

   "The present spectrum allocation criteria, pricing methodology and the management system suffer from a number of deficiencies and therefore the Authority recommends that this whole issue is not to be dealt in piecemeal but should be taken up as a long-term policy issue. There is an urgent need to address the issues linked with the spectrum efficiency and its management."

8. TRAI therefore cannot be said to have overlooked the aspect of availability of Spectrum and no intention can be imputed to TRAI of recommending grant of licences to everyone irrespective of availability of Spectrum. In fact, even earlier by letter dated 22.02.2003 and the recommendations dated 27.10.2003 TRAI had clearly stated that additional mobile service providers in various service areas can be considered if there is adequate availability of Spectrum both for existing service providers and for new players. Not only this the NTP, 1999 in clear terms states as below:-

   "It is proposed to review the Spectrum utilisation from time to time keeping in view the emerging scenario of Spectrum availability, optimal use of Spectrum, requirements of market, competition and other interest of public. The entry of more operators in a service area shall be based on the recommendation of the TRAI who will review this as required and no later than every two years."

   This policy is binding on everyone including TRAI under Section 25(2) of the Act.

9. The issue of fixing cut-off date and the subsequent alteration by pre-dating the cut-off date has no relation whatsoever to the recommendation of "No Cap" as explained above.

10. In fact, based on TRAI's recommendations of 2007, the first step should

have been to assess the availability of Spectrum, to lay down Spectrum allocation criteria and pricing methodology as a matter of policy and to place the same in public domain. Thereafter, the Central Government should have sought a specific recommendation from TRAI for issuing new licence to a service provider as envisaged by the second and fourth proviso of Section 11(1) of the TRAI Act. However, this was not done. Thus, the grant of licence in large number in January, 2008 is clearly contrary to Section 11(1) of the Act.

11. TRAI had written letter dated 02.03.2007 (**Annexure C herein**)to the DoT drawing its attention to compliance with Section 11(1) of the Act. Subsequent to the grant of licences, TRAI again wrote to DoT on 01.07.2008 (**Annexure D herein**). The DoT replied that this provision applies to "new licence" and it means "something being brought/ introduced for the first time as a new category of licence." DoT's letter dated 02.07.2008 (**Annexure E herein**)is enclosed.
12. It is submitted that the mandatory seeking of recommendation contemplated by the two provisos are in the context of Section 11(1) (a)(i) and (ii), which prescribe the subject matter: -
"(i) need and timing for introduction of new service provider"
"(ii) terms and conditions of licence to a service provider."
The DoT is not right in avoiding the seeking of specific recommendation as per the provisos. Thus, the grant of licences suffers from illegality.

Allocation of Spectrum:

1. Allocation of Spectrum is part of Spectrum management. There are 4 aspects of allocation of Spectrum which are being considered:
Non-holding of Auction.
Allocation at 2001 price.
Application of first come – first serve principle.
Issue of alteration of cut-off date and the mode of implementation of FCFS.
2. On the first aspect, the writ petitioners have submitted relying on CAG report that TRAI in its recommendations dated 28.08.2007 recommended that market price of 2G Spectrum licenses be determined through a competitive mechanism by auction and that DoT did not comply with this. It is submitted that in para 2.71, 2.72, 2.76, 2.78 and 2.79 TRAI did not recommend holding of auction for

grant of new licenses in 2G bands up to 10 MHz. To this extent there is no breach of the recommendations.

3. The learned Attorney General has contended that the Government committed no error in not holding auction as TRAI had not recommended auction and this was for good reasons. It is also contended that whether auction should or should not be held is a matter of policy and since the Government has taken the decision on basis of recommendation of expert body, statutorily constituted for the purpose, no fault can be found on this account.

3A. There is a complete lack of pleading and factual basis in the writ petitions for questioning the non holding of auction. The issue is only based on an assumption that TRAI recommended grant of licence through auction. Hence this issue should not be examined on account of paucity of material, and absence of challenge to TRAI's recommendation as regards no auction.

The respondent licences also made similar submissions as regards non-holding of auction.

4. If nevertheless we examine it, then the following needs to be noted. Section 4 of the Indian Telegraph Act, 1885 treats the establishment, maintenance and working of telegraphs as an exclusive privilege of the Central Government. It also provides that this privilege can be parted in favour of any person by granting a license "on such conditions and in consideration of such payments as it thinks fit". Act 8 of 2004 has inserted an Explanation. The Explanation provides that the payment made for the grant of a license shall include such sum attributable to the USO as may be determined by the Central Government after considering the recommendations made in this behalf by TRAI. USO is defined by Section 3(1A) of the Indian Telegraph Act, 1885, which is as below: -

> "Universal Service Obligation means the obligation to provide access to basic telegraph services to people in the rural and remote areas at affordable and reasonable prices."

Clause (1A) was also inserted by Act 8 of 2004 w.e.f. 01.04.2002. The Rules for administration of the USO Fund known as IT (Amendment) Rules 2004 were notified on 26.03.2004. By IT (Amendment) Act 2006 the word "basic" in Section 3(1A) was deleted to cover mobile service.

The Rules were again amended in the year 2006 by Notification dated 17.11.2006. They were again amended in the year 2008 by notification dated 18.07.2008 to provide subsidy support to eligible operators for operational sustainability of rural telephony. The USOF is created by a Universal Service Levy of 5% of AGR. In addition Government may give grants. The Funds can, inter alia, be used for creation of infrastructure for provision of Mobile Services in rural and remote areas.

5. So far as TRAI Act, 1997 is concerned, its power to make recommendations in connection with license granted under Section 4 of the ITA, 1885 is contained in Section 11(1)(a) as below: -
“ (i). need and timing for introduction of new service provider;
(ii). terms and conditions of licence to a service provider;
(iii). revocation of licence for non-compliance of terms and conditions of licence.”
Further, in the same clause it is prescribed that TRAI can recommend measures to facilitate competition and promote efficiency in the operation of telecom services so as to facilitate growth in such services; technological improvements; type of equipment to be used; and efficient management of available Spectrum. When considered along with regulatory function under Section 11(1)(b), the entire gamut of powers would include the making of recommendations with respect to allocation of Spectrum. But while doing so TRAI has to focus on facilitating competition, efficient operation of Telecom Services and growth of Telecommunications in the light of available Spectrum. The preamble of the TRAI Act, 1997 also requires TRAI, “...to protect the interests of service providers and consumers of the telecom sector, to promote and ensure **orderly growth** of the telecom sector.”

7. Section 11(1)(b)(ix) mandatorily requires TRAI to “ensure effective compliance of Universal Service Obligations.” Thus, it is a statutory obligation to provide access to basic telegraph services to people in the rural and remote areas at affordable and reasonable prices. And mobile services were included in USO in December, 2006.

8. The Statement of Objects and Reasons of the TRAI Act, 1997 “stresses on achieving the universal service, bringing the quality of telecom services to world standards, provisions of wide range of services to meet the customers demand at reasonable price, and participation of the companies registered in India in the area of basic as well as value

added telecom services as also making arrangements for protection and promotion of consumer interest and ensuring fair competition."

9. The NTP, 1999 sets out the main objectives as under:
   - Access to telecommunication is of utmost importance for achievement of the country's social and economic goals. Availability of affordable and effective communications for the citizens is at the core of the vision and goal of the telecom policy.
   - Strive to provide a balance between the provision of universal service to all uncovered areas, including the rural areas and the provision of high level services capable of meeting the needs of the country's economy;
   - Encourage development of telecommunications facilities in remote, hilly and tribal areas of the country;
   - Create a modern and efficient telecommunications infrastructure taking into account the convergence of IT, media, telecom and consumer electronics and thereby propel India into becoming an IT superpower;
   - Convert PCO's, where justified, into Public Teleinfo centers having multimedia capability like ISDN services, remote database access, government and community information systems etc.
   - Transform in a time bound manner, the telecommunications sector to a greater competitive environment in both urban and rural areas providing equal opportunities and level playing field for all players;
   - Strengthen research and development efforts in the country and provide an impetus to build world- class manufacturing capabilities.
   - Achieve efficiency and transparency in spectrum management .
   - Protect defence and security interests of the country.
   - Enable Indian Telecom Companies to become truly global players.

10. The NTP, 1999 goes on to provide as under:
    "It is proposed to review the spectrum utilization from time to time keeping in view the emerging scenario of spectrum availability, optimal use of spectrum, requirements of market, competition and other interest of public. The entry of more operators in a service area shall be based on the recommendation of the TRAI who will review this as required and no later than every two years.

CMSP operators would be required to pay a one time entry fee. The basis for determining the entry fee and the basis for selection of additional operators would be recommended by the TRAI. Apart from the one time entry fee, CMSP operators would also be required to pay license fee based on a revenue share. It is proposed that the appropriate level of entry fee and percentage of revenue share arrangement for different service areas would be recommended by TRAI in a time-bound manner, keeping in view the objectives of the New Telecom Policy."

11. While referring to "Spectrum management" it provides as under: - "With the proliferation of new technologies and the growing demand for telecommunications services, the demand on spectrum has increased manifold. It is therefore, essential that spectrum be utilized efficiently, economically, rationally and optimally. There is a need for transparent process of allocation of frequency spectrum for use by a service and making it available to various users under specific conditions."
12. There is a need to have a transparent process of allocation of frequency spectrum which is effective and efficient. This would be examined further in the light of ITU guidelines. For the present, the following course of action shall be adopted.
    - Spectrum usage fee shall be charged.
    - Setting up an empowered Inter- Ministerial Group to be called as Wireless Planning Coordination Committee (WPCC) as part of the Ministry of Communications for periodical review of spectrum availability and broad allocation policy.
13. The NTP, 1999 records the commitment of the Government "to provide access to all people for basic telecom services at affordable and reasonable prices" (Para 6) and states that TRAI was formed with a view to provide an effective regulatory framework and adequate safeguards "to ensure fair competition and protection of consumer interests".
14. Chartering the course of development and strategies for growth of telecom when tele-density is small, the thrust is to expand in semi urban and rural areas and provide access at affordable and reasonable price, robust competition is to be sustained, with USO in view and the Spectrum being finite and scarce is an extremely complex task. It also has its own dynamism arising on account of the developments which take place in implementation of policy and advancement of new

technologies. Therefore, the strategies have to be periodically evolved in the light of various factors. There is neither any constitutional nor statutory compulsion to hold an auction for allocation of Spectrum. In the following cases even this Hon'ble Court has taken the view that public auction/tender is one of the methods of securing the interest and though it is the ordinary rule, it is not an invariable rule. There may be situations where there are compelling reasons necessitating departure from the rule. But then the reasons for the departure must be rational and should not be suggestive of discrimination. Nothing should be done which gives an appearance of bias, jobbery or nepotism.

i) **1987 (2) SCC 295** (Pr. 34-41, 43) Sachidanand Pandey and Anr. v. State of West Bengal and Ors.

In this case land was allotted for establishment of a modern five-star hotel at a negotiated price. This court observed, while distinguishing the case of *C.R. Reddy* that "the difference between sale of land and other readily saleable commodities and the allotment of land for establishing a modern five-star hotel of international standards is so obvious as to need no more explanation."

ii) **2000 (8) SCC 262** (Pr. 19 – 26) Netai Bag & Ors. v. The State of West Bengal & Ors.

iii) **1980 (4) SCC 1** Kasturi Lal Lakshmi Reddy v. State of Jammu and Kashmir and Anr.

iv) **1986(4) SCC-566,** State of M.P. Vs. Nand Lal Jaiswal

v) **1997(7) SCC-592,** M.P.Oil Extraction Vs. M.P. (Pr. 41,45,46)

15. TRAI while not recommending auction in 2G band had acted fairly and reasonably in public interest, keeping in mind that Spectrum was scarce and finite and also keeping in mind the various goals and factors set out in TRAI Act, 1997; ITA, 1885; the NTP, 1994 and NTP, 1999 and the stage of development. The decision was taken *bonafide* and reasonably in public interest hence it is not liable to be interfered with in exercise of judicial review for the following reasons:

    i) Allocation of Spectrum, which includes holding or non-holding of auction, is a matter of public policy and the courts do not ordinarily interfere unless the policy is found to be unconstitutional or *malafide*.

ii) While exercising power of judicial review, the courts do not sit in appeal and do not substitute the decision. The courts are only concerned with the decision making process i.e. the manner in which the decision is made. If all relevant factors have been considered and nothing that is irrelevant is taken into consideration and the decision is *bonafide* then the courts would not interfere.

iii) It has been held that in economic matters the executive is given wide latitude and policy-making is empirical. Especially in complex policy making, involving development of telecom services and with USO obligations and promotion of competition and orderly growth the courts ordinarily defer to the executive decisions and if two views are possible then the courts would not interfere.

2001(3) SCC-635, Ugar Sugar Works Vs. Delhi Admn.
1990(3) SCC-223, Sitaram Sugar Co. Vs. UOI
(Pr.48,49,50,57,58,59,60,
1997(7) SCC-592, M.P. Oil Extraction vs. M.P.(Pr. 41)
2002(2) SCC-333, Balco Employees Union Vs. UOI
(Pr. 34,36,37,38,39,40,41 to 47,92,93,98)
2007(8) SCC-418, Dhampur Sugar Vs. Uttaranchal
2011(1) SCC-640,BAJAJ Hindustan Limited vs. Sir Shadi Lal Enterprises Ltd.

16. The TRAI notes that the telecom industry in India has seen phenomenal growth in the recent past and that the annual growth in 2006-07 almost out paced total combined growth from the beginning of telephony in India up to March 2004 and that at the time of recommendations being presented the Industry had already achieved the goal of 15% tele-density set for the year 2010 in NTP, 1999. The industry was poised to surpass DoT's target of 250 Million subscribers by 2007. This was mainly due to policy of liberalization of the Indian telecom market.

17. TRAI notes that for further growth there is an urgent need for a clear, fair, predictable, transparent and stable policy, especially with regard to spectrum, licensing, investments and competition. It favoured a robust competitive environment wherein service providers and technologies compete to deliver vide variety of telecom services to the end user for sustained growth. (Para 1.4)

18. It is noted that growth in wireline services is minimal and the exponential growth is largely in the wireless segment, and this trend

was likely to continue. (Pr.1.11)

(iv). Spectrum is the single most important input, but the spectrum management policy has not kept pace with the dynamism of this sector. It is not predictable. TRAI states that, "The future growth of wireless services will receive a set back unless spectrum issues are addressed on emergency basis." (Pr. 1.13)

(v). "As new spectrum technologies unfold and proliferate, spectrum management should evolve in a responsible, fair, transparent, predictable and technology neutral manner." (Pr. 1.15)

(vi). Apart from considering the above aspects maximization of consumer interest, ensuring availability of adequate spectrum, maintaining level playing field and facilitating technological developments were kept in mind for facilitating further growth. (Pr. 1.16)

(vii). In para 2.2 the wireless market shares of various operators is noted. The growth of number of subscribers and fall of tariffs during the period of one decade since 1994 is depicted in a graph. (Pr. 2.1). A comparison is made with other selected countries in relation to mobile penetration (Pr. 2.3). The mobile penetration in India was 16.3% and was far behind Malaysia, Thailand, Brazil, Philippines, China and even Pakistan. Even this 16.3% penetration was on account of the urban tele-density of 48%. The rural tele-density was only 6%. There was a widening gap between the urban and rural areas. (Pr. 2.4)

(viii). In para 2.11 it is mentioned that the conflicting viewpoints during consultation process were examined in the light of NTP, 1999, growth objectives, sector experience, principles of fair competition and technological developments.

(ix). While recommending no cap the TRAI notes that growth continues to remain the top priority of the Government and to achieve the target of 500 million subscribers by 2010, and for increasing penetration in rural areas huge capital investment was required, and this was not possible by relying upon few operators. There was tremendous potential for further growth. (Pr. 2.14). It is also noted that the Capex to Sales ratio was one of the highest for Indian service providers (as highest as 70-80% in some cases). Since Indian market was in the high growth phase, therefore the Capex requirement would be much higher during this phase as compared to other markets (Pr. 2.15 and 2.16).

(x). From Pr. 2.17 to Pr. 2.37 the Authority emphasized the importance of preserving potential threat of competition. In para 2.38 to 2.40, 2.47 TRAI emphasized predictability and transparency in spectrum management and recommended that information regarding availability of spectrum and allocation criteria should be in public domain. It was recommended that long term policy be drawn on urgent basis.

(xi). In para 2.55, the Authority reiterated its earlier recommendation for de-linking spectrum from the licensing regime. In this context it was emphasized that entry fee determination in 2001, bears no relationship to the present spurt in telecom market.

(xii). In para 2.57 and 2.59 recommendations were made for spectrum efficiency and tightening of subscription criteria. Importantly, Constitution of a multi-disciplinary committee was recommended to frame a new Spectrum allocation criteria (Pr. 2.61). But in view of paucity of time it was suggested that at present the existing criteria may be continued. (Pr. 2.62)

4. In para 2.73 to 2.79 following reasons are evident for concluding that there should not be any auction :

(i). Telecom sector is witnessing dynamism and unprecedented growth. Since after the 4th license was granted in 2001, the prevailing practice is to grant a license on the basis of the entry fee discovered by the bidding process for grant of license to the 4th Cellular operator. (51 Licenses had been so granted in year 2004, 2006 and 2007).

(ii). The overriding consideration was of providing a level playing field to a new entrant. Different licensees were at different levels of operation in terms of the quantum of spectrum. This means that a new entrant who will be having a higher Capex today for roll out based on start–up Spectrum of 4.4 MHZ will have to compete necessarily with the existing operators who were covering 48% urban tele-density. The Urban market was likely to get saturated in a year or two (and it has). The new entrant would have to focus more on semi-urban, rural areas and hill areas and that further enhances Capex requirements.

(iii). The Spectrum in 800 and 900 MHZ bands had already been issued to the first, second and third cellular operators. The 800 and 900 MHZ band is very valuable and supports the provision of 3 G and LTE services. They are far more efficient both technically and economically than 1800 MHZ which is being used for spectrum allocation since year 2001. The new entrants were to get spectrum in 1800 MHZ band only.

So all operators in this band were to be given a level playing field.

(iv). The spectrum fee regime comprised a). entry fee b). license fee as a percentage of AGR and c). Spectrum usage charges as a percentage of AGR. In view of the objective of growth, affordability and penetration in semi-urban and rural areas, the authority was not in favour of changing the spectrum fee regime for a new entrant.

(v). By reference to past practice the Authority was referring to the allowing of migration to UASL on the basis of 2001 price and even new UASL licenses had been granted on that basis in year 2004 and 2006 and in January, 2007. These licenses had been granted without holding any auction for new entrants. The authority felt that the holding of auction would therefore, result in denying level playing field to the new entrant. This was considered to be not advisable for achieving the objective of growth, affordability and penetration of wireless services.

(vi). It is submitted that TRAI has kept the objectives set out in TRAI Act and NTP, 1999 in view while making the recommendation of not holding auction in 2G band. It has considered all relevant factors and no irrelevant factor has been taken into consideration. Nobody has suggested that recommendations made by TRAI are not *bona fide* and there are no pleadings in this regard in any of the Writ Petitions. Even the CAG says that role of TRAI is to foster competition and ensure level playing field. (Pg 92 Para 3.2.2). It is also not possible to condemn the recommendation as arbitrary or perverse given the complexity of the determinations.

(vii). Prior to the grant of impugned licenses the application for license were not many and the demand was comparatively less and therefore whoever applied was given spectrum. The criteria and methodology of selecting the new entrant assumes importance where the demand grows beyond the availability of spectrum. In 2007 DoT had not assessedthe availability of spectrum and actual demand. Most applications were submitted after the recommendation was given. If DoT found that demand was more than the availability of spectrum and it wanted to issue many new licenses it should have indicated the positon to TRAI and sought its recommendation under Section 11(1) proviso. This was not done.

Determination of Entry Fee;

1. While TRAI was not in favour of holding auction for 2G bands it has nowhere suggested or recommended that the entry fee should be kept pegged at 2001 level. Further, having recommended that spectrum fee regime should not be changed TRAI has made two important statements. **First**, for additional grant of spectrum above 4.4 MHZ, it recommended enhancement of spectrum charges by 1% (Pr. 2.83). Spectrum usage charge is in the form of a royalty and it captures the economic value of spectrum that is used. **Second,** in para 2.55 and 2.73 it has been clearly observed, "it is also a fact that entry fee determination in 2001 does not bear any relationship to present spurt in telecom market", and again that "The entry fee as it exists today is, in fact, a result of the price discovered through a markets based mechanism applicable for the grant of license to the 4th Cellular operator. In today's dynamism and unprecedented growth of telecom sector, the entry fee determined then is also not the realistic price for obtaining a license. Perhaps, it needs to be reassessed through a market mechanism." Thus, while TRAI wanted "the dual- charge", "methodology" and "spectrum fee regime" to continue unchanged it did recognize that the entry fee needed to be re-assessed through a market mechanism. Thus TRAI was not in favour of auction based entry fee but recognized reassessment through market mechanism.
2. It is noteworthy that the aspect of spectrum pricing had not been referred by Central Government to TRAI by letter dated 13th April, 2007 and this part of the recommendation has been made *suo motu* as the letter of the Government mentioned that the Government was contemplating to review its policy. TRAI expected that the pre-requisite exercise would be conducted in the context of predictability and transparency. However, this part of TRAI's recommendation including para 6.7 were not considered by Central Government (**See Counter Affidavit TRAI Vol.I Annex-R-3**). The Government's decision communicated by letter dated 08.11.2007 said that "these recommendations are beyond scope of present reference and hence not considered." (**Counter Affidavit TRAI Vol. I Annex-R-3 Pg. 193-207**) Vol. I). Importantly, the Government has adverted to para 5.23 which is not covered in the summary recommendations (Pg. 207). But the decision is silent about Pr. 2.38-2.40 and Pr. 2.55, 2.73. In this context before finalizing the

price Government should have complied with NTP-99 and Sections 11(1) Vth Proviso by seeking TRAI recommendation for grant of licence to a new service provider. TRAI had written a letter dated 15.10.2007 (Rejoinder Affidavit Pg. 278-281), to the DoT drawing its attention to this aspect and had also referred to TDSAT judgment dated 07.07.2006 in Petition No. 7 of 2003 as well as its judgment dated 27.09.2003 (Pg. 278). Another letter was written on 19.10.2007 (Pg. 281).

Annexure 4

Rajeev Chandrasekhar's Letter to SP, CBI

From: Rajeev Chandrasekhar, MP.

My dear Priyadarshi, 20th June, 2011

Sub: Evidence of illegal acts and conspiracy for issuance of new UASL licenses without bidding in 2003-2004, in violation of the TRAI Act and Cabinet decision. Additional evidence also cited from CAG Report of 16/11/2010 and the Justice Shivraj V. Patil Patil One man Committee (OMC) report of 31/01/2011.

This is further to my letters dated 22/12/2010 and 10/01/2011, and my meeting with you on 14/06/2011.

There is conclusive and undeniable evidence that there were big beneficiaries of illegal acts by TRAI/DoT which caused a corresponding loss to the exchequer in violation of Cabinet decision of 31/10/2003, UASL guidelines of 11/11/2003, NTP'99 as amended on 11/11/2003, established procedure of multi-stage auctions, extant policy and the TRAI act, Section 11(1)(a)(i), Second proviso and Section 11(1)(a)(i), Fifth proviso.

The events and actions leading to these issuance of licenses/spectrum in Telecom are often complex and it is easy for even the most informed to be mislead and confused. This letter attempts to clarify the real situation, in as simple as simple a way as possible, to allow the process of investigation and justice to be pursued and all the illegal actions and wrongdoers to be identified.

2003-04 (26 New UAS licenses Granted illegally to 4 companies):

It seems that the prevailing view with regard to the issuance of new UAS licenses (not migration) to the private companies during this period is sought to be justified by the potential accused/involved parties by citing the 'Note for Cabinet' – F.No. 808-26/2003-VAS, section 2.4.6(i0 and (iii), which state:

"2.4.6 Based on the above the GoM has recommended the following course of action:

i) The scope of NTP'99 may be enhanced to provide for licensing of Unified Access Service for basic and cellular license services and Unified Licensing comprising all telecom services. Department of Telecommunications may be authorized to issue necessary addendum to NTP-99 to this effect.
ii) The recommendations of TRAI with regard to implementation of Unified Access Licensing Regime for basic and cellular services may be accepted. DoT may be authorized to finalize the details of the implementation with the approval of the Minister of Communications & IT in this regard including calculation of entry fee depending o the date of the payment based on the principles by the TRAI in its recommendations.

The reality is this: The contention that there was a Cabinet Decision which approved the grant of New UAS licenses is utterly, completely false and is an attempt to divert attention from the real perpetrators of this illegal act.

To understand the scams in 2003-04, it is most crucial to distinguish, in clear terms, between (a) an existing BSO/limited mobility operator and (b) a new UASL operator, specifically:

i) An existing BSO/limited mobility operator has to be viewed on a circle-wise basis only. An existing BSO/limited mobility operator in, say 6 circles (e.g. Tatas) as on 11/11/2003, does not qualify as an existing operator for the remaining circles where it did not have a BSO license. The status of existing versus new has to be evaluated on a circle-wise basis only.

ii) TRAI recommendations of 27/10/2003, GoM approval of 30/10/2003, Cabinet decision of 31/10/2003 and UASL guidelines of 11/11/2003 – only pertain to migration for existing BSOs/limited mobility operators to the UASL regime. There is not a single word about new UASL operators in any of these four said documents/approvals.

iii) As the CBI has cited in its charge sheet of 02/04/2011 (page16/17), under the TRAI Act, Section 11(1)(a)(i) and (ii), second Proviso, the Central Government needs to mandatorily seek recommendations before "new license to be issued to a service provider". This statutory provision cannot be overrun by any decision of GoM, Cabinet or MoCIT/DoT officials.

With the above background as a basis of evaluating the contention of the potential accused/involved parties, kindly evaluate the following evidence:

i) The cabinet approved the TRAI recommendations and TRAI recommendations approved migration of existing BSO/limited mobility operators to UASL ONLY in CIRCLES where they were already licensed as BSOs. Cabinet note refers to "date of payment based on principles given by TRAI in its recommendations". This only refers to existing BSOs and consequently excludes new UASL applicants:

The authorization provided by the cabinet is not unfettered. It can go neither beyond the subject of the TRAI recommendations (bound by TRAI Act. If this authorization was meant for new UAS licenses, then there would be no need/meaning to the phrase "calculation of entry fee depending upon the date of payment based on the principles given by TRAI". The concept of date of payment only arises with regard to existing licenses who migrate on a circle-wise basis, and not to new UAS licensees.

A plain reading of the TRAI recommendations of 27/10/2003, page 42, Annexure III shows that the date of payment is critical and linked to the calculation of entry fee, but relates only to BSO operators with limited mobility pertaining to the circles where they seek migrations, i.e. Reliance (18 circles), Tatas (6 circles), Bharti (6circles), and Shyam and HFCL (1 circle each). New UAS licenses (i.e. UAS licenses for new circles), on the other hand, have no relevance to the phrase 'date of payment'. Nor can this be calculated by the TRAI in its recommendations since the TRAI would not have known on 27/10/2003 when which new entrant will pay for which circle or enter through which process – First Come, First Serve (FCFS) or multi-stage bidding etc.

In conclusion, this section is entirely restricted to migrating licensees in those specific circles, and in case of Tatas, it is specifically limited to the 6 circles of Gujarat, Maharashtra, Karnataka, Andhra Pradesh, Tamil Nadu and Delhi only. The 12 new UAS licenses which they received in January/February 2004 are not covered by this authorization.

ii) TRAI recommendations only refer to 'migration' or 'existing BSOs'. No mention of new UASL licenses for operators:

A plain reading of the TRAI recommendations, which is basis of the GoM and Cabinet approvals of 30/10/2003 and 30/10/2003 respectively, shows that the recommendations only use the words 'migration' or 'migrating' or existing BSOs' in all the relevant sections, including but not limited to sections 7.4, 7.5, 7.7, 7.8, 7.12, 7.13, 7.14, 7.16, 7.17, 7.18, 7.19, 7.20, 7.21, 7.22, 7.23, 7.24, 7.26, 7.29, 7.30, 7.31, and 7.37. there is no use of the phrase 'new unified access license' anywhere and surely the GoM/Cabinet could not have approved (consequent upon the statutory restrictions) beyond what the TRAI had recommended for existing BSOs/CmSPs migrating UASL.

iii) UASL guidelines dated 11/11/2003 issued by DoT make no mention of new UAS licenses'. They neither provide the application format nor the process to grant new UAS licenses:

The entire UASL guidelines of 11/11/2003 relate to migration for existing BSOs/limited mobility operators (which can only be on a circle-wise basis). It neither speaks about new UAS licenses nor does it prescribe the format for applying for such licenses. Most importantly, UASL guidelines of 11/11/2003 do not mention FCFS anywhere as a process for grant of new UAS licenses. That is because the guidelines were not meant to address new UAS licenses. It merely mentions that future applications will be received under the UASL regime without any hint of the format or the process/timing of allocation.

iv) The letter by Shri Pradip Baijal, former TRAI Chairman, dated 14/11/2003, which is the basis for 26 new UAS licenses – including

12 to the Tatas – granted between January and April 2004, is patently illegal:

Under the TRAI Act, The Chairman has no authority whatsoever to clarify statutory recommendations through a personal letter – that too based on a telephonic conversation – written other GoM approval, Cabinet decision and issuance of UASL guidelines of 11/11/2003. The letter by itself is patently illegal. If it is treated as a fresh recommendation, then it violates section 11(4) (Transparency) since neither can such recommendations be generated without public consultation nor can they be given without being placed in public domain. In the current instance, there was no consultation for new UAS licenses or even UAS licenses in the first place. Moreover, the letter of 14/11/2003 has never been placed on the TRAI website and is in fact missing from TRAI's files – as per their reply to an RTI enquiry. This was a surreptitious move by the Chairman to benefit companies such as Tatas who had already applied for 7 new UAS licenses on 12/11/2003 in the BSO format. I am sure you are aware that the then TRAI Chairman went on to work with and consult for some of the beneficiaries of these licenses – this fact is already in the public domain.

For collaborative evidence, please see CAG Report of 16/11/2010, sections 3.1.6 and 3.1.7 and the Justice Shivraj V. Patil OMC Report, sections 2.51-2.55 and section 3.2(iv).

v) The DoT accepts that Chairman TRAI's letter is over and beyond the TRAI Recommendations approved by Cabinet on 31/10/2003:

A reading of the file notings within the DoT beginning 20/11/2003 till 24/11/2003 clearly shows that senior-most members of the Telecom Commission and officials of the DoT, including legal advisors, do not agree with the contention that the Cabinet had authorized the grant of new UAS licenses with the approval of the then MoCIT. The handwritten note on file dated 21/11/2003 by D(LF) which remains uncontested on files till date) states:

"the matter was discussed in a meeting with M(P), M(F), LA(T) and DDG (LF) in the chamber of M(F) today. It emerged in that:

In view of the letter dated 14th November 2003 from TRAI, it is to be presumed that the entry fee for new applicants would be equal to the entry fee paid by the fourth cellular operator and the entry fee of the existing BSO fixed by the Government (based on TRAI recommendations) where there is no cellular operator.

Further the new applications would submit PBG equivalent to fourth cellular operator (however the quantum of PBG may need to be decided where there are no fourth cellular operator). The above is over and above the recommendations of TRAI on unified licensing which was approved by the Cabinet as the same was about migration of only existing, cellular and basic service licensees to the unified access service license.

It is presumed that such new licenses in the category of UASL would be on a first come, first serve basis on basis of applications submitted for consideration.

Important Notes:

- All the highlighted sections above show that the UASL guidelines did not prescribed even basic information such as PBG etc. and therefore, could not have been applied to new UASL operators.
- The basis of this note is the letter of 14/11/2003 and that leads to the presumption of entry fee.
- It clearly states that this is over and above the TRAI recommendations which were approved by the Cabinet as the same was about migration of existing CMSPs, BSOs to UASL only (not new US licensees).
- Even the process of grant of such licenses i.e. FCFS has to be presumed since nothing is stated in the UASL guidelines of 11/11/2003.
- This note is based on the meeting of member of the Telecom Commission and is signed by DDG (LF), senior DDG (VAS), Director AS (II), Member (P) Member (F), Chairman – Telecom Commission and eventually by the then MoCIT – between 21/01/2003 and 24/11/2003. Not one single signatory has contradicted the handwritten note which is the basis of originating the approval for grant of new UAS licenses.

vi) The decision to grant new UAS licenses in 2004 violates the TRAI Act, Section 11(1)(a)(i), Second Proviso:

The TRAI Act, as cited by the CBI in its chargesheet of 2/4/2011, recognizes the need for mandatory recommendations to be sought by the central government from the TRAI while issuing licenses to new service providers. By example, since Tatas would be considered 'new service providers in the 12 circles, as would others who received licenses in January/February 2004, a specific and separate set of recommendations would have to be received as per the statute – which in turn will have to follow a process of public consultation compliant with section 4 of the TRAI Act. Since no sch consultation ever took place and no such consequent recommendations were made/placed in the public domain, any grant of licenses to 'new service providers' or 'new UASL operators' is a blatant violation of the TRAI Act. The compliance should have been followed for all 26 licenses granted.

vii) Substantial evidence in the CAG Report which shows that the TRAI Chairman's letter was unauthorized, including that the TRAI recommendations of 2003 regarding bidding of fourth/fifth cellular operator were violated:

As it is well known that the fourth/fifth cellular operator, as per the TRAI recommendations of 27/10/2003, was to enter through a process of multi-stage bidding (section 7.37 and 7.39). As per the DoTs own admission (Justice Shivraj Patil OMC Report – Annexure 27, Page 313, Section 7), grant of new UAS license was nothing but the grant of new CMSP licenses.

Consequently, the then TRAI Chairman, Shri Pradip Baijal, in conspiracy with the then DoT, allowed a backdoor entry inti cellular mobile telephony (under the garb of UASL) to certain operators, bypassing the process of tendering and bidding that was the norm for new cellular licenses till that point. This was in violation of the TRAI Act and while deliberately delaying implementation of the bidding for the fourth and fifth cellular mobile operator or UASL operator. So in effect, the nomenclature was changed to grant spectrum without the auction process in blatant violation of TRAI's own recommendations and the Cabinet approval of 27/10/2003 and 31/10/2003 respectively.

viii) The OMC Report provides collaborative evidence of the violation of the TRAI Act in the grant of the new UAS license and the benefits that accrued to these private companies:

Relevant sections of the Justice Shivraj Patil OMC Report include

Sections 3.2(i)-(iv), Sections 2.51-2.55, and most importantly Section 6.1 (i), which state:

"this report, the decision so taken was not notified to public for the benefit of all prospective applicants. Without there being any notified procedure to be followed for the grant of UASLs and without applications having been invited from all, the procedure thus formulated was applied to facilitate consideration of applications made by Tata Tele Services limited in the forms prescribed for grant of BSLs."

"...said officials appear to be responsible for deviation brought out in formulation of the procedure."

Conclusion:

The only set of licenses who could have legally received UAS licenses as a consequence of the TRAI Recommendations of 27/10/2003, Cabinet decision of 31/10/2003 and UASL guidelines of 11/11/2003, are the 31 migration licenses (7 licensees) that have been identified in Annexure III of TRAI Recommendations of 27/10/2003 and annexure I of UASL guidelines of 11/11/2003.

All other new UAS licenses (not migration) granted since January 2004, till the announcement of the new UASL guidelines of 14/12/2005 (being investigated independently) are blatantly illegal, and explicitly violate TRAI Act, section 11(1)(a)(i) , second and fifth proviso. If this was not the case, there was no need whatsoever for both the TRAI Recommendations and the UASL guidelines to attach such detailed annexures identifying the date of payments and the additional entry fee that will not be paid for migration to UASL in each of these 31 circles only.

In fact, the "date of payment" and resultant "calculation of entry fee" indicated in these annexures for migrating licenses directly identifies itself with the language used in the Cabinet approval of 31/10/2003, section 2.4.6(ii) – which is being falsely cited by the potential accused to masquerade as a Cabinet approval for grant of new UAS licenses.

With all the evidence above, it is clear that in 2003-04, serious illegalities were committed to ensure UASL licenses were issued in 2004/2005 at

2001 prices – to benefit private companies, cause loss to exchequer and in contravention to the Cabinet approvals, existing policy and TRAI Act.

Copy of all relevant annexures is being attached herewith for your ready reference.

I hope that the above-mentioned evidence and facts will lay to rest any impression that new UAS licenses in 2003-04 wer in accordance with Cabinet approval. Rather, they were issued in violation of cabinet approval and law.

Yours Sincerely
RAJEEV CHANDRASEKHAR

Shri Vivek Priyadarshi
Superintendent of Police
Central Bureau of Investigation
CGO Complex
Lodi Road
New Delhi

Encl. List of Annexures and Actual Annexures

Annexure	Description
1	Letter from Shri M.S. Verma, Chairman TRAI to Shri Vinod Vaish, Secretary – DoT Dated 20/02/2003 regarding issuance of licenses to additional cellular mobile operators
2	TRAI Recommendations on Unified Licensing (in reality, UASL) dated 27/10/2003
3	Cabinet Note dated 10/09/2003 for constitution of GoM on Telecom Matters
4	Cabinet Approval dated 31/10/2003, of TRAI Recommendations of 27/10/2003 and other telecom issues
5	Note from Dr. Ashok Chandra, Deputy Wireless Advisor on the subject "Group of Ministers on Telecom matters - setting up the 'Task Force'on modalities for release of spectrum for growth of telecom services
6	Office Memorandum dated 11/11/2003 from Shri A.S. Verma, Director (VAS –II) on "Addendum to the New Telecom Policy – 1999 (NTP-99)"
7	UASL guidelines dated 11/11/2003 for migration of existing BSOs and CMSPs to the Universal Access Service regime
8	Letter from Shri Pradip Baijal, Chairman TRAI to Shri Vinod Vaish, Secretary –DoT dated 14/11/2003 separating TRAI Recommendations of 27/10/2003 as applicable to new unified licenses also
9	DoT file notings regarding grant of new UASL license based on applications received after the announcement of UASL guidelines dated 11/11/2003
10	DoT internal note on issuance of new cellular mobile licenses in face of new UASL guidelines of 11/11/2003 equating UASL with CMSPs
11	DoT note dated 23/03/2001 by Shri Arvind Chawla, Director (BS-II) on the subject "Procedure for allocation of spectrum on first come first served basis"
12	Second letter from TRAI dated 19/11/2003 on the subject "Recommendation of the TRAI on issues relating to spectrum" – referring to Shri Pradip Baijal's letter of 14/11/2003.

Acknowledgements

I am grateful to Ashok Desai, former Attorney General, and Prof. Littlechild, former power regulator of the UK, who advised me that given all the work I was doing, it was possible that there may be inquisitions against me and papers may be found missing, or not given to me. Hence it was critical that I keep copies of all important papers when I retire. And this is precisely what happened eight to twelve years after the events. For any other bureaucrat taking bold decisions today, I volunteer the same advice.

I want to express my gratitude to Sumit Majumdar, professor of technology and regulation at the University of Texas in Dallas, who met me often when he came to Delhi while writing his book, *India's Late, Late Industrial Revolution*, and helped me with my book drafts at each stage. I also want to express my gratitude to B.M. Vaish, my class-mate from Roorkee, for the immense moral support during all my inquisitions.

I am grateful to D.P.S. Seth, former CMD of BSNL and a member of TRAI, without whose help and guidance I could not have moved forward in bringing the 2003 reforms. Seth also helped me in the numerous inquiries I faced. I am also grateful to P.K. Sarma, member TRAI, who helped us most by his mature reaction to numerous issues we faced. The TRAI team, headed by Harsh and later Rajendra Singh, did an incredible job in the three years I was there. Hajela, TRAI's advisor, always gave independent advice on tricky issues and helped me write this book.

I'd like to express deep gratitude to my erstwhile colleagues P.K. Basu, Rakesh Kakkar, Sanjiv Ahluwalia and Vishwanath Anand. Their help and inputs were invaluable. Vinod Vaish, a colleague turned lifelong friend, helped me with the contents of this book. S.D. Saxena, Arvind Kumar, Asish and Smita Tripathy—thank you all for your edits, inputs and complete support.

I'd like to especially thank Veeresh Malik for giving me the idea of a self-published e-book. Not only did I receive numerous responses, it also helped me write a more detailed and improved book.

During all the inquiries against, and then in writing the book, my son Utsav helped beyond his responsibility to the father. My wife, who had to jointly bear the brunt of all the adverse media publicity, allegations and repeated visits by CBI, always stood by me. Her silent strength and loyalty were very important to me, even though I may not have expressed this, as I should have.

And then without Arun Shourie being my minister, I would never have achieved so much in life; nor got into so much trouble.

And lastly, I am very grateful to those who worked with me in TRAI and the power and disinvestment ministries. I would also like to thank my colleagues in Noesis. Stung by all the allegations, they stood by me and helped me through my difficult times.

NOTES

Chapter 2: Chapter India's Unusual Telecom Growth

1. InfoDev's *Telecommunication Regulation Handbook Module 1 – Overview of Telecommunication Regulation*, pp. 1, 2. https://www.itu.int/ITU-D/treg/Documentation/Infodev_handbook/1_overview.pdf (accessed on 12 July 2014).
2. The basic concern of this group was to accelerate universal access of telecom services at affordable rates, especially in the rural areas. Report of the Group on Telecom & IT Convergence on Limited Mobility, p. 13. http://pib.nic.in/focus/foyr2001/foapr2001/rg_tit.pdf (accessed on 1 April 2014).
3. Cabinet note: "Note for the Cabinet", F.No. 808-26/2003-VAS dated 31 October 2003. The approval contained in R. Poornalingam, additional Secretary, Cabinet Secretariat's approval letter DC No. 30/CM/2003 dated 3 November 2003 approving DoT proposals.

Chapter 3: The State Conspires in TRAI Cases

1. 'Performance Audit Report of CAG on the Issue of Licences and Allocation of 2G Spectrum by the Department of Telecommunications', p.14., http://www.performance.gov.in/sites/default/files/departments/telecom/CAG%20Report%202009-10.pdf (accessed on 14 April 2014).
2. Joint Parliamentary Committee (JPC) to examine matters relating to allocation and pricing of telecom licences and spectrum (Fifteenth Lok Sabha), para 10.26, p.161, http://164.100.47.134/New_Events_LS/

writereaddate/JPC_ReportL.pdf (accessed on 1 May 2014).

3. *Corruption and Corporate Governance in India: Satyam, Spectrum and Sundaram*, Subramanian Swamy, New Delhi: Har-anand Publications, 2009 is a book written based on the JPC report. Swamy's book also picks up a lot of material from the draft PAC (Public Accounts Committee) report. I have not repeated the entire analysis of these parliamentary committee reports, books and articles, but have concentrated on the fraudulent enquiries that UPA-II pursued after removing or misinterpreting facts and documents in all scam cases trying to shift the blame to the NDA government functionaries.
4. TRAI Recommendations on Unified Licensing, p.24, http://www.trai.gov.in/WriteReadData/Recommendation/Documents/Recomodifiedfinal.pdf (accessed on 2 February 2014).
5. '2G scam money went to tax safe havens via Surat', ED, 10 July 2015 http://www.business-standard.com/article/pti-stories/2g-scam-money-went-to-tax-safe-havens-via-surat-ed- 115071000769_1.html (accessed on 11 July 2015).
6. Subramanian Swamy, *2G Spectrum Scam*, p. 7, New Delhi: Har-Anand Publications (2011). Subramanian Swamy had written a detailed letter to the prime minister, and when that was not heard, he filed a PIL. India against Corruption, an NGO with association with Sri Sri Ravi Shankar, Anna Hazare, Ramdeo, Prashant Bhushan, Santosh Hegde, Arvind Kejriwal, Kiran Bedi and others, then took over this movement against corruption.
7. 'ED unearths India's biggest hawala trail in 2G case', 10 July 2015, http://www.moneycontrol.com/news/business/ed-unearths-indias-biggest-hawala-trail2g-case_1889741.html (accessed on 11 July 2015).

Chapter 4: Unraveling the Conspiracy

1. Justice Patil Committee Terms of Reference : http://leagueofindia.com/Shivaraj_Patil_Report.pdf (accessed on 10 July 2015).
2. Patiala House Court Judgment in additional spectrum case on Shyamal Ghosh IN THE COURT OF O. P. SAINI: SPL. JUDGE, CBI (04) (2G SPECTRUM CASES), NEW DELHI. RC No. 24(A)2011CBI-ACB CC No. 01/12, CBI Vs. Shyamal Ghosh and other 15.10.2015,

Paragraphs 278 and 279, p.220 http://judis.nic.in/Daily_Orders/DDC/list_new2.asp?DO_Pdf_Name=po19715102015.pdf (accessed on 13 July 2015).

Chapter 5: The Value of Judicial Guidance

1. Videsh Sanchar Nigam (Tata) vs. TRAI, Item no 6, Appeal No.10 of 2005, p.37 onwards, http://tdsat.nic.in/judgements2005.htm (accessed on 20 April 2015).

Chapter 7: Reforms in a Hurry – Power Sector Reforms in Post-1991 India

1. Open Access, Electricity Act 2003, p.7 http://www.cercind.gov.in/Act-with-amendment.pdf (accessed on 20 April 2015).

Chapter 8: Disinvestment: New Learnings (2000–03)

1. See, Chapter 6, 'Selling the family silver to pay the groceries bill?', p.164, in the book *Reforms and Economic Transformation in India*, edited by Jagdish Bhagwati and Arvind Panagariya, New Delhi: Oxford University Press, 2012.

Chapter 9: The CBI Falters

1. The PNGRB story is dated 9 August 2013 as the front-page article in the print edition but the article titled 'Re-opening Radia Tapes, CBI wants probe into corporates, ex-judges, politcians', the online edition of *The Indian Express* has dated it 10 August 2013. http://epaper.indianexpress.com/146097/Indian-Express/10-August-2013#page/1/2 (accessed on 20 March 2016).
2. 'FM Arun Jaitley criticises CBI for raking up old issues; says such actions can damage investment climate', *Economic Times*, 1 September 2014, http://economictimes.indiatimes.com/news/economy/policy/

fm-arun-jaitley-criticises-cbi-for-raking-up-old-issues-says-such-actions-can-damage-investment-climate/articleshow/41381959.cms (accessed on 21 March 2016).

3. 'Make CBI liable for malicious charges', Kanchan Gupta, *Mid-day*, 6 September 2014, http://www.mid-day.com/articles/make-cbi-liable-for-malicious-charges/15581175 (accessed on 23 March 2016).
4. 'Is this the way to energise civil servants?', Arun Shourie, *The Indian Express*, 5 September 2014, http://indianexpress.com/article/opinion/columns/is-this-the-way-to-energise-civil-servants/ (accessed on 20 March 2016).

Chapter 12: Looking into the Future: Disruptive Changes

1. *Straight from the Gut*, Jack Welch with John A. Byrne, pp. 309, 310 and 311, New York: Grand Central Publishing; Reprint edition, 2003.

Bibliography

Baijal, Pradip. 2007. *Disinvestments in India: I Lose and You Gain*. New Delhi: Pearson Publications.

Bedi, Iqbal Singh, Ian Brown, Urs Grasser, Mercy Wanjau and Malcom Webb. 2016. *Trends in Telecommunication Reform 2016: Regulatory Incentives to Achieve Digital Opportunities*. Edited by John Walden. Geneva: International Telecommunication Union.

Bhandari, Bhupesh. 2012. *Spectrum Grab: Inside Story of the 2G Scam*. New Delhi: BS Books.

Blackman, Colin and Lara Srivastava (Ed). 2011. *Telecommunications Regulation Handbook (Tenth Anniversary Edition)*. Washington: InfoDev, World Bank.

Blumsack, Seth, Jay Apt and Lester B. Lave. 2005. 'A Cautionary Tale: US Electricity Sector Reform'. *Economic & Political Weekly*, Vol. 40, Issue No. 50.

Choudary,T.H. 2004. *Information and Communication Technologies for Classes and Masses*. Hyderabad: CTMS Publication.

Debroy, Bibek, Ashley J. Tellis and Reece Trevor. 2014. *Getting India Back on Track*. New Delhi: Vintage Books.

Desai, Ashok V. 2006. *India's Telecommunications Industry: History, Analysis, Diagnosis*. New Delhi: Sage Publications.

Dobbs, Richard, James Manyika and Jonathan Woetzel. 2015. *No Ordinary Disruption*. New York: BBS Public Affairs.

Dossani, Rafiq. 2003. *Telecommunications Reform in India*. Kolkata: Viva Books Pvt Ltd.

Dubash, Navroj K. and Daljit Singh. 2005. 'Of Rocks and Hard Places: A Critical Overview of Recent Global Experience with Electricity Restructuring'. *Economic & Political Weekly*, Vol. XL, Issue No. 50.

Dubash, Navroj K. and D. Narasimha Rao. 2007. *The Practice and Politics of Regulation: Regulatory Governance in Indian Electricity*. New Delhi: NIPFP and Macmillan India Ltd.

Forbes, Naushad. 2001. 'Doing Business in India: What has liberalization changed?' Working Paper No. 93. California: Centre for Research on Economic Development and Policy Reform.

Gill, S.S. 2004. *Information Revolution in India: A Critique*. New Delhi: Rupa Publications.

Haldea, Gajendra. 2011. *Infrastructure at Crossroads*. New Delhi: Oxford University Press.

Haldea, Gajendra. 2004. *Introducing Competition in Generation of Electricity*. New Delhi: NCAER.

Hsueh, Roselyn. 2011. *China's Regulatory State*. New York: Cornell University Press.

Kessides, Ioannis N. 2004. 'Reforming Infrastructure: Privatization, Regulation and Competition – A World Bank Policy Research Report'. Co-publication of World Bank and Oxford University Press, Report Number 28985, Vol. 1.

Khanna, Sushil. 2012. *State-Owned Enterprises in India: Restructuring and Growth*. The Copenhagen Journal of Asian Studies, Vol. 30, No. 2.

Kim, Yongsoo, Tim Kelly and Siddhartha Raja. 2010. *Building Broadband: Strategies and Policies for the Developing World*. Washington: Global Information and Communication Technologies (GICT) Department, World Bank.

Kumarapathirana, R.B. 2012. *Regulatory Compendium – APT*. Bangkok: Asia-Pacific Telecommunity

Levy, Brian and Pablo T. Spiller. 1996. *Regulations, Institutions, and Commitment: Comparative Studies of Telecommunications*. New York: Cambridge University Press.

Majumdar, Sumit, Ingo Vogelsang and Martin Cave. 2002. *Handbook of Telecommunications Economics, Vol. 1: Structure, Regulation and Competition*. Holland: Emerald Group Publishing Limited.

Mukherji, Rahul, Sumit Ganguly. 2011. *India since 1980*. New Delhi: Cambridge University Press.

Mukherji, Rahul. 2014. *Globalization and Deregulation Ideas, Interests, and Institutional Change in India*. New Delhi: Oxford University Press.

Parakh, P.C. 2014. *Crusader or Conspirator? Coalgate and other Truths*. New Delhi: Manas Publications.

Pearson, Prof. Peter and Prof. Jim Watson. *UK Energy Policy 1980–2010: A History and Lessons to be Learnt*. London: The Parliamentary Group for Energy Studies.

Pottruck, David S. and Terry Pearce. 2000. *Clicks and Mortar: Passion Driven Growth in an Internet Driven World*. California: Jossey-Bass.

Raghavan, Vikram. 2007. *Communications Law in India: Legal Aspects of Telecom, Broadcasting and Cable Services*. New Delhi: LexisNexis Butterworths.

Rai, Vinod. 2014. *Not Just an Accountant: The Diary of The Nation's Conscience Keeper*. New Delhi: Rupa Publications.

Saxena, S.D. 2009. *Connecting India: Indian Telecom Story*. New Delhi: Konark Publishers Pvt Limited.

Shapiro, Carl and Hal R. Varian. 1999. *Information Rules: A Strategic Guide to the Network Economy*. Boston: Harvard Business School Press.

Sharma, Dinesh C. 2009. *The Long Revolution: The Birth and Growth of India's IT Industry*. Noida: HarperCollins Publishers India.

Singh, Joginder. 2012. *CBI and 2G*. New Delhi: Har-Anand Publications.

Swamy, Subramanian. 2011. *2G Spectrum Scam*. New Delhi: Har-Anand Publications.

Swamy, Subramanian. 2009. *Corruption and Corporate Governance in India: Satyam, Spectrum and Sundaram*. New Delhi: Har-Anand Publications.

Swamy, Subramanian. 2010. *Economic Development and Reforms in India and China: A Comparative Perspective*. New Delhi: Har-Anand Publications.

Telecom Sector in India. A Decadal Profile. 2012. Telecom Regulatory Authority of India.

Thomas, Stephen. 2005. 'British Experience of Electricity Liberalisation: A Model for India?' *Economic & Political Weekly*, Vol. XL, No. 50.

Wade, H.W.R. and C.F. Forsyth. 2004. *Administrative Law – Ninth Edition (Indian Edition)*. New Delhi: Oxford University Press.

Welch, Jack. 2001. *Straight from the Gut*. New York: Warner Books.

Wellenius, Bjorn and Peter A. Stern. 1994. *Implementing Reforms in the Telecommunications sector: Lessons from Experience*. Washington: World Bank Regional and Sectoral Studies.

Index